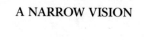
A NARROW VISION

A NARROW VISION

*Duncan Campbell Scott
and the
Administration of Indian Affairs
in Canada*

E. Brian Titley

UNIVERSITY OF BRITISH COLUMBIA PRESS
VANCOUVER 1986

A Narrow Vision: Duncan Campbell Scott and the Administration
of Indian Affairs in Canada

This book has been published with the help of a grant from the Social Science
Federation of Canada, using funds provided by the Social Sciences and
Humanities Research Council of Canada.

Canadian Cataloguing in Publication Data

Titley, E. Brian.
A narrow vision

Bibliography: p.
Includes index.
ISBN 0-7748-0261-8

1. Scott, Duncan Campbell, 1862-1947.
2. Canada.   Indian Affairs Branch—History.
I. Title.
JL103.I53T58 1986   354.710681'497
C86-091444-5

International Standard Book Number 0-7748-0261-8

Printed in Canada

Contents

Acknowledgements

I am grateful to a large number of individuals whose encouragement, advice and support helped to bring this project to a successful conclusion. The following are acknowledged in particular: Donald H. Akenson, Robert Carney, Jane Fredeman, Karen Hissett, Bennet McCardle, J.R.Miller, Donald B. Smith, Sally Weaver, and Lyle Weiss.

Introduction

Duncan Campbell Scott is best known as a literary figure. He is frequently mentioned in the company of Wilfred Campbell, Bliss Carman, Archibald Lampman, and Charles G.D. Roberts—a group of poets and essayists who were distinctly Canadian in their choice of subject matter, if not in style. Scott the civil servant is comparatively unknown. That he was head of the federal Indian Department for almost two decades is occasionally alluded to in passing. His role in that capacity, however, has escaped the attention of serious scholarship.

A biographer undertaking this neglected task might pose a number of intriguing and legitimate questions. How did a celebrated poet function in the highest echelons of the civil service? How did he reconcile the demands of his artistic spirit with the mundane routine of the office? Could he serve his muse and Caesar with equanimity?

The study that I have chosen to engage in, however, is not a biography. I do not attempt here to perform the biographer's delicate balancing act between psychology and literature or to fathom the inner soul of D.C. Scott. Someone well versed in Canadian literature will undoubtedly sooner or later shoulder that burden, and I hope the material explored here will prove useful.

I have chosen to examine Scott the civil servant, an approach which requires little justification. Scott would have been a significant historical figure had he never penned a stanza of poetry. This book is essentially a study of the personnel and policies of the Department of Indian Affairs in a particularly turbulent and eventful era. As the leading official of the department and the principal arbiter of policy during that time, Scott provides a convenient focus.

The administration of Indian Affairs was (and still remains) a complex and many-faceted enterprise. A multitude of responsibilities ranging from the management of schools to the disposal of timber from reserve lands came under its auspices. Therefore, any analysis of the department's activities must be selective. My criteria have been significance and interest—criteria which are admittedly susceptible to the whims of subjectivity. Conscious of my own predilections, I have attempted to select issues which reflected the peculiarities of Indian administration in a number of regions of Canada, as well as those which were of overall national importance. In all of the topics examined, Scott played a pivotal role in seeking resolutions satisfactory to the department and within prevailing policy guidelines.

Scott, Duncan Campbell (1862-1947)

As a youth, this poet found secure employment as a copying clerk for the Department of Indian Affairs and stayed with that department for the next fifty years, occasionally winning promotions by attrition. To judge from photographic evidence, Scott spent much of that time at his desk, his right hand draped over an open book, his left hand supporting his head as he gazed pensively into the middle distance. As a government official, he ensured that his native charges always got a fair shake, usually by the scruff of the neck. By doing his Christian and civic duty to ensure the rapid decline of native culture in Canada, he conveniently provided himself with sunset-tinged images of the "tragic savage" to enrich his bland versifying, while at the same time enriching his private collection with filched Indian art, now worth a bundle.

National Lampoon,
June 1983

1

Indian Administration:
Origins and Development

The fundamental principles governing Canada's Indian policy were first developed during the century prior to Confederation. The imperial administration was largely responsible for determining its main features in the early stages, but much of the initiative passed to the colonial legislatures as the nineteenth century progressed.

The Colonial Office in London never adopted a consistent set of principles for dealing with the Indians in Britain's North American possessions. Policy varied from region to region and was characterized by pragmatism and *ad hoc* arrangements.[1] In the Maritimes and in the colonies of Vancouver Island and British Columbia, for example, matters were generally left in the hands of the local governors and assemblies. In the Canadas, however, the imperial administration continued to supervise relations with Indians until 1860. It was here also that the greatest body of legislation affecting Indians was developed— legislation that was borrowed heavily by the new Dominion government as it began to formulate its own Indian policy. Indian administration in the Canadas provides the key to many post-Confederation developments. In fact, it is necessary to return to the period prior to the conquest of New France to seek out the origins of some of the principles upon which that administration was based.

The nucleus of an Indian department appeared in the late seventeenth century when Indian commissioners were appointed in the Thirteen Colonies to regulate the fur trade and suppress the liquor traffic. When the Seven Years' War broke out, relations with the Indians took on a greater sense of urgency. The Indian department was divided into two branches in 1755. Two superintendents were appointed, Sir William Johnson in the north and John Stuart in the south, and both reported to the British military commander in North America.[2] As far as the colonial administration was concerned, the Indians, or more precisely, those of the Iroquois Confederacy, were vital military allies in the struggle with the French for domination of the continent. Johnson, whose headquarters lay in the Mohawk Valley, had the important role of sustaining their friendship by distributing presents and protecting their lands from encroachment by whites.[3] The practice of maintaining a distinct branch of government with responsibility for relations with the Indians was therefore well established prior to the conquest.

Following the fall of Quebec, the Indian alliance continued to be valued. The Royal Proclamation of 1763 was designed to retain native goodwill by establishing a boundary between their lands and those of the whites. And it enunciated the principle that Indian lands could be surrendered only to the Crown and for compensation in each instance.[4] It at once tacitly acknowledged aboriginal land title and suggested procedures of surrender that were later incorporated into the treaty system. The wisdom of this policy was subsequently confirmed when the Indians generally remained loyal to the British cause during the American Revolutionary War.

In the aftermath of that upheaval, the Indian department was removed to Canada where its role continued as before. It became necessary to find lands for the Loyalists who fled northwards and also for the Iroquois allies of the British whose territories were now in American hands. These lands were secured north of Lakes Erie and Ontario in what was to become the colony of Upper Canada in 1791. Colonial authorities purchased them in a series of treaties with the Mississauga Indians.[5] As the colony expanded and more land was needed, further purchases were made until all of what is now southern Ontario was surrendered. These agreements provided for reserves, cash payments, and annual presents. The process culminated in the Robinson treaties of 1850 whereby the Indians gave up their title to lands north of Lakes Superior and Huron. Meanwhile, ill-advised sales and surrenders considerably reduced the tract of land granted to the Six Nations on the Grand River. A similar fate befell the lands of the Mohawks of the Bay of Quinte. The Indian department greatly encouraged such surrenders; lands so acquired could be sold to raise money for administrative purposes.

The aggressive policy of the colonial authorities towards Indian land is best explained by changing circumstances. The successful defence of British North America during the War of 1812 and the more settled times that followed brought the military usefulness of the Indians to an end. Officials of the Indian department no longer felt it necessary to appease them by protecting their lands. And transfer of the department from military to civilian control in 1830 signified that the relationship between the two peoples had changed fundamentally.[6]

The Indian department was organized in a haphazard and unsystematic way, reflecting its relative unimportance. The Colonial Office in London was largely responsible for its operations, but the Treasury and Army Commissariat also had roles to play. It was financed in part by an imperial grant, which was rarely generous. Additional monies came from a number of funds created by the sale of Indian lands and of resources therefrom.[7] The tradition of subsidizing Indian administration from such trust funds continued long after Confederation.

Many Indians fared poorly after coming into contact with white civilization. Their numbers were often decimated by the ravages of diseases to which they had no immunity. And they lost their economic independence as the fur trade moved the centre of its operations to distant territories in the northwest. As their lands were taken for settlement, their plight became increasingly unenviable.

This situation attracted the attention of the British Colonial Office in the 1830s, and it was decided that a policy of assimilation would solve the "Indian problem." Under the guidance of government agents and evangelical missionaries, the Indians were to be settled in permanent villages and instructed in the English language, Christianity, and agricultural methods. The hoped-for result would be self-supporting individuals who were indistinguishable from their fellow citizens.

The Indian department was strongly behind the civilization program, although its enthusiasm was largely inspired by self-interest. The department needed a new purpose or its days might be numbered. After all, voices were already being raised in London calling for its abolition.

But Sir Francis Bond Head, who arrived as lieutenant-governor of Upper Canada in 1836, had his own views on the problem at hand. Convinced that the Indians were a doomed race, he resolved to relocate them on the islands of the Manitoulin area where they could live out their final days in relative peace. Large-scale land surrenders were secured as a prelude to this removal. Native unrest and protests by missionaries followed, and Head's operation was halted by the Colonial Office.

By 1838 the program of civilization was again in effect, but with few state resources allocated to it. The task of cultural transformation was placed almost entirely in the hands of the missionary churches. As a result of their endeavours, a number of industrial schools and model villages made their appearance. The money and manpower at the disposal of the missionaries was limited, however, and "progress" was necessarily slow. Those engaged in the work came to realize that the period of protection and guidance might be a prolonged one.[8]

The historical experience of the Indians of Lower Canada was substantially different. While the French regime had often implicitly recognized native sovereignty in its dealings with the various tribes, no land surrenders or treaties in the British tradition had taken place. A number of reserves were created, nonetheless, at the initiative of the church and the state. Some Indians settled on them in an experiment at sedentary living. These reserves were confirmed by the British in the Articles of Capitulation, 1760.[9] In the post-conquest era, the treaty system was not extended to the colony, but additional reserves were granted over the years. Under both regimes, the pressure to conform to European ways was applied to the Indians relentlessly.

Prior to 1850 there was no legislation in either Upper or Lower Canada for the protection of Indian lands. As settlement intensified, reserves were increasingly encroached upon by squatters, and resources such as timber were taken at will. To offer the Indians some measure of protection, the assembly of the United Canadas passed two pieces of legislation in 1850, "An Act for the better protection of the Lands and Property of the Indians in Lower Canada" and "An Act for the protection of the Indians in Upper Canada from imposition and the property occupied or enjoyed by them from trespass and injury."

The Lower Canada legislation vested all Indian land and property in a commissioner of Indian lands, who had control over leasing and the collection of rents. But what was most interesting about the statute was that it offered the first definition of an Indian—someone of Indian blood reputed to belong to a particular tribe. The spouses, children, and adopted children of such individuals were also included in the definition. The legislation was amended in the following year to exclude non-Indian males married to Indian women.[10]

In Upper Canada the statute prohibited the conveyance of Indian lands without crown consent. In addition, Indians were declared not liable to taxation or for the payment of debts under certain circumstances.

While these measures were designed to offer a modicum of protection, it was envisaged that such tutelege would not always be required, and so a mechanism enabling Indians to take on the responsibilities of full citizenship was soon put into place. The "Act for the Gradual Civilization of the Indian Tribes in the Canadas," 1857, specified that an adult male Indian who was of good character, free of debt, and fluent in either English or French, would be eligible for enfranchisement, that is, full citizenship. As an inducement to take this step, he could be offered up to fifty acres of reserve land in fee simple and a share of band funds.[11]

The Indians objected vigorously to this legislation which they correctly perceived as a threat to the integrity of their lands. Between 1857 and 1867 only an insignificant number applied for enfranchisement, and only one was accepted. The authorities blamed tribal councils for organizing resistance to the measure.[12]

The initiative of the Canadas in passing such legislation showed that responsibility for dealing with Indians was passing out of the hands of the imperial administration, and in 1860, the Indian department was transferred officially to colonial control. It was one of the last services to be so transferred, and it was only reluctantly accepted by the Canadian authorities. Upon this transition, Indian administration became one of the many branches of the Crown Lands Department and the commissioner of crown lands acquired the title of superintendent general of Indian affairs. Two years later, William Spragge, a long-serving employee of Crown Lands, was elevated to the position of deputy superintendent general of Indian affairs,[13] the title by which the permanent head or chief civil servant of the Indian department would be known until 1936.

By the creation of the new Dominion in 1867, a clearly identifiable branch of the public service had thus been developed for dealing with Indians. In addition, a body of legislation was in place which placed the Indian in a distinct legal category, protected his lands, granted him a number of privileges, and imposed certain disabilities. A mechanism for eliminating all such distinctions between Indians and non-Indians had also been devised.

The tradition of Indian administration that emerged in the Maritimes differed in a number of important respects. The Micmacs and Malecites of that region came into contact with the French during the early years of their exploration and colonization of the continent. The French presence in Acadia was never substantial, and they did not subdue or destroy the native population. They did, however, succeed in converting the Indians to Catholicism and in winning their support in the struggle with the English.[14]

After the loss of Acadia in 1713, the French, from their bastion at Louisbourg, attempted to retain the friendship of the Indians by distributing presents and using the influence of missionaries. It was believed that they would be useful allies in future contests with the English.

During the first half of the eighteenth century, the English did not commit extensive forces to the defence of Nova Scotia. With only a fort at Annapolis and a fishing station at Canso, they too were obliged to seek the goodwill of the Indians. But with the construction of Halifax in 1749, the expulsion of the Acadians in the 1750s, and the conquest of New France and Louisbourg a few years later, the English position became secure and that of the Indians increasingly precarious.[15] The change was more evident as thousands of Loyalists, fleeing the American republic in the early 1780s, made the colony their destination.

Prince Edward Island had had its own government since 1769, and in 1784 Nova Scotia was partitioned to create the colony of New Brunswick with its capital at Fredericton. Indian policy was now in the hands of three colonial jurisdictions. But attitudes towards the native population in Halifax, Fredericton, and Charlottetown did not differ substantially, and the policies adopted were more remarkable for their similarities than for anything else.

In Nova Scotia and New Brunswick aboriginal title was not recognized, and all land was presumed to belong to the Crown. Consequently, no surrenders or treaties were considered necessary. As their traditional domains were invaded by settlers, the Indians had to petition the colonial governments for lands of their own. As a result, a number of reserves were granted. These were constantly invaded by squatters, and the authorities seemed unwilling or unable to take remedial measures. The Indians were gradually demoralized and impoverished, and many were forced to resort to begging or peddling artifacts to make a living. Relief was voted intermittently by the colonial governments in cases of extreme need.

It was not until the 1840s that some effort was made to find a place for the Indians in society. Largely because of intervention by London, an Indian commissioner was appointed in Nova Scotia. His goal was to lead the native population to self-sufficiency through education and training in agriculture. The education program was frustrated by a variety of factors. School boards were generally unwilling to accept Micmac children into their classrooms, and the assembly refused to pay the expenses involved. The Indians themselves were suspicious of the whiteman's schools, and they were reluctant to part with their children. The promotion of agriculture was hampered by widespread potato blight in the second half of the decade. By the 1850s, almost all initiatives had been abandoned, and Indian administration confined itself to the distribution of relief and dealing with squatters on reserves.[16]

In New Brunswick around the same time Moses H. Perley advocated a similar program. The sale and leasing of surplus Indian lands would finance education in trades and agriculture and self-sufficiency and assimilation would be achieved at no great cost to the taxpayer. As in the neighbouring colony, the scheme foundered. Reserve lands were sold cheaply or on credit, and very little money was raised for the benefit of the Indians.[17]

On Prince Edward Island the native experience was equally discouraging. In 1767 the entire island was granted to absentee British proprietors. Nothing was left for the Indians, and they survived by squatting on land to which they held no title, fishing a little, and selling handicrafts. The assembly continued to ignore their plight, and it was only on the initiative of some well-meaning individuals that Lennox Island was purchased for them in 1870. Here they were able to make some progress in agriculture and fishing. When P.E.I. entered Confederation in 1873, there were 302 Micmacs to be brought under the jurisdiction of the federal Indian department. Lennox Island and a small lot on the Morell River were their only reserves.[18]

By Confederation the Indians of the Maritimes had experienced a century of indifference at the hands of the settler population, the local assemblies, and the Colonial Office. They had been deprived of their lands without compensation. And even where reserves had been granted, they had been whittled away by encroachment or by ill-advised sales and leases. Indians were denied the vote and other civil rights. However, at least in Nova Scotia, they were allowed to hold land individually and were liable for debts.[19] No body of protective legislation or special department with exclusive jurisdiction over their affairs had appeared. These they were to experience for the first time after Confederation.

In the Pacific Northwest, sustained contact between Indians and Europeans began with the maritime-based fur trade of the late eighteenth century. In the early decades of the nineteenth century, the trade became increasingly centred at forts established on the coast and in the interior by the North West Company, and this tendency became more pronounced after its merger with the Hudson's Bay Company in 1821. The combined company proceeded to secure a virtual monopoly by forcing out its Russian and American competitors.

Robin Fisher maintains that the fur trade was an enterprise of mutual benefit to Indians and whites during both its maritime and land-based phases. The Indians quickly came to realize the value of the pelts they had for sale and were prepared to negotiate at length to secure the best possible prices. It was a profitable business for them, and their standard of living improved. Of course, there were also disadvantages such as the introduction of respiratory diseases, smallpox, and other maladies.[20] Relations between Indians and whites were generally good. The traders knew that antagonism would be bad for business and that their isolated forts could be eliminated easily in the event of hostility.

The establishment of the colony of Vancouver Island in 1849 heralded change. The charter granted to the Hudson's Bay Company seemed to imply that settlement would not be pursued with such vigour as to hinder the fur trade. Indeed, settlers were slow to arrive, but that was largely owing to the unattractiveness of the Island compared to such places as California.

James Douglas, the chief factor at Fort Victoria, was appointed governor of the colony in 1851 after the departure of the ineffectual first appointee, Richard Blanshard. The Colonial Office left relations with Indians very much in Douglas's hands. London was justifiably confident that this experienced fur trader could maintain native goodwill. As settlers arrived during the 1850s, the governor signed fourteen treaties with the Indians around Fort Victoria, Fort Rupert, and Nanaimo. In return for surrendering their lands, the Indians were offered small reserves, a few blankets, the right to hunt on unoccupied land, and the right to fish as hitherto.[21]

A large influx of gold seekers in 1858 meant the end of the fur trade era. The mainland, known until then as New Caledonia, was transformed into the colony of British Columbia, and Douglas was chosen as its first governor. He retained the governorship of Vancouver Island, and in the same year that colony severed its special relations with the Hudson's Bay Company.[22]

Miners and settlers had little time for Indians, and conflicts between the two races became frequent. What the Indians resented most was the occupation of their lands without compensation. While Douglas wanted both colonies to be settled by whites, he did not want the Indians to be swept aside in the process. But his policy of purchasing aboriginal title on the Island soon ran into difficulty with an unsympathetic House of Assembly that refused to vote money for such purposes. The Colonial Office proved equally unsympathetic, and after 1859 no compensation was offered when Indian lands were occupied. Reserves continued to be laid out, but there were no more treaties or payments. A similar policy was adopted on the mainland.

Douglas insisted that the Indians should be granted reserves adequate for their needs and the allotments were sometimes generous, at least by later standards. The Crown retained title for fear that their inhabitants might be swindled out of their holdings by unscrupulous settlers. And so reserves remained secure during Douglas's regime. In fact, Indians were allowed to add to their property by pre-emption and purchase under the same conditions as whites.

After Douglas's retirement in 1864, Indian policy fell into the hands of J.W. Trutch, who was appointed chief commissioner of lands and works for British Columbia, a position he was to hold until 1871. An engineer and surveyor by trade, Trutch was unsympathetic to Indians, whom he regarded as lazy and dangerous and as an impediment to the progress of the colony. Much of the reserve land granted in Douglas's time was taken away as a result of his initiatives. Reserves were "adjusted," which meant that large valuable tracts were cut off and opened to white settlement. A land ordinance in 1866 prevented Indians from pre-empting land without the written permission of the governor. While they were thereby virtually denied the possibility of acquiring individual holdings and while their reserves were being reduced in such a way that a family was expected to exist on about 10 acres, whites were permitted to pre-empt 160 acres and purchase an additional 480.[23]

Trutch's policies were in harmony with settler demands. Indian protests were futile, and when restlessness and violence predictably appeared, harsh repression followed, including the bombardment of coastal villages by British warships.[24] When British Columbia entered Confederation in 1871, Victoria's concept of reserve entitlement and its refusal to acknowledge aboriginal title constituted major grievances on the part of the native population. They were to continue as major sources of contention between the federal and provincial governments and the Indian people for many decades thereafter (see Chapter Eight).

The British North America Act of 1867, which established the Dominion of Canada, granted responsibility for "Indians and lands reserved for Indians" to the federal government. Rather than initiate original or innovative policies, the Dominion chose to continue with and to build upon the patterns that had been established in the Canadas. Consequently, existing Indian legislation was confirmed by the new federal government.[25]

The Indian department was initially attached to the department of the secretary of state. In 1873, however, the Department of the Interior was created, and Indian affairs came under its jurisdiction as the Indian Branch. The title superintendent general of Indian affairs automatically accrued to the incumbent minister of the interior.[26]

A number of important additions were made to existing Indian legislation in 1869. The superintendent general was empowered to grant "location tickets" to specific tracts of reserve land. This was designed to encourage Indians in the practice of private property and in land use in the white man's manner. It was seen as a first step to enfranchisement.[27] Legislation also allowed for the election of chiefs and councillors by male band members twenty-one years of age or older.[28]

One of the immediate challenges facing the Indian Branch was the extension of its jurisdiction to all areas of the Dominion. An administrative structure based loosely on what had evolved in Upper and Lower Canada was decided upon. At that time Ontario was divided into seven superintendencies, each containing a number of reserves, with officials bearing the title of visiting superintendent or agent in charge. Quebec also had seven superintendencies.

The same type of administrative structure was soon created in the Maritimes. One agency was created on Prince Edward Island and three in New Brunswick, each with full-time officials in charge. In Nova Scotia, nineteen administrative units were created. There the agents were usually local farmers, physicians, or clergymen who only attended to Indian affairs on a part-time basis. The native population of the Maritimes was by this time so small that it posed no threat to the dominant society. Thus, Ottawa tended to ignore it and concentrated its efforts instead on the Indians of British Columbia and the Prairies who were not just a majority in their respective regions, but who were also viewed with a certain apprehension.[29]

The creation of the federal bureaucracy in British Columbia began with the appointment of Israel Wood Powell as superintendent of Indian affairs in 1872. Powell was a local politician and physician who, by all accounts, knew little about Indians upon his appointment. His office was located in Victoria, and he continued to maintain his medical practice while attending to his new responsibilities. In 1874 a second superintendency headed by James Lenihan was created with headquarters at New Westminster. Powell remained the senior official with primary responsibility for Vancouver Island and the coastal region, while Lenihan was mainly concerned with the interior.[30]

The division into two superintendencies was abolished in 1880 to pave the way for the establishment of six agencies the following year. The position of superintendent of Indian affairs for the province was retained, however, and Powell remained in office until 1890.[31]

The prairie region undoubtedly presented the greatest difficulty to Ottawa in its efforts to establish a uniform system of Indian administration. The area had long been under the exclusive jurisdiction of the Hudson's Bay Company—part of its fur empire of Rupert's Land and the North-Western Territory. These domains were transferred to the federal government in 1870, the same year in which the "postage stamp" province of Manitoba was created. The balance of the area, the Northwest Territories, remained relatively unorganized. However, it was obvious that if Ottawa were to establish its claim on a firmer footing, the fertile lands, already attracting the attention of covetous eyes south of the border, would have to be occupied by settlers as soon as possible. A railway connecting the disparate parts of the sprawling Dominion was also deemed necessary, and it was promised as part of the agreement under which British Columbia entered Confederation in 1871.

The railway and settlement would go hand in hand, but before they could proceed, Ottawa was obliged to seek the surrender of the Indian title. This procedure had a long history in Upper Canada, and it was now to be transferred to the west in a more elaborate form. The western Indians had already been demoralized by the ravages of epidemics and the illicit whiskey trade, and as the 1870s passed, they witnessed the rapid disappearance of their principal means of sustenance, the buffalo. The treaty system appeared to offer at least the prospect of survival, and most Indian leaders were prepared to accept it.

Between 1871 and 1877 the first seven of the "numbered" treaties were signed. These agreements secured for the federal government the Indian title to all of the fertile lands in the southern part of what are today the prairie provinces. In addition, Treaty No. 3 achieved the surrender of that part of the Canadian shield lying between the Manitoba border and Lake Superior, an area later incorporated into Ontario. Its surrender, along with that of the fertile belt, paved the way for the construction of the transcontinental railway.

In return for the surrender of their lands, the treaties granted the Indians reserves; a gratuity upon signing; annuities of five dollars per person; supplies of tools, ammunition, and similar commodities; free schooling; and the right to hunt on unoccupied lands. Chiefs received additional considerations such as flags, medals, suits of clothing, and larger cash payments. The provisions varied from treaty to treaty, but they were similar in most important respects. Treaty No. 6, for instance, was the only one in which allowance was made for medical treatment. It was provided that the Indian agent should keep a "medicine chest" in his house for the benefit of the Indians.[32]

Treaties No. 1 and 2 were conducted in 1871 on behalf of the federal government by Wemyss Simpson and A.G. Archibald, the first lieutenant-governor of Manitoba, whose jurisdiction also extended to the Northwest Territories. His successor, Alexander Morris, officiated at Treaties Nos. 3, 4, 5, and 6 between 1873 and 1876. The presence of the North-West Mounted Police on the Prairies from 1874 onwards facilitated the process of treaty-signing and further legitimized the Dominion's authority in the region.

In 1873 a Board of Indian Commissioners was appointed to supervise relations with the native population of Manitoba and the Northwest Territories. It accomplished little, however, and in 1876 superintendents and agents were appointed. J.A.N. Provencher became superintendent of Indian affairs for Manitoba while in the Northwest Territories the title went to David Laird,[33] who had served as minister of the interior in Alexander Mackenzie' s Liberal administration since 1873. He was also made lieutenant-governor of the Territories.

With his headquarters at Battleford, the new capital, his immediate task was to establish a form of government. The Indians were one of his major responsibilities, and it was he who conducted Treaty No. 7 with the Blackfoot in 1877.

Provencher was dismissed from office in 1878, and in the same year Laird asked to be relieved of his Indian superintendent's duties. In the following year Edgar Dewdney, Conservative M.P. for Yale and a favourite of John A. Macdonald, who was now back in power, was appointed to replace both men. His initial title was Indian commissioner for the Northwest Territories, but early in 1880 his mandate was expanded to include the province of Manitoba and the district of Keewatin. When Laird's term of office as lieutenant-governor came to an end in 1881, he was succeeded by Dewdney, who retained the position of Indian commissioner.[34] The position of Indian commissioner was subsequently held by Hayter Reed (1888-93), Amedee E. Forget (1893-98), and David Laird (1898-1909), when it was abolished in a general re-organization of Indian Affairs.

The commissioner of Indian affairs was the principal official of the Indian Branch (later, the Department of Indian Affairs) on the Prairies. Under his guidance the provisions of the treaties were administered. He organized the surveying of reserves and the settlement of Indians on them. A complex bureaucracy of Indian agents and agency inspectors was created to carry out his instructions in the far-flung corners of his domains. The commissioner, in turn, reported to the headquarters of the Indian Branch in Ottawa.[35]

As an Indian administrative structure was being created in the new provinces and territories, it also became necessary for the Dominion to introduce order and consistency to the legislation affecting Indians. This was accomplished largely by the Indian Act of 1876, which consolidated existing legislation and allowed for its uniform application across the country, with some minor exceptions.

The Indian Act continued the tradition that had developed in Upper and Lower Canada by placing the Indians in a distinct legal category. They were regarded as minors—special wards of the federal government who were deprived of the privileges of full citizenship.

It was naturally imperative that those falling into this special class be carefully identified. An Indian was defined as a male of Indian blood "reputed to belong to a particular band." The wives and children of such persons were also included. Indian women who married non-Indians were excluded, although they were allowed to continue receiving their share of band revenues and annuities. A band itself was defined as a body of Indians holding lands or a reserve in common or for whom funds were held in trust by the federal government.

Special measures were written into the act to protect the integrity of reserve lands. They were held in trust by the Crown for the benefit of the Indians, and they could not be mortgaged or seized in lieu of a debt. Clause 26 did allow for the surrender of such properties, but only upon agreement by a majority of male band members over twenty-one at a meeting specially called for that purpose. The surrender had to be approved by the superintendent general of Indian affairs, and it could be made only to the Crown. The consent of the band was required before the superintendent general could issue licences for the removal of timber or stone from a reserve. And again, it was only with band consent that the superintendent general could issue location tickets to specific reserve lots. What these measures meant was that the Indians were always to be consulted on the question of disposing of their lands and resources. Revenue from the sale of such properties was to be held in trust for the band by the government. Up to 10 per cent, however, could be paid directly to the Indians.

Clauses 61 to 63 allowed for the election of chiefs and councillors by adult male band members. Chiefs were to hold office for three years, but they could be deposed at any time by the governor-in-council for "dishonesty, intemperance, immorality, or incompetency." Chiefs-in-council were granted the power to make regulations regarding the maintenance of roads and bridges; the construction and repair of schools and other public buildings; the granting of reserve lots; and the suppression of "intemperance and profligacy." These powers were later extended to include such matters as the "repression of noxious weeds." These measures were designed to encourage the Indians to adopt some responsibility for their own affairs and to give them experience in the democratic process. Clauses 64 to 69 dealt with the privileges of Indians. Perhaps the most important of these was exemption from taxation on reserve property.

A number of disabilities were listed under Clauses 70 to 73. For instance Indians in Manitoba, the Northwest Territories, and Keewatin were forbidden to acquire land by the homestead or pre-emption method. A similar piece of legislation already existed in British Columbia, and it was therefore unnecessary to mention that province. This was one of the instances in which the act differentiated between western and eastern Indians.

"Intoxicants" required seven clauses in all (79 to 85). It was forbidden to sell liquor to Indians, and they were forbidden to manufacture it, to be in possession of it, or to be in a state of intoxication. Selling liquor to Indians could bring a jail sentence of one to six months, and, in addition, the "barrell, keg, case, box, package, receptacle or vessel" which contained the offending substance could be seized and destroyed.

Clauses 86 to 94 outlined the procedures for enfranchisement, or the relinquishment of Indian status. The candidate for enfranchisement was required, first of all, to receive the permission of his band and an individual allotment of reserve land. He then could make application to the superintendent general, who would investigate his suitability in terms of sobriety and civilization. If the superintendent general were satisfied on those accounts, he would grant a location ticket to the candidate, who would then enter a probationary period of not less than three years. If all went well, the candidate would be eligible for title to his land in fee simple, a share of band funds, and enfranchisement. Western Indians were excluded from taking advantage of this procedure.[36] Presumably they were considered insufficiently advanced on the road to civilization. An amendment in 1880, however, permitted the governor-in-council to apply the enfranchisement provisions to any band of Indians.

The Act of 1876 created the legislative framework for an Indian policy that was applied more or less uniformly across the country. It granted considerable powers to the superintendent general and his representatives and ensured that Indians were increasingly subjected to bureaucratic regulation.[37] The act was amended over the years, but in its general thrust and intent, it changed little. It was designed to protect the Indians until they acquired the trappings of white civilization. At that point, they were supposed to abandon their reserves and their special status and disappear into the general population.

In an amendment to the Indian Act in 1880, the Indian Branch was elevated to the status of a department in its own right—the Department of Indian Affairs. It remained, however, under the direction of the minister of the interior, who continued to hold the title of superintendent general of Indian affairs.[38] Indian administration was usually regarded as a minor component of that minister's portfolio, and, in practice, effective decision-making lay in the hands of the deputy superintendent general, the head of the department. This practice became well established during the tenure of Lawrence Vankoughnet, who served as deputy superintendent from 1874 until 1893.[39] Vankoughnet was a lifelong friend of John A. Macdonald, and when the Conservative leader returned to power in 1878, retaining the interior portfolio in his own hands, the deputy superintendent was given virtually a free hand in running his department.

The department was organized into an inside and outside service. The inside service consisted of the headquarters staff in Ottawa. By the early 1880s it comprised the deputy superintendent general, a chief clerk, an accountant, a small clerical staff and a number of messengers, packers, and other unskilled personnel. The total number of employees was less than forty. Most of the clerks were engaged in copying letters into letter books before typewriters arrived in the middle of the decade.[40]

The outside service was by far the largest component of the department, amounting to 460 employees by 1890. These were the workers in the field—the men and women who dealt with Indians directly and who were responsible for policy implementation at the local level. The most important of them were the Indian agents, whose administrative units contained one or more reserves. Their responsibilities were extensive: they directed farming operations where appropriate; they administered relief when necessary; they inspected schools and health conditions; and they ensured that the rules of the department and the provisions of the Indian Act were complied with. They were also authorized to preside over band council meetings, and while they could not vote, they were often able to influence the decisions made. Their powers were increased considerably in 1881 when an amendment to the Indian Act made them justices of the peace under the act. They could then prosecute and hand down sentences for violations of its provisions.[41]

The outside service was ultimately responsible to headquarters. Nevertheless, through the offices of the Indian commissioner for Manitoba and the North-west Territories and that of the Indian superintendent for British Columbia, some initiative was left to the men in the field. Vankoughnet was, however, an inflexible bureaucrat who attempted to centralize all decision-making in his own hands. This was bitterly resented by western officials, who felt, reasonably enough, that their knowledge of local conditions made them better judges on questions of policy implementation and procedure. Since communication between the west and Ottawa was slow, attempts at centralizing made for very inefficient administration. Nevertheless, the tendency towards the centralization continued after Vankoughnet's departure.

John A. Macdonald's "national policy" involved the location of the western Indians on reserves and the settlement of the Prairies by those who would till the soil. Settlement was slow at first, but it began to accelerate in the early 1880s when the CPR reached the west. This development was a further harbinger of doom for the region's native population. The buffalo were gone, and the Indians were finding the transition to agriculture and a sedentary existence difficult to make. The sight of their former hunting grounds being occupied by newcomers only added to their sense of grievance. And grievance turned to unrest as it became clear that the government's promise to look after them in times of hardship was not being kept. Supplies sent west were frequently inadequate to avert starvation and destitution. Vankoughnet's policy of keeping expenses at a minimum was largely responsible for the growing native discontent, and it was a major contributing factor to Indian participation in the North-West Rebellion of 1885.[42] The rebellion tended to confirm in the minds of department officials that the western Indians constituted a potential menace and that they would have to be watched carefully. Edgar Dewdney and Hayter Reed, who had been obliged to deal with the rebels directly, blamed Vankoughnet's obsession with economy and centralization for the episode. After the death of John A. Macdonald in 1891, they began to move against him. They found a sympathetic ear in T. Mayne Daly, minister of the interior in John Thompson's administration, and in 1893 Daly forced Vankoughnet to retire. The deputy superintendent left on 27 July of that year, and Duncan Campbell Scott, an ambitious young man who had recently been promoted to chief clerk and accountant of the department, was chosen to act in his place while a permanent successor was being chosen.[43] The choice turned out to be Hayter Reed, Indian commissioner for Manitoba and the Northwest Territories since 1888.[44]

The departure of Vankoughnet did not usher in an era of lavish spending on the "Indian problem." Indian administration continued to be circumscribed by an obsession with economy. This was an inescapable by-product of the relative insignificance attached to such matters in successive governments' budgetary allocations, but it also reflected an almost universal conviction on the part of department officials that "gratuitous aid" should never be granted to "able-bodied Indians." Bringing the native population to self-sufficiency was one of the principal aims of the department. In fact, his ability to make the Indians under his charge economically independent was often the measure of success or failure of an Indian agent. This was especially so on the Prairies where expenses were particularly high because of the destitution which followed the destruction of the buffalo, the difficulties encountered by the Indians in adopting agriculture, and the promises made in the treaties.

Education had long been viewed as an effective instrument for the transmission of new economic habits to the Indians, and, of course, it was also seen as the key to their cultural transformation. During the decades following Confederation, a network of department-sponsored "Indian schools" (both day and residential) was established across the country to accelerate the accomplishment of these ends. This involved major capital and on-going operating costs, but by working in conjunction with the principal Christian missionary churches, substantial savings were effected (see Chapter Five). The Indians were often not enthusiastic about the prospect of their children being re-socialized in the white man's classroom. Some measure of coercion was therefore found necessary. The Indian Act was amended in 1894 to allow the governor-in-council to make regulations regarding attendance of Indian children at school. Deputy Superintendent Reed, who had had personal experience of Indian hostility to schooling in the Northwest, was largely responsible for this measure.[45]

Co-operation between the churches and the state was also evident in other aspects of Indian administration. The missionaries were frequently frustrated in their efforts at evangelization by the persistence of certain aspects of native culture which they regarded as fundamentally incompatible with Christianity. It was missionary agitation that led to the proscription of some of these customs under the Indian Act. Under an 1884 amendment, Clause 3 prohibited the celebration of the potlatch and the dance known as "Tamanawas," with penalties ranging from two to five months' imprisonment for violations.[46] In 1895, this prohibition was extended to dances in which the "wounding or mutilation" of persons or animals was involved[47] (see Chapter Nine).

When existing legislation had been consolidated and refined in 1876, specific guarantees had been written into the act for the protection of Indian lands and property. But as time passed, the federal government found itself under increasing pressure to modify them. The advancement of settlement, especially in the west, meant that reserves attracted the attention of those who sought cheap land and who felt that the Indians were not using their property to its maximum advantage. Slowly and almost imperceptibly at first, the Indian Act was amended to accommodate their demands. In 1894, for example, an amendment allowed the superintendent general to lease the lands of Indians unable to work it themselves because of illness or disability, without first securing a surrender. This clause was amended, it should be noted, in the following year to require the consent of the location ticket holder to the lease, but not that of the band.[48] It represented the thin end of the wedge of confiscation. For the first time, reserve lands became available for the use of non-Indians without the acquiescence of the band. Amendments of a more substantial nature followed as settlers, municipalities, and railway and resource companies demanded access to what they regarded as "surplus" and "idle" Indian lands. Official disillusionment with the reserve system, which came to be seen as a hindrance to assimilation, accelerated this trend.

In 1896, after several years of decline following the death of John A. Macdonald, the Conservatives lost power to Wilfrid Laurier's Liberals. The new minister of the interior was the energetic maverick from Manitoba, Clifford Sifton. While Sifton's principal preoccupation during his term of office was the settlement of the west, he did give some attention to the Indian component of his portfolio. Upon appointment, he observed that there were almost as many officials as there were Indians and that this situation would not be allowed to continue.[49] And gross inefficiency within the department also came to his attention. He noted, for instance, that a "deluge" of letters remained unanswered, some of which had been received several years previously.[50]

The Liberals had been critical of government spending while in opposition, and now that they were in power, they felt obliged to take measures of economy. Sifton applied drastic surgery to Indian Affairs, reducing staff and budgets and reorganizing its structure. Hayter Reed, the deputy superintendent general of Indian affairs, and A.M. Burgess, the deputy minister of the interior, were removed from office and replaced by a single deputy, James A. Smart, an old political ally of Sifton's.[51]

The greatest savings were to be expected in Manitoba and the Northwest Territories, where by far the largest proportion of the department's expenses were incurred. Western administration was the responsibility of the Indian commissioner, whose office was located in Regina. The incumbent at the time was Amedee E. Forget, a native of Quebec who had originally gone west as secretary to Sifton's Lieutenant-Governor David Laird in 1876.[52] Shortly after appointment, Forget made a number of suggestions to effect greater efficiency. He proposed the centralization of decision making in Ottawa and a corresponding reduction in the commissioner's role. The commissioner's office should be moved from Regina to Winnipeg and its staff reduced from fourteen to three. Some agencies could be consolidated, allowing for a further reduction in manpower.[53] Sifton was generally in agreement with these proposals, and the reorganization was implemented. The commissioner's role was reduced to inspecting agencies and schools.

Forget did not hold the position much longer. In 1898, he resigned to become lieutenant-governor of the Northwest Territories. A new Indian commissioner had to be found, and the man who had filled the post in the 1870s, David Laird, offered his services once more. Laird had left the west in 1881 and had spent the intervening years in his native Prince Edward Island. Success eluded him in the newspaper business and in his efforts to return to politics. By the time the commissioner's position became available, he was in some financial difficulty, and he appealed to Laurier for the appointment. Being a prominent Liberal, he was not denied, and by October 1898, he was on his way west to the commissioner's headquarters in Winnipeg.[54]

The reorganization of the department enabled Sifton to dispense with many employees. Some positions were cancelled permanently, but many of those dismissed were replaced by Liberal supporters. Patronage was customary in public service appointments, and the government defended its actions by claiming that certain agents were guilty of political partisanship during the general election and deserved dismissal.[55]

Further measures of economy were effected by reducing salaries. Those of Indian agents, for instance, which had ranged up to $1,400 per annum, were reduced to around $900 or $1,000. Clerks and farming instructors also received decreases.[56]

These reforms did result in some savings, but many of the department's expenditures were for fixed items such as treaty payments and the maintenance of schools, and these obligations limited the reductions that could be made. After initial cuts, salary levels and the size of the department began to grow again. The centralization of decision-making meant greater authority for headquarters officials such as secretary J.D. McLean and accountant Duncan Campbell Scott. Neither had much experience in dealing directly with Indians, but they shared Sifton's concern that expenses be minimized.

In 1902 Sifton abandoned his experiment of placing the Interior and Indian Affairs departments under one deputy. The responsibilities attendant upon immigration policy were proving to be more than enough for one man. Sifton's choice as the new deputy superintendent general of Indian affairs was Frank Pedley, a Toronto lawyer who had no previous experience of working with Indians. Evidently, petty rivalry between department officials prompted the appointment of an outsider.[57] The arrival of Pedley did not adversely affect the growing influence of D.C. Scott as decision-maker within the department. Since the new deputy superintendent was generally ignorant of existing practices and policies, he tended to rely on Scott's expertise, and a considerable proportion of his correspondence was actually prepared by the accountant.

The poor health and unacceptably high death rate of the native population was a source of concern both within and outside the department in Sifton's day.[58] The population continued to decline, and those critical of the government cited this fact as evidence of the failure of department policy. Yet instituting a comprehensive health scheme was resisted because of its high cost. Instead, the department relied on the services of local physicians on an *ad hoc* basis. And Sifton pointed out that they employed only those who could be relied on "not to attend the Indians except in cases of necessity," since free treatment led to demands for further treatment, and if proper judgment were not exercised, "the medical bill would run up to a very high figure."[59] In 1904, however, Sifton responded to the mounting criticism by appointing Dr. P.H. Bryce as medical inspector for both the Interior and Indian Affairs departments (see Chapter Five).[60]

Agriculture and ranching were promoted as ideal occupations for Indians, especially those on the Prairies, around this time. Annual reports of the department gave special attention to the numbers of cattle owned and to the acreages under cultivation. In Frank Pedley's opinion, agriculture was important because it secured "fixity of tenure," which was "the first and essential step towards any form of civilization." It also had the advantages of fostering "habits of industry" and being a means of economic self-sufficiency.[61]

Sifton expressed similar sentiments, and he was prepared to increase expenditure to encourage ranching and farming because of the benefits he believed would accrue. As he explained in the House of Commons in 1903:

> The Indians in the Calgary district, the Bloods, Piegans and Blackfeet, the most dangerous and difficult Indians to manage, have been induced to go into cattle raising to a very considerable extent, and I think that in five or six years perhaps we shall be able to discontinue the practice of giving rations altogether.[62]

One experiment in encouraging the Indians to use their land in the white man's manner appeared to be particularly successful—the File Hills colony, an experiment in radical social engineering initiated by W.M. Graham, agent at the Qu'Appelle agency near Regina in 1901. At that time boarding and industrial schools were viewed by both secular and ecclesiastical authorities as the great crucibles in which young Indians would shed their ancestral ways. But a major fear of missionaries and government officials was that upon graduation native boys and girls would return to their parents, losing those painfully acquired advances in civilization and Christianization. Graham established his colony to prevent this "retrogression."

File Hills was a farming settlement made up of carefully selected boys and girls who had graduated from boarding and industrial schools in the area.

Graham was involved in the selection of the colonists, and he was assisted by the principals of the File Hills Boarding School and the Lebret Industrial School. The young Indians were married off and settled in houses equipped with appropriate effects. They were also assigned individual tracts of land which they were expected to farm. Nineteen thousand acres on the Peepeekisis reserve were granted by the government for that purpose.

Graham carefully supervised the entire experiment. There was to be no contact between the colonists and the older Indians who adhered to traditional culture. And social interaction among the colonists themselves was closely monitored to prevent any lapse into tribal ways. For example, visits between households were strictly limited. Pow-wows, dances, and any other form of native ceremony considered "a hindrance to progress" were forbidden.

The objective of the colony was to produce a group of Indians who had internalized the white man's religion and culture and who were self-sufficient farmers. The economic aims were advanced not only by the activities of department farming instructors, but also by the deliberate promotion of the work ethic. Competition between colonists was encouraged by an annual exhibit at which prizes were awarded for achievements in grain-growing, cattle-breeding, cooking, and sewing. Competitive sports also helped to foster individualism and provided alternatives to traditional recreation practices. A brass band served a similar purpose.

In 1907 Graham wrote a report on the File Hills experiment. Its success in preventing cultural "regression" was, in his opinion, "phenomenal." At that stage there were twenty young families in the colony producing good crops and raising their children in the English language. One of the colonists, Fred Dieter, had even hired white men as farm help.[63]

Sifton was evidently impressed with Graham's work and cited his achievements in the House of Commons on a number of occasions as evidence of the progress that was being made. In 1902, for example, he credited Graham with the following state of affairs: "instead of having a horde of savages in the North-West, as we had a few years ago, we shall soon have an orderly, fairly educated population, capable of sustaining themselves."[64] In 1904, he was again praising Graham's accomplishments. Noting that the agent had been promoted to inspector, he observed that the agencies under his charge had shown the "greatest improvement" in the Northwest. In fact, things were so good that the distribution of rations had ceased to be necessary.[65]

Canada's jurisdiction in the north was gradually extended during Laurier's administration. Perhaps the most dramatic developments took place in the Yukon, which was organized as a district in 1895 and elevated to the status of territory three years later. The Mounted Police established a presence there during that decade as increasing activity by American miners demanded the assertion of Canadian authority.[66]

The excitement of the gold rush affected the native population of the territory very little. While some Indians found profitable employment during the boom years, most avoided the new towns and carried on in their traditional pursuits. The Church of England had been active in missionary work among them since the 1890s, and early in the new century, Bishop O.I. Stringer began to call upon the federal government to protect Indian rights, recognize their status, and offer treaties. Ottawa greeted these appeals with little enthusiasm. Nevertheless, the police were permitted to distribute relief in times of need, and some small grants were made to mission schools. In 1910, after a visit to the Yukon by Interior Minister Frank Oliver, Indian Affairs granted $30,000 for improvements to the boarding school at Carcross. This act of generosity was followed in 1914 by the appointment of the Rev. John Hawksley, an Anglican missionary, as the first superintendent of Indian affairs for the territory.[67] The extension of the Indian bureaucracy to other regions north of the sixtieth parallel was not accomplished until the 1920s, when Treaty No. 11 made such arrangements necessary.

Clifford Sifton's years in office are often remembered as a time of large-scale immigration to Canada—a phenomenon actively encouraged by the minister himself. The prairie region and British Columbia were the destinations of most of those who arrived, and the availability of farmland was the major attraction. As the best lands were occupied, settlers began to cast envious eyes on those held by Indians. Some argued that the Indians had been granted land far in excess of what they could use and that it should be "opened up" for settlement. Such demands were often made in parliament by MPs on behalf of their constituents.

In 1903, for example, W.A. Galliher, MP for Yale and Cariboo, asked Sifton if the reserve at Salmon Arm, which contained rich agricultural land, and that at Similkameen, which had "valuable deposits of precious metals," could be opened up. The minister observed that such a demand arose from "the natural feeling in human nature which causes one man sometimes to covet his neighbour's goods." He pointed out that reserves had been set aside in solemn arrangements between the Crown and the Indians and that they could not be disturbed.[68]

It was not widely known outside of the department that a formal surrender by the majority of adult male band members was required before reserve lands could be sold. Sifton was obliged to explain this in Parliament on a number of occasions. It was possible, however, for agents to put pressure on Indians to secure a surrender, and this happened frequently enough. Nevertheless, the minister refused to entertain amendments to the Indian Act which would have facilitated the process.

Sifton resigned in 1905 in a dispute with Laurier over the separate schools question in the new provinces of Alberta and Saskatchewan. His successor was Frank Oliver, who soon demonstrated that he had little regard for the integrity of Indian lands. When pressed in the Commons in March 1906 by Opposition leader Robert Borden on the question of large "unused" reserves which were hindering development in the prairie provinces, Oliver responded sympathetically. He conceded that, while Indian rights ought to be protected, they should not be allowed to interfere with those of whites—"and if it becomes a question between the Indians and the whites, the interests of the whites will have to be provided for." He assured the House that the department was making every effort to secure the surrender of "surplus" Indian land.[69]

Shortly afterwards, Oliver introduced an amendment to the Indian Act which was designed to facilitate the process. Speaking on the second reading of Bill 194, he pointed out that the prevailing regulations permitted the distribution of up 10 per cent of the purchase price of surrendered land to the Indians, while the remainder was put into band funds. This arrangement offered little incentive to the Indians to give up their land. Therefore, he proposed to allow up to 50 per cent of the purchase price to be distributed immediately to band members. The minister confidently predicted that the measure would accelerate the surrender process, and this was vitally necessary since the Indians on the Prairies held vast surpluses of land. In his opinion the allocation of one square mile per family of five under most of the western treaties had been excessive and ill-advised.[70] The amendment was adopted without dissent.

This amendment made it easier for department agents to persuade Indians to dispose of their lands, but band consent was still necessary. Nevertheless, the process of securing surrenders did not proceed with the haste that was anticipated. In 1911, Oliver successfully introduced two more amendments to the Indian Act which gave the department greater powers of coercion. Section 46 allowed portions of reserves to be taken by municipalities or companies for roads, railways, or similar public purposes without a surrender, but with the consent of the governor-in-council. Section 49a was even more controversial. It permitted the removal of Indians from any reserve next to or partly within a town of eight thousand inhabitants or more if the Exchequer Court of Canada so ruled.[71] This was the notorious "Oliver Act," which alarmed Indian leaders. They correctly perceived it as a major step in the erosion of band control of reserve lands.

In adopting these amendments, the government was acceding to the demands of those who coveted Indian land. But the measures also reflected the opinion of leading officials within Indian Affairs. Most amendments were initiated, after all, in the department.[72] For instance, Commissioner David Laird shared Oliver's opinion that western reserves were "much in excess" of what the Indians could use and that it was in their best interests to surrender such lands and to have the proceeds invested on their behalf.[73] In fact, department officials were increasingly coming to the view that reserves had outlived their usefulness. Frank Pedley suggested that they resulted in the isolation and segregation of Indians and thereby hindered progress. And in some instances they encouraged the perpetuation of the tribal form of government.[74]

During Laurier's term of office, the surrender and sale of Indian lands began to pick up momentum. Oliver told the House of Commons that between 1 July 1896 and 31 March 1909 the department had sold 725,517 acres of land surrendered from reserves for a total sum of $2,156,020. During the same period 1,020 Indian islands had been disposed of for $74,353.[75]

Securing the surrender of Indian lands was a policy approved of by politicians of every persuasion. Nonetheless, there were always some who found fault with either the price secured or the manner of disposal. Opposition members of Parliament were particularly critical of the way in which St. Peter's reserve near Selkirk, Manitoba, was surrendered. The surrender was obtained on 24 September 1907 in the presence of Frank Pedley, who evidently arrived with a briefcase bulging with $5,000 in cash. G.H. Bradbury, MP for Selkirk, accused the department of using bribery and trickery to secure the surrender. He also declared that potential purchasers were discouraged from making bids on the land while friends of the government staked out their claims. And the land was sold at five dollars an acre, while its true value was around twenty dollars.[76] Indian discontent over this transaction carried on for years. In 1911, the Manitoba government conducted an investigation which showed that irregularities of a substantial nature had indeed taken place.[77]

Further reorganization took place within the department before the end of Laurier's regime. In 1909, the commissioner's office in Winnipeg was closed, and David Laird was transferred to Ottawa where he continued to work in an advisory capacity until shortly before his death in January 1914.[78] In 1909 also, the department created the position of superintendent of education, and Duncan Campbell Scott was given the appointment, while retaining his accountant's responsibilities. It showed at once the increasing importance attached to education as far as policy was concerned and Scott's rising star within the department.

The Liberals were defeated in the general election of 1911, and Robert Borden's Conservatives formed a government in October of that year. The interior portfolio was held initially by Robert Rogers, but by December 1912, W.J. Roche was given the position. Among his first responsibilities as superintendent general of Indian affairs was to investigate the activities of Deputy Superintendent Frank Pedley. Pedley had become involved in speculation on the sale of Indian lands, and he was forced to resign in October 1913.[79] His successor was Duncan Campbell Scott, who for many years had been the real decision-maker within the department. Scott was to hold the position of deputy superintendent until 1932. During this period he was to be the principal architect of Indian policy.

2

The Poet and the Indians

The man who was to direct the federal Indian department for almost twenty years was a complex figure whose activities and influence extended far beyond the civil service. In fact, Duncan Campbell Scott's reputation is based largely upon his contributions to the world of *belles lettres*, while his role as government mandarin has been relatively ignored. But his career in the latter capacity and, in particular, his "attitude" to the native population has been the subject of much conjecture by commentators who have been evidently entranced by his poetic skills. A critical reassessment of Scott's worldview is long overdue.

Duncan Campbell Scott was born on 2 August 1862 in a parsonage near Parliament Hill in Ottawa. His father, William Scott, was a Methodist preacher who had emigrated from England in the 1830s, spending a number of years in the United States along the way.[1] His mother, Isabella Campbell McCallum, had been born in Lower Canada of Scottish parents.[2]

Though Ottawa was his birthplace, Scott spent his early years in the small towns and villages of Quebec and Ontario, which brought him into contact with French Canadians and Indians. They remained objects of curiosity to him throughout his life, and they were both featured prominently in his literary endeavours.

In spite of the financial constraints which the religious profession made inevitable, Scott's parents introduced him and his sisters to the arts as a matter of course. William Scott was better read than the average preacher and possessed a library of standard literary classics which he made available to his son. Scott's lifelong interest in music came from his mother, who encouraged him to study the piano from the age of seven.[3]

In 1877 the family settled for a while in Stanstead, Quebec, where Scott completed his formal education at the local Wesleyan college. He was by then fifteen, and he was giving some thought to a career in medicine. His mother's brother, Duncan Campbell McCallum, was a professor of medicine at McGill University, and this undoubtedly was a factor influencing his choice.[4]

With the impending retirement of his father, however, there was no money for medical studies. But William Scott had been a supporter of John A. Macdonald for many years, and in December 1879 he arranged for his son to have an interview with the prime minister with a view to employment in the civil service. No examination was necessary. The young Scott had merely to submit a specimen of his handwriting. It was found acceptable, and he was hired as a copy clerk in the Department of Indian Affairs. "It was a very efficient system," he remarked late in life. "You just had to be a friend of someone in the government."[5]

He came to enjoy his work, and on 8 October 1880 his appointment in the civil service was made permanent. During the decade that followed, he was promoted steadily as he demonstrated business acumen and a gift with figures. His devotion to organization aims undoubtedly also accelerated his advance. By the end of the 1880s, he was bookkeeper with an annual salary of $1,350, a substantial sum in those days. In 1891, he became the clerk in charge of the accountant's branch, a division of the department that was becoming increasingly important. Among its responsibilities was the administration of the Indian trust fund which continued to expand as reserve lands were sold and leased. On 1 July 1893, Scott was promoted to the position of chief clerk and accountant upon the superannuation of the incumbent, R. Sinclair.[6] In this role he monitored all department expenditure, and his influence on the direction of policy was thereby enhanced.[7]

Further evidence of Scott's rising star appeared in 1905 when he was appointed as one of the commissioners to negotiate Treaty No. 9 in the James Bay area of northern Ontario (see Chapter Four). His other promotions have already been alluded to: superintendent of education in 1909; deputy superintendent general in 1913. The latter advancement evidently came unexpectedly. His predecessors as department head had been political appointees, and Scott himself had never been active politically. Nonetheless, he had coveted the position and seemed to believe that it was rightfully his. Nor did he have any difficulty serving Conservative and Liberal governments with equanimity. Fortunately for him, the successive interior ministers/superintendents general tended to regard Indian Affairs as a minor component of their responsibilities, and Scott was given considerable freedom in determining the direction of policy and in mundane matters of administration.

While Scott's ultimate promotion had nothing to do with party politics, it did not mean that he was a man of no political opinions. Perhaps as a consequence of family tradition, he preferred the Conservatives to the Liberals.[8] The pro-British sentiments of the Tories undoubtedly appealed to him, and his views reflected that peculiar blend of imperial pride and patriotic attachment to the homeland that characterized English-Canadian nationalism.

Scott firmly believed in the great civilizing mission of the British Empire, and he saw Canada's international role as an integral component of that entity. The men who had built the Empire were among his great heroes. In his "Mermaid Inn" series, for example, he extolled the exploits on England's behalf of Sir George Grey in "less civilized quarters of the empire."[9] Grey's actions as a military commander and colonial administrator subduing aboriginal peoples helped to extend and strengthen British hegemony in Australia, New Zealand, and southern Africa during the nineteenth century. Similarly, in writing for an American audience in the *Bookman* of New York in 1896, Scott explained that the "manifest destiny of Canada is to be one of the greatest powers in the Federated Empire of England."[10]

Scott's imperialist sentiments were complemented by his chauvinism. He was a strong advocate of the teaching of Canadian history in school, and for overtly political reasons. It should be taught as a series of the "great deeds" and "heroic sufferings" of those who had founded the nation so that the young would be inspired to emulate them. Students should be made conscious of the country's roots; they should understand how "all its life flowed either from the old world or New England."[11] The native population, presumably, had contributed nothing to the life of the country.

Carl Berger, in his acclaimed study of Canadian political thought, *The Sense of Power*, argues that in the period 1867-1914, imperialism was the dominant form of nationalism. Those who adhered to this ideology longed for the day when their country would become an equal partner in a British imperial federation. In fact, some believed that Canada, because of its vigour (in comparison to the decadence that was observed in England) would ultimately become the dominant partner. The greatness of their country would thus be assured.[12] While Berger does not mention Scott specifically, his political ideas were virtually identical to those of Sir George Parkin, Col. George Taylor Denison, George Munro Grant, Stephen Leacock, and other contemporaries.

Scott's rise in the civil service was mainly the result of the attitudes and skills he brought to the job. Nonetheless, it is conceivable that his advancement was aided by the growing reputation he was acquiring for himself in the world of literature.

Scott's literary activities began at a relatively early stage in his career. In the service he met men who shared his interests in the arts. Most important among them was Archibald Lampman, who had entered the Post Office in 1883. Lampman had already published some poetry by the time they met, and he began to influence Scott in the same direction. The two men spent much of their leisure time together in the countryside surrounding Ottawa. Nature had been Lampman's principal source of inspiration, and it began to stir Scott's

imaginative powers as well. It had not occurred to him that he should write
poetry, or even prose, until then. Music had always been his principal means of
artistic expression. In fact, he had become quite an accomplished pianist, and
he had even begun to learn the violin. But as soon as he began to write, music
quickly took second place.[13]

One of Scott's first poems, "The Hill Path", was published in *Scribner's
Magazine* in May 1888. In 1893 his first collection of poems appeared—*The
Magic House and Other Stories*. These early efforts and his subsequent activities
during the 1890s helped to establish his reputation as a man of letters. Between
February 1892 and July 1893, he joined with Lampman and another civil
service poet, William Wilfred Campbell, to write a weekly column entitled "At
the Mermaid Inn" in the Toronto *Globe*. In this series, Scott and his companions
were intent upon creating an atmosphere supportive of the arts in Canada.
They deplored the tax on books, for example, which showed how misguided
official opinion was on the matter. They were particularly interested in fostering
Canadian talent and appealed for the establishment of a national literary
journal which would serve this purpose.[14]

During that decade Scott became a regular contributor to *Scribner's Magazine*.
The American monthly tended to publish material by established writers from
Britain and the United States, but it also gave an occasional opportunity to
newcomers. Quaint stories of French-Canadian life were already popular with
its readers, and when Scott began to experiment in this genre, his works found
immediate acceptance.[15] The success of his sketches of rural Quebec led
ultimately to the publication of *In the Village of Viger* in 1896.

In 1898 Scott's second volume of poetry, *Labour and the Angel* appeared.[16] The
first of his Indian poems, "Watkwenies" and "The Onondaga Madonna" were
featured in this collection.

Scott's lifelong friendship with Pelham Edgar also began in the 1890s. Edgar
was a bright young scholar and literary critic; later, he was to teach in the French
and English departments at Victoria College, Toronto. Scott often sent him his
latest poetry for evaluation before submitting it for publication. He regarded
Edgar's criticisms highly, and the changes he proposed were frequently adopted.[17]

Scott and Edgar worked closely together during the opening decade of the
new century when they were chosen as the joint editors of George Morang's
Makers of Canada. This twenty volume series of biographies was executed in the
"great man" tradition of history. In fact, the choice of editors was a strange one
since neither possessed credentials as historians. The Scott-Edgar correspondence shows that the two men were more concerned that their contributors
express themselves in elegant prose than that they adhere to the canons of
historical scholarship.[18]

Nevertheless, in the major controversy that surrounded the publication of
the series, Scott defended the right of authors to their own interpretation. The

controversy in question involved the selection of W.D. Le Sueur as the biographer of William Lyon Mackenzie. W.L. Mackenzie King, deputy minister of labour in Laurier's government and grandson of the rebel leader, opposed the choice of Le Sueur, whom he suspected would be critical. Scott became aware that King was putting pressure on Morang, and he denounced this interference to Edgar as "impertinent." He assured Edgar that Le Sueur's account would be "strictly impartial":

> There is no reason why the book should be designed simply to please Mackenzie King. His Grandad is part of his stock in trade and of course he is jealous that that stock should not become damaged on his hands in any way.[19]

But Scott's concern for fairness was of little avail. George Morang succumbed to King's pressure. When the publisher received the completed manuscript from Le Sueur early in 1908, he rejected it as unsuitable on the grounds of its negative conclusions. To compound matters, he refused to return the manuscript even though Le Sueur offered to repay his advance of $500. The author had to go to court to recover his work. In further court cases in 1912 and 1913 Mackenzie King successfully sought an injunction preventing Le Sueur from publishing his book at all by claiming that he had acquired access to the family papers under false pretences! A condensed version of Charles Lindsay's bland biography of Mackenzie, which had originally appeared in 1862, replaced Le Sueur's work in the series.[20]

Scott's own contribution was a volume on John Graves Simcoe, the first lieutenant-governor of Upper Canada. He saw much to admire in his subject, especially his "purity of purpose and his lofty rectitude." In fact, Scott suggested that the aim of the biography was to redirect the reading public to such neglected virtues. However, he was critical of the lieutenant-governor's plans to establish the Anglican church in Upper Canada, and he was not above employing a little sarcasm when discussing the narrowness of Simcoe's loyalism and his undemocratic tendencies.[21] But when it came to handling Indians, especially the troublesome Iroquois, Scott was not stinting in his praise:

> He was an ideal representative of that firm, true and uniform policy that has made the Canadian Indian believe the British sovereign his great parent and himself a child under beneficent protection.[22]

No doubt Scott saw himself carrying on in that great tradition of Indian administration.

In 1905 another of Scott's volumes of collected poetry, *New World Lyrics and Ballads*, was published. The dominance of Indian themes in these works was conspicuous. "The Forsaken," in particular, has attracted considerable attention over the years, and it continues to be the subject of controversy among both admirers and critics. Scott's literary output continued, even when he was burdened with the responsibility of directing the Department of Indian Affairs. *Lundy's Lane and Other Poems* appeared in 1916, and it was followed by *Beauty and Life* in 1921. By this time his reputation as a man of letters was firmly established. He had been admitted to the Royal Society of Canada in 1899 and in 1921-22, he served as its president.[23] It was in 1922 also that the University of Toronto awarded him an honorary D. Litt., the first it had ever conferred.

Scott led an extremely busy literary life. For example, he worked consistently at promoting the poetry of his friend Archibald Lampman after the latter's untimely death in 1899. In fact, Lampman's reputation is largely owing to Scott's untiring efforts.[24]

Nothing would have pleased Scott more than the establishment of an internationally recognized Canadian literary tradition. His interests, however, extended to all forms of artistic expression. Ottawa was a dull town in his day, and it was poorly served by the cultural amenities associated with national capitals. Scott played an important role in generating and sustaining some cultural life. He was president of the Ottawa Symphony Society for a number of years. He was also a founding member of the city's Little Theatre and wrote a play, *Pierre*, that was performed there.[25]

Scott was an avid and knowledgeable collector of art. He owned two Emily Carr paintings, one of which had been presented to him by the artist herself. The painter Edmund Morris, who was noted for his Indian portraits, was a close friend, and accompanied Scott on several of his wilderness journeys on department business. When Morris drowned in the St. Lawrence in 1913, Scott wrote "Lines in Memory of Edmund Morris" as a mark of appreciation. Scott was also on close terms with the painter Clarence Gagnon and served as his sales agent between 1925 and 1931 when Gagnon was abroad.[26] His pamphlet on Walter J. Phillips, another painter, is further evidence of the poet's abiding passion for this form of aesthetic expression.[27]

Scott's house at 108 Lisgar Street, now torn down, became a favourite meeting place for writers, artists, and musicians in the Ottawa area. These gatherings were limited to small groups who shared the poet's interest in the arts. The Hart House Quartet played there on occasion, and Alfred Noyes gave a number of readings. Scott himself would sometimes entertain his guests at the grand piano or with readings of his own verse.[28]

The poet's personal life, though marred by tragedy, was generally tranquil. In October 1894, he married Belle Warner Botsford of Boston. She was a professional violinist who had studied in Paris and enjoyed a brief concert career in Britain, the United States, and Canada. They met in Ottawa when Scott performed as her accompanist at a recital. She was vivacious and energetic and tended to dominate the socially self-conscious poet. But they shared mutual interests that more than compensated for any personality incompatibility.[29]

Their only child, Elizabeth Duncan, was born in July 1895. Scott was devoted to her, as his personal letters show. In 1907 the parents decided that she should attend a school in France for a year. In April Scott received a four-month leave of absence and went to Europe to join his wife and daughter who were already there. Leaving Elizabeth in Paris, the Scotts journeyed to Spain at the end of May. But upon their arrival in Madrid they were greeted with the shocking news of the girl's sudden death. This major blow aggravated the nervousness and gloom which already characterized Scott. Some of those who knew him claimed that he never fully recovered from the effects of this tragedy, and he kept some of Elizabeth's toys in the music room until his own death.[30]

In April 1929 Scott's wife died. But within two years, in March 1931, he took as his new bride Elise Aylen of Ottawa, the niece of his old friend and neighbour, Arthur S. Bourinot. She was an aspiring poet, and Scott had written the introduction to her *Roses of Shadow* which had appeared shortly before.[31] By this time, he was sixty-eight and was to retire from the federal service in the following year. Elise shared many of his interests, and the marriage gave him another lease of life which sustained him throughout his lengthy retirement.

In appearance, Scott was tall and lean. He wore old-fashioned spectacles and conservative clothes. Madge Macbeth remembered him as slow-moving and soft-spoken. Nor, in her recollection, did he ever swear or lose his temper. He had "a rather aloof and even forbidding exterior." He did not make friends easily or adapt well to new surroundings. By his own admission, he was reticent and difficult to communicate with on any degree of intimacy. Even though he was a member of many organizations of a cultural nature, he disliked the meetings and socializing that they entailed.[32] Desmond Pacey has suggested that the poet's Scottish mother may have been responsible for "the somewhat dour quality of his personality".[33]

Wilfred Eggleston's wife painted a vivid portrait of Scott and his second bride:

> But sitting across from them in that room that night, even so, I was not prepared to see such an elderly man (in my estimation) with such a young wife! . . . Why, he was old enough to be her grandfather! He was tall, very thin, craggy, his face deeply lined. To me he looked very austere and cold. I found him very forbidding. Still he was a Victorian gentleman, very courtly, very nice. But I was never able to get accustomed to him. Neither could I to Elise. On that first meeting I thought her pretty, but withdrawn. She had a very sweet smile, albeit fleeting, and she spoke little. Like myself, she stayed in the background.[34]

In spite of appearances and his heritage, Scott was no religious fanatic or joyless puritan. In adulthood, he severed connections with his father's Method-ist church though he retained his personal faith.[35] He enjoyed an occasional drink and was critical of the "fuss, canting and general expenditure of breath" surrounding the prohibition debate of the 1890s. He blamed the bishops and "the meaner sort of Evangelical persons" for the agitation. In his opinion, it would be better to ensure that liquor laws were respected than to impose prohibition.[36] Nor was he enamoured of censorship. As he explained to Professor E.K. Brown:

> Puritanism I dislike as much as you do and I decry the Censor. In Canada we have had our censoring done for us and have merely followed the lead in banning. I hope your remark that puritanism is diminishing is true.[37]

That Scott was a leading figure in two worlds—literature and the civil service—has been a source of fascination to both his admirers and detractors. It is intriguing that Indians, with whom he dealt in a professional capacity, should also make appearances in his poetry and prose. Is it possible to discern in his writings his true feelings about the native population? This obvious question has given rise to much speculation and on-going debate.

Scott's admirers in the world of literature are legion. As one of the Confedera-tion poets, he is often accorded uncritical acclaim, which sometimes extends to his work in the government. E.K. Brown probably ranks foremost among Scott's admirers. The Toronto English professor came to know the poet during the 1940s and did much to promote his reputation. In Brown's opinion, Scott was "an administrator of rare imaginative sympathy and almost perfect wisdom." And he treated native people favourably in his writings. They were depicted as "complex yet intelligible persons" and not as noble savages. "The Forsaken," one of Scott's more controversial poems, in which an old Indian woman was abandoned to die by her tribe, Brown says, did not represent a moral commen-tary on an unacceptable custom; it was nothing more than a universal tragedy—a tale of the strong grown weak and disgarded.[38]

Susan Beckman writes in a similar vein. She attributes to Scott "a strong concern, affection and respect for the Indian" which arose from his work. And his humanitarianism was coupled with "the keen eye of the experienced observer who has made some efforts to immerse himself in the culture he [was] describing."[39]

Scott's compassion for the Indians is also alluded to by Roy Daniells:

> His concern with Indians as wards of the Canadian government was sincere and deep; within the somewhat narrow limits set by government policy he laboured unceasingly for them.[40]

This passage implies that Scott was a pawn whose actions were constrained by government policy but who, nevertheless, worked for the benefit of the Indians. Such an assumption overlooks the critical role that Scott actually played in directing government policy.

Melvin Dagg is more reticent in his appraisal of Scott. He admits that in his more popular works, Indians were frequently portrayed as "doomed figures." Dagg argues, however, that this was not always the case. For example, in "Lines in Memory of Edmund Morris," Crowfoot, the Blackfoot chief, is honoured. And in "Watkwenies" the old Indian woman weighing her "interest-money" symbolizes Indian dissatisfaction with the treaties and is obliquely critical of government policy.[41] This is an improbable hypothesis, however, considering the role Scott played in determining the actual terms of these settlements (see Chapter Four).

Keiichi Hirano, a Japanese observer, is less apologetic. He perceives that Scott's attitude to the Indians lacked "critical insight." He also notes the negative tone of "a weird and waning race" and similar celebrated phrases.[42]

Gerald Lynch enters the realm of Scott's non-fiction in an attempt to discern his "attitude". He finds contradictions that he is unable to resolve, but he nonetheless concludes that the poet was compassionate towards the Indians:

> Finally, I do not doubt that Scott was, in the poems as well as the prose writings, resigned to the inevitability of assimilation, though certainly not the cold-hearted assimilation that critics of the socio-political school of Scott criticism read into the Indian poems.[43]

One of the more astute critics, John Flood, demonstrates the advantages of a broader perspective, which points out the inferior role to which Indians are assigned in Scott's short stories.[44] The natives are used as props, backdrops to the main events. Nor are they ever depicted as equal to the white man. They are invariably caricatured as drunken, stupid, or "pagan."[45]

Historian E. Palmer Patterson II also attempts to view Scott and his ideas as products of their time and comes to conclusions similar to Flood's. He notes, for example, that the graphic violence in Scott's writing is almost always the work of Indians. In fact, the brutality of their past is a constant theme. In "The Onondaga Madonna," the line "her rebel lips are dabbled with the stains of feuds and forays" offers a subtle hint of cannibalism. In "Watkwenies," Iroquois history is similarly depicted: "Vengeance was her nation's lore and law; the long knife flashed, and hissed, and drank its fill." And "At Gull Lake: August 1810" describes the torture and mutilation of the unfaithful wife of a Saulteaux chief. In Patterson's opinion, Scott's association of violence with Indians reveals his belief that they represented the irrational, brutal element in man. And their behaviour is somehow genetically determined. The pure-blooded Indian is a relentless savage; the half-breed, however, shows traits of civilization. Only by interbreeding with the whites can they hope to advance themselves. In "The Onondaga Madonna," the native woman is of mixed blood herself and is bearing the child of a white man. Therein lay the seeds of progress.[46]

As these varying remarks show, Scott's poetry is a highly unreliable guide to his feelings regarding the native population. Nor is it really necessary. Scott's pronouncements on Indians in readily comprehensible prose, in both an official and unofficial capacity, are legion. Because of their frequency and unwavering consistency, they are by far the best guide to what the private and public man really believed.

The Indian past is an appropriate starting point. As an historian, Scott was little more than an amateur. His biography of Simcoe and his contributions to Shortt and Doughty's *Canada and its Provinces* were his most noteworthy accomplishments. But he claimed to believe that historians of his day relied rigidly on documentary evidence in their attempt to "unfold the truth." And he also noted with relief that "the partisan historian fortified with bigotry and blind to all evidence uncongenial to his preconceptions" had become an extinct species.[47]

Yet when it came to analysing the Indians' role in Canadian history, Scott showed that partisanship was far from dead. In describing the Indian contribution in the American Revolutionary War, for example, his emphasis is on their savagery and brutality: "then began a lurid chapter of warfare in the Indian manner, with episodes of flame and the torture stake." To compound matters, the Indians' "treachery" rendered them unreliable as allies.[48]

Nor could he acknowledge that Indians had contributed anything to the establishment and development of the country. In fact, it was quite the opposite. He noted that in the early years "the Indians were a real menace to the colonization of Canada." He depicted this menace in what is a revealing passage:

> The Indian nature now seems like a fire that is waning, that is smouldering and dying away in ashes; then it was full of force and heat. It was ready to break out at any moment in savage dances; in wild and desperate orgies in which ancient superstitions were involved with European ideas but dimly understood and intensified by cunning imaginations inflamed with rum.[49]

This flourish of the pen must have been a favourite, for Scott used it to describe the Indians in his biography of Simcoe and also incorporated it into his essay, "The Last of the Indian Treaties." His penchant for hyperbole is clearly evident. Engaged in what he called the "Science of History," he gathered the most emotionally charged adjectives he could muster to attach to the Indian. "Savage," "wild," "desperate," "cunning," "treacherous," "superstitious," and "brutal" are prominent in this catalogue of abuse.

Here is a further illustrative passage from the Simcoe work. Scott is describing the Iroquois after their settlement in Upper Canada:

> The savage nature was hardly hidden under the first, thinnest film of
> European customs. Scalps were hung up in their log huts, and arms that
> had brained children upon their parents' door-stones were yet nervous
> with power.[50]

In Scott's opinion, the Indians had not only exhibited these characteristics in
the dim and distant past, but also had continued to do so within his own living
memory. He explained that it had been "the promise of plunder" that had
caused some of the western Indians to join in the Metis rebellion of 1885, totally
ignoring the circumstances of despair and frustration in which Big Bear,
Poundmaker, and their followers found themselves.[51]

As for the disappearance of the buffalo on the Prairies, Scott apportioned
blame equally among Indians and whites.

> For years these animals had been carelessly butchered by Indians and
> whites alike for the sake of their hides, and the plains were covered with the
> bleached bones lying where their carcasses had rotted in the sun.[52]

It would have been more accurate to note that the buffalo had been systematically slaughtered by whites to amass quick profits in the robe trade. It had also at
the same time deprived the plains Indians of their principal means of sustenance rendering them incapable of resisting the encroaching tide of settlement.
The Indians had always lived off the buffalo, and they had used all parts of the
animals, not just the hides. To blame them for a landscape dotted with rotting
carcasses and bleached bones was hardly fair.

If the Indian in the past was prone to savagery and superstition, what of his
future? Scott was convinced that aboriginal economic activities such as hunting,
trapping, fishing, and food-gathering would have to be abandoned. The Indian
should learn how to cultivate the soil or prepare himself for employment in the
"industrial or mercantile community." This economic transformation would
have to be accompanied by "the substitution of Christian ideals of conduct and
morals for aboriginal concepts of both."[53]

A change of this magnitude was not impossible, according to Scott. In fact, it
had been achieved in the past, in specific cases. He noted in one of his
contributions to *Canada and its Provinces* that the authorities of Upper Canada
had successfully settled Indians in villages in the 1830s. These efforts had been
accompanied by education, Christian evangelization, and encouragement to
adopt agriculture. Such a policy had changed the Mississaugas from "a wander-
ing and dissolute band to a contented and progressive community" in just four
years.[54]

Scott saw this case as exceptional. Passing on the advantages of white civilization to the Indians would be a slow and tedious process. This was inevitable
since they harboured primitive instincts that would take generations to eradicate.
He observed on one occasion, for instance, that as far as the Indian was concerned, peaceful occupations were "foreign to his natural bent."[55] He also
declared that "Altruism is absent from the Indian character."[56]

Education would be a key element in the cultural transformation. While still
young and impressionable, the Indian child would be introduced by the school
to a superior set of behaviours and values. One outcome would be Indian
adults who had internalized the work ethic and a sense of civic responsibility. As
Scott pointed out, "without education and with neglect the Indians would
produce an undesirable and often a dangerous element in society."[57]

But he felt that the school alone would prove inadequate to the task of
civilization. If the savage impulses he attributed to the Indians were deep-
rooted in their collective psyche—primeval instincts that were somehow genetically transmitted—it followed that if the group remained endogamous these
inherited disabilities would never be purged. Therefore, advancement could
only take place through the injection of a superior strain of blood. Intermarriage with the more advanced caucasian race would provide the Indians with
the best prospect for progress. As Scott put it:

> The happiest future for the Indian race is absorption into the general
> population, and this is the object of the policy of our government. The
> great forces of intermarriage and education will finally overcome the
> lingering traces of native custom and tradition.[58]

In other words, the Indian would ultimately disappear as a cultural and
biological entity. Of course, the pursuit of this aim was already under way as the
twentieth century dawned, and some mixed results were available. Although
Scott frequently generalized about Indians, he was also prepared to differentiate among them, especially when it came to assessing progress.

He was least optimistic about the plains Indian. In his opinion, they were a
people "whose hatred of work [was] proverbial."[59] They had only been in
constant contact with white people for a short period of time, and they were
finding the transition from hunting to agriculture extremely difficult in spite of
vigorous government efforts on their behalf.

On the other hand, Scott noted that the Indians of southern Ontario and
Quebec had been advancing steadily, mainly because of their close and frequent association with white society. In one of his contributions to *Canada and
its Provinces*, he reported with satisfaction that "one band [had] fully worked out
its problem and become merged into the white population." He was referring to
the Wyandottes of Anderdon who had become enfranchised in 1881. "By
education and intermarriage they had become civilized."[60]

Scott had an almost equally good opinion of the Indians of British Columbia. They had adjusted well to the arrival of the white man and were proving to be economically useful to their new masters. Many of them were engaged in "congenial employment" in the salmon canneries, hop-fields, and fruit farms, and some were even taking on "the more arduous toil of the packer, miner, or navvy."[61] He observed that many of the men were excellent fishermen, "but not without the usual native failing, lack of steadiness." He was evidently happy that the Indians were being transformed into an unskilled or semi-skilled labour force and that their traditional way of life was disappearing:

> The outlook in British Columbia is certainly encouraging; there is fine material among the natives to make good British citizens, and in two or three decades we may expect that a large number of Indians will have been absorbed into the ordinary life of the Province.[62]

The main obstacle to further progress in British Columbia, according to Scott, was the persistence of "degrading native customs" such as the potlatch, although it seemed to be weakening as a result of the efforts of missionaries and teachers. He was certainly optimistic:

> Anyone who desires to understand the social progress of which these Indians are capable, and also the strength of their attachment to an adopted religion, should study the history of the Metlakatla settlement under the Rev. George [sic] Duncan.[63]

Here Scott was referring to the radical experiment in social engineering conducted by the Anglican missionary William Duncan following his arrival at Fort Simpson in 1857. Appalled at most aspects of coastal Indian life, Duncan resolved that total cultural transformation would be required. Having secured a small following, he decided to create an isolated community.

In 1862 Duncan led his "catehumens" to Metlakatla where the new zion was established. It became a model village in which almost everything, from rules and regulations to architecture, and was based on the standards of Victorian England. Indian customs were forbidden, and strict rules were imposed requiring religious observance, school attendance, cleanliness, industriousness, abstinence from alcohol, and other trappings of the Protestant ethic. Duncan ruled Metlakatla in an autocratic manner with the assistance of a force of Indian constables and succeeded in imposing astonishing behavioural changes on those under his sway. In fact, the transformation was so dramatic that it drew the wondrous admiration of visitors, one of whom remarked that they were no longer Indians, but white men![64]

Scott viewed missionaries such as Duncan as playing a vital role in carrying the beacon of white civilization to the unfortunate aborigines. However, the government had an equal, and an increasingly dominant, part to play in the noble enterprise. But the task was an onerous one for the state. Scott once observed that the British North America Act had given to the federal government "the burden of the Indian,"[65] and the acquisition of the western territories had "largely increased the burden."[66] Here was an unmistakable echo of the rhetoric of nineteenth-century imperialism. Like Kipling, Scott rationalized the subjugation of colonized peoples by cloaking it in the aura of "responsibility" and "duty."[67]

In making these observations, Scott was writing in his capacity as deputy superintendent general of Indian affairs, but there is no evidence to suggest that his private views differed. He saw the Indians as primitive, child-like creatures in constant need of the paternal care of the government. With guidance, they would gradually abandon their superstitious beliefs and barbaric behaviour and adopt civilization.

To some observers, the persistence of the reserve system appeared to inhibit the achievement of the ultimate objective of Indian-white intermarriage and represented a "contradiction" or "inconsistency" in Scott's policies. This is not really the case. Scott did not see the reserve system as a permanent feature of Indian administration, but as transitional. He believed that it was only necessary where continuous contact between Indians and whites was a relatively recent phenomenon. In southern Ontario and Quebec, for instance, he could see no further justification for its continuation, since the Indians inhabiting those regions had mixed and intermarried with whites for over two centuries.[68] Scott believed that such individuals ought to be enfranchised, against their will if necessary (see Chapter Three). While the end result for all Indians would be the same—disappearance as a distinct people—all would not accomplish it simultaneously.

Because of his literary skills and the sheer volume of his writings, Scott best articulates the assumptions that underlay Canadian Indian policy in his day. The views he espoused in both his official reports and his other writings display a remarkable resilience to change over time. As specific aspects of policy are examined in subsequent chapters, this stubborn consistency will become increasingly evident.

3

General Aspects of Policy and Administration

By the time of Scott's promotion to deputy superintendent, the Department of Indian Affairs had grown into a substantial bureaucracy. Its jurisdictional network covered the entire country with the exception of the Northwest Territories. Decision-making was centralized in the Ottawa headquarters. In fact, centralization had been a growing feature of administrative practice over the years, epitomized by the closing of the commissioner's office in Winnipeg in 1909. It meant that power was concentrated in the hands of the deputy superintendent and the officers in charge of the various branches of the inside service.

The inside service itself was divided into six branches with a total of seventy-six employees. The secretary's branch continued to be headed by John D. McLean, who held the titles of secretary and assistant deputy superintendent. It had become the largest of the administrative subdivisions with twenty-five employees. The accountant's branch was now under Frederick H. Paget. William A. Orr was both clerk of lands and timber and registrar of land and was in charge of the lands and timber branch. The survey branch was under the supervision of Samuel Bray, the chief surveyor. George M. Matheson, the registrar, headed the record branch and Martin Benson, the clerk of schools, directed the schools branch. In addition to these officers there were an architect and a law clerk. The majority of the other employees were clerks, but a number of draftsmen, surveyors, and messengers were included.[1] An architect's branch was added in 1916.

By 1913 the outside service comprised 651 employees engaged on a full-time or part-time basis. The most important field officers were the agents and the inspectors of agencies. Agencies usually had a clerk or two at their disposal and a medical officer. The latter was invariably a physician with a practice in the vicinity of Indian communities whose services were called upon on an *ad hoc* basis. In the prairie provinces, where a special effort was being made to encourage the Indians to adopt agriculture, farming instructors, stockmen, and blacksmiths were frequently employed. A number of Indians also appeared on the department's payroll. They were usually engaged as constables, interpreters or labourers.[2]

This growing and cumbersome bureaucracy was making increasing demands on the public purse, a tendency Scott had attempted to discourage while serving as the department's accountant. Now that he was in charge, financial restraint became all the more evident. But the penny-pinching mind of the bookkeeper was not the only factor at work. By the spring of 1913 Canada was sliding into an economic recession after years of growth and prosperity. The recession lasted well into the war years when the munitions industry and other accoutrements of the imperial military effort stimulated the economy once more.[3] During these years Indian Affairs was accorded even less significance in government circles than was customary. Its parliamentary appropriation of $2,195,319.20 in 1915 was cut to $1,980,552.17 in 1916 and to $1,749,031.51 in the following year. The 1915 vote was not surpassed until 1920.[4]

Shortly after his promotion to deputy superintendent, Scott made clear a renewed emphasis on accountability and spending restraint. On 25 October 1913, he sent a circular to all agents for the purpose of assisting them in the "efficient management" of their agencies. The circular advised agents that the suppression of vice, and the liquor traffic in particular, was one of their most important duties. They were reminded that they had magisterial powers under subsection 161 of the Indian Act and could impose fines or prison terms for liquor offences. They were also authorized to hold preliminary investigations when Indians violated the criminal code. They were urged to take full advantage of these powers. And the circular noted that the department had "no objection to Agents or other outside officers of the Department acting as informers in cases of prosecutions under the Indian Act."

Agents were also told to take an active interest in education in their agencies. They ought to visit the schools regularly and submit monthly reports to headquarters on the appropriate forms. Particular attention was to be given to truancy.

Scott expressed his eagerness that the Indians adopt agriculture, or at least cultivate gardens, and that "habits of industry and thrift" be encouraged. When expenditure did become necessary, agents were required to keep accurate accounts and to justify every penny. When band funds were available, it was preferable to use them rather than to make demands on the public coffers. In cases of destitution, the department was willing to provide support in order to prevent suffering. But, the circular noted, the Indians "must be trained to rely upon their own exertions." The same principle applied in the case of medical expenses. If Indians could afford to pay physicians' fees, they should be forced to do so.[5]

Scott's circular was not designed to provide friendly advice, but rather to point out a number of strict principles that agents were obliged to adhere to or risk the loss of their jobs. This soon became evident when, in January 1914, the deputy superintendent wrote to his minister recommending the dismissal of M. Miller, who had served as Indian agent at Crooked Lakes, Saskatchewan, since 1904. Miller had refused to move his family on to the reserve and continued to reside in Moosomin. His absence, especially on weekends, had afforded the Indians opportunities for "debauchery." His lack of supervision allowed the illegal liquor traffic to flourish, and ploughing had been neglected. It was therefore "advisable to obtain control by the appointment of a new Agent who [would] reside at headquarters and pursue the policy of the Department with vigour."[6]

Throughout his incumbency, Scott constantly sought to replace incompetent and insubordinate agents with those whose dedication to department aims were not in question. This was not always possible, however, since political patronage still played a role in appointments. Nonetheless, he frequently reminded officers of their duties and of the possibility of dismissal.[7]

The effects of the First World War were felt in native communities as in the rest of the country, and that conflagration gave rise to a number of innovations in Indian policy. The government encouraged Indians to enlist, and between 3,500 and 4,000 of them served with the Canadian Expeditionary Force. They mainly served in the infantry, and they suffered the same dangers and casualties as everyone else. However, by an order-in-council dated 17 January 1918, they were exempted from the provisions of the Military Service Act which had introduced conscription the previous year. The exemption was made on the grounds that they were not full citizens. Indian participation in the forces, then, was purely voluntary, and those who served were rewarded with the federal franchise without loss of status.[8]

The sacrifice of their young men in the trenches of the western front was not the only contribution expected of Indians in the war effort. The production of extra food was considered vital to the success of the Entente powers, and the Indians held land that could be employed to that end. On 29 September 1914, Scott wrote to agency inspectors in the prairie provinces proposing that Indians make "strenuous efforts" to produce as much wheat as possible so that Britain's needs would be met and a great service rendered to the Empire.[9] Such exhortations continued throughout the war, and the amount of reserve land brought under cultivation increased considerably. But Scott remained convinced that more could be done. On 12 February 1918, he wrote to all agents to observe that those who were producing food were "literally fighting the Germans." And those agents who were unable to show satisfactory results would have their services terminated.[10] He also wrote to the principals of boarding and industrial schools informing them that all boys fifteen and older were to be released to work for local farmers. The per capita grants would be maintained for those so engaged.[11]

Undoubtedly, the most curious feature of the agricultural endeavours was a scheme initiated by W.M. Graham, the enterprising agent who had established the much-lauded File Hills colony. In 1904 he had been promoted to the position of inspector of agencies in the South Saskatchewan inspectorate, a post he had held ever since. He acquired considerable influence in Ottawa in 1917 when Arthur Meighen, who was related to his wife, became minister of the interior and superintendent general of Indian affairs in Borden's Union government. In January 1918, Graham wrote to Meighen outlining a plan to increase food production by the efficient use of "idle" Indian land. Graham claimed that in the South Saskatchewan inspectorate alone there were 340,000 acres of pasture land of which only about 120,000 acres were being used by the Indians. Those lands could raise cattle production to three times the existing level. And the maximum utilization of Indian lands all over the Prairies would bring untold benefits. Indian bands also had "idle funds" which could be invested in the scheme.[12]

Meighen responded favourably to this proposal, and he arranged to have Graham appointed Commissioner for Greater Production for the provinces of Manitoba, Saskatchewan, and Alberta, effective 16 February 1918. The new commissioner, whose office was to be located in Regina, was granted extensive authority. He was empowered to formulate a policy for each reserve; to direct the implementation of such policies; to lease Indian lands; to market grain and livestock; to engage or dismiss employees as he saw fit; and to make recommendations to the superintendent general with regard to the "greater efficiency" of the Indian service in the west.[13]

Graham's greater production scheme, which was financed by a grant of $362,000 from the war appropriation, had three distinct components:

1. Encouraging individual Indians to increase their crop production.
2. Leasing reserve lands to non-Indian farmers. 16,374 acres were leased for cultivation and 297,024 acres for grazing.
3. Establishing and operating "greater production farms" on Indian land. These were unusual experiments in state agricultural entrepreneurship— farms directed by the department's agents using Indian labour. They were set up on the Assiniboine, Blackfoot, Blood, Crooked Lakes, and Muscowpetung reserves and occupied a total area of 20,448 acres.[14]

The scheme presupposed that Indian lands would be readily available. Scott inquired of the Justice Department and was assured that under the War Measures Act of 1914 as much land as necessary could be expropriated without band consent for temporary use. He communicated this information to Graham, and on that basis initial steps were taken to launch the scheme.[15]

In the meantime, however, it was considered advisable to amend the Indian Act, not only to legitimize the expropriations but also to make available "idle" band funds for investment in the scheme. Subsection 2, section 90, chapter 36 was added to the act in April to permit the superintendent general to spend band funds for public works on reserves without the consent of the Indians. In commenting on this amendment, Scott observed that it had been necessary to deal with the cases in which "the council of a band, through some delusion, misapprehension or hostility, [acted] in a manner contrary to the best interests of the band" such as refusing to sanction expenditure on drainage systems or other measures to improve productivity.[16]

A further subsection (3) authorized the superintendent general to lease non-productive reserve lands to persons who would bring them under cultivation or use them for grazing, without a surrender. When he introduced the measure in the Commons, Meighen was asked how the Indians would fare if some of their best lands were taken under the scheme. He replied: "I do not think we need waste any time in sympathy for the Indian, for I am pretty sure his interests will be looked after by the Commissioner."[17] This amendment showed clearly that the gradual erosion of Indian control of their reserve lands, which had begun almost imperceptibly in the 1890s, would continue and with greater intensity.

The greater production farms did not live up to their sponsors' expectations. The winter of 1919-20 was particularly severe in Alberta, resulting in considerable livestock losses to both Indians and whites. In some cases up to 40 per cent of herds perished. The scheme was hardly responsible for the vicissitudes of climate, but the losses aggravated what was already an unsatisfactory situation from the Indians' perspective.

The Blood Indians of southern Alberta were especially aggrieved by some of the results of Graham's plan. On 31 May 1920, they presented a memorandum to the department outlining their complaints. They pointed out that on 30 May 1918 about 4,800 acres of their reserve had been taken for the creation of a greater production farm. Indian labour was used and so was Indian farm machinery, which had been virtually commandeered by the agent at great inconvenience.

The Indians complained about gross mismanagement and about official highhandedness. They disclosed that a wheat crop had been left unfenced during the summer of 1919 and that cattle and horses had destroyed most of it. There were further instances of incompetence. In September 1918, for example, a mixed herd of cattle had been sold for $44,000. The Indians were told that their share of the profit would be $50 per head. But some of this money was subsequently used to purchase more cattle, which were later sold at $20 a head—a considerable loss.

Headquarters asked Graham to respond in detail to these complaints. He attempted to dismiss most of the allegations as being either exaggerated or absurd, but he did admit some mismanagement. He blamed the destruction of the wheat crop, for example, on the slow delivery of fencing materials by a railway company. And he blamed the ill-advised cattle sales on the local agent, who had since been fired.[18]

Nor were the financial returns all that impressive. In March 1921 Scott requested a statement and received the following figures from Graham:[19]

SUMMARY OF RECEIPTS AND EXPENDITURES
RE: GREATER PRODUCTION FARMS, 23 MARCH 1921

Amount advanced from war appropriation	$362,000.00
Revenue from sales as of 28 February 1921	$572,192.07
Total	$938,192.07
Expenditures	$826,838.94
Balance on hand	$111,353.13

After three years of operation, total expenditure far exceeded the revenue from sales. And the balance on hand was less than one-third of the initial investment from the war appropriation. Such figures led Scott to doubt the wisdom of carrying on with the farms, especially as their *raison d'etre*, the war effort, was past. Yet there was little he could do as long as Arthur Meighen remained an enthusiastic supporter of the scheme. The interior minister (and later prime minister) described the results as "exhilarating" and boasted in the House of Commons that the federal government was the "largest farmer in the Dominion."[20]

With the fall of the Meighen administration at the end of 1921, it became possible to phase out the experiment. The order-in-council appointing Graham as commissioner of greater production was rescinded on 16 January 1922. On 23 February, Scott wrote to Graham informing him that it was the department's policy to close the greater production farms as soon as possible. Nor would there be further leases of reserve lands to white farmers. Such lands had often been neglected, abused, and rendered useless. The department would, however, continue to secure the surrender of "surplus Indian lands" and sell them to settlers.[21] Graham was disappointed, but he was allowed to retain about 400 acres of the Muscowpetung operation as an experimental or demonstration farm. The remainder of the farms were turned over in time to graduates of Indian residential schools.[22]

When all factors are considered, the greater production scheme did prove profitable. But most of the profits were generated from the leases of reserve lands to neighbouring farmers. By April 1920 these leases had generated in excess of $200,000.[23] Such revenues offset the sluggish performance of the _ government farms. By the time the scheme was terminated, the war appropriation had been repaid, and a profit of $57,329.03 lay on the books. There were also some permanent benefits. Much of the money invested had been spent on agricultural equipment, barns, fences and so forth, and these ultimately became the possessions of the Indians.

The demise of Graham's grand plan did not result in his demotion to his previous status of inspector. In July 1920, Meighen secured his appointment as Indian commissioner for the prairie provinces.[24] It meant the resurrection of the position that had been abolished in 1909 when David Laird had been transferred to Ottawa, and Graham remained in the position throughout the 1920s.

The greater production scheme and the amendments to the Indian Act that accompanied it represented extraordinary intrusions by the state into the management of Indian lands and funds. It was argued that the times demanded such measures. Winning the war overshadowed all other considerations, and the federal government was prepared to use its powers in an unprecedented manner. The introduction of income tax, conscription, and prohibition, the outlawing of strikes, the regulation of prices and of the sale of wheat were the most conspicuous examples of that phenomenon.[25] In this light, the greater production scheme was not an exotic flirtation with Bolshevism, but something that could be understood, if not condoned, in an atmosphere of regulation and control. However, the power to lease Indian lands and invest Indian funds without band consent remained on the books even when the crisis was over.

The end of the war brought its own problems, and the Indians were much affected by the arrangements made in the transition to more settled times. Undoubtedly, the major task facing the government was demobilizing 350,000 soldiers and re-establishing them in civilian life. In fact, it had become necessary to begin such operations long before the conflict ended. The Military Hospitals Commission was created in 1915 to deal with the injured and disabled soldiers who were already returning to Canada, and in February 1918, the new Department of Soldiers' Civil Re-establishment was set up with Sir James Lougheed as minister. The disabled veterans were granted pensions and were reasonably well looked after.

The able-bodied, on the other hand, were relatively neglected. The average gratuity paid to veterans upon discharge was a mere $240. And a vigorous campaign for a $2,000 bonus ended in failure. The fact that the public debt had risen to over two billion dollars during the war tended to discourage a policy of generosity.[26] For a minority who qualified, however, a land settlement scheme was offered.

The Soldier Settlement Act of 1917 (assented to 29 August) launched the scheme. It authorized the establishment of a three-member Soldier Settlement Board responsible to the minister of the interior. The board was empowered to grant up to 160 acres of land owned by the dominion government to qualified returning veterans in addition to normal homestead entitlements. Loans of up to $2,500 were also made available for the purchase of stock, equipment, and other effects.[27]

As the war ended, the number applying for participation in the scheme rose beyond initial expectation, and special measures were taken to accommodate them. An order-in-council of 11 February 1919 permitted the Soldier Settlement Board to purchase privately owned land and sell it later to returning veterans at the purchase price. The board could make loans not exceeding $4,500 to qualified veterans for such purchases. To qualify, a downpayment of 10 per cent was required, and the candidate had to satisfy the board that he was capable of working the land. Additional loans of $2,000 were made available for the purchase of stock and equipment. And another $1,000 could be borrowed on improvements. The land purchase loan was repayable over twenty-five years at an interest rate of 5 per cent. The other loans accrued no interest during the first two years, but they were then repayable in four annual installments.[28]

These changes were incorporated into a new and far more elaborate Soldier Settlement Act which was assented to on 7 July 1919. The most unusual feature of this legislation was that it empowered the board to acquire by compulsory purchase as much agricultural land as it deemed necessary. Indian lands were excluded, but the board was permitted to acquire those parts of reserves that had been surrendered under the Indian Act.[29]

During the summer of 1918, there was some discussion within the department regarding the possibility of extending the benefits of the settlement scheme to Indian veterans. The Soldier Settlement Board was willing to co-operate if administrative and jurisdictional difficulties could be overcome. One of the major problems was that section 102 of the Indian Act prohibited non-Indians from holding mortgages on reserve lands. It was also necessary to determine whether the scheme would best be directed by the board or by Indian Affairs.

Scott was of the opinion that the problem of dual authority over reserve lands could be overcome were the department to take over operations as far as Indian veterans were concerned. He favoured making the land grants on reserves only; other lands were best left for non-Indian soldiers. And he believed that enfranchisement should be a condition of participation. After all, the Indian soldiers had proven their manhood, and full citizenship would be a "fitting recognition of their services and would be an object lesson to the other Indians indicating to them that their best interests [lay] in moving forward and supporting the Government rather than in lagging behind and being indifferent or hostile to the administration of their affairs."[30]

Meighen agreed that it was advisable to locate the Indian soldiers on reserves and that the department should administer the scheme. But he had serious doubts about Scott's enfranchisement proposal. He had heard from Commissioner Graham that the veterans were no more ready for responsibility than those who had stayed at home. If they were going to be successful farmers, they would continue to need the guidance of the department.[31]

In February 1919 meetings took place between Scott and W.J. Black, chairman of the Soldier Settlement Board, and they agreed that the department would administer the scheme as far as Indian veterans were concerned. An amendment to the Indian Act (part 3, sections 196-99), assented to on the same day as the new Soldier Settlement Act (7 July 1919), granted the necessary powers to the deputy superintendent general. Not only did he thereby acquire the authority to supervise the loans, but he was also empowered to grant location tickets to common reserve lands without band consent. He could also purchase non-reserve lands.[32]

In the administration of the scheme, funds were advanced by the Soldier Settlement Board to the deputy superintendent upon request. Based upon the judgment of its agents about the suitability of applicants, the department granted loans to Indian veterans on identical terms to those offered by the board to other veterans. Land could be allocated either on or off a reserve, but the department strongly favoured the former arrangement. In the event that an Indian was located on a reserve other than his own, he would remain a member of his original band. No mortgages could be taken on reserve lands, and the loans were therefore secured by assets such as buildings, equipment, and stock. And the department took out insurance to provide further security. In the event of a default, the soldier's interest in the land could be sold to another Indian and the assets disposed of as the department saw fit.[33]

This was not clear in the phrasing of the Indian Act amendment of 1919, and many Indian spokesmen were under the impression that loan defaults could lead to the alienation of reserve lands. Considerable agitation followed, and Scott himself admitted that the "verbiage" of the legislation was a source of legitimate complaint.[34] Consequently, a new amendment to the act was introduced in 1922 eliminating the ambiguity.[35]

There was an immediate demand for participation in the settlement scheme by returning Indian veterans. As early as April 1919, Commissioner Graham was sending urgent appeals to Ottawa for assistance in enabling the soldiers to take up farming. Even though a number of administrative difficulties remained, Scott authorized emergency expenditures so that a year's work would not be lost. The granting process picked up momentum during the autumn of 1919 and continued throughout the following year. By 30 August 1919, 26 loans had been made. The number had risen to 80 by November and to 130 by May 1920. Scott described the results as "gratifying."[36] By April 1924 the total number of loans had risen to 218. Four had been repaid in full, while twenty-three had been defaulted on. Expenditures had amounted to $458,983.83, of which

$49,207.53 had been repaid. Scott reported that the Indian settlers were meeting their obligations "fairly satisfactorily."[37]

The majority of the settlers were located in Ontario, and in that province two full-time agricultural advisers, E.J. Sexsmith and E. Moses, were appointed to supervise operations. On the Prairies, the work was under the direction of W.M. Graham, who regarded the scheme as yet another opportunity to turn the Indians into farmers.

As the 1920s progressed, loan repayments continued to be made at a steady, if unimpressive pace. The Depression which began towards the end of 1929 brought a precipitous drop in the price of agricultural products and created serious problems for both Indian and non-Indian settlers. An amendment to the Soldier Settlement Act in 1930 attempted to deal with their dilemma by reducing all existing debts by 30 per cent. At the time of Scott's retirement in 1932, the majority of the Indian settlers were still on the land and attempting to pay off their loans under difficult circumstances.

One further aspect of the soldier settlement scheme must be alluded to. The close relationship that existed between the board and the department was partly a result of the latter's willingness to make Indian lands available for settlement by non-Indian veterans. About 26,000 former soldiers wished to participate in the scheme, and finding enough land for them all was a major task in spite of the board's expropriationary powers. Early in 1919, Indian Affairs agreed that it would no longer offer for sale to the public reserve lands that had been surrendered. They would be offered instead to the Soldier Settlement Board. And the department resolved to seek further surrenders for the same purpose, especially in the west.[38]

The expropriationary powers granted to the board did not, of course, extend to Indian lands. In the discussion surrounding the Soldier Settlement Act of 1919 in Parliament, this feature was regretted by F.B. Stacey, M.P. for Fraser Valley. He deplored the fact that a great surplus of "unused" Indian land was available in British Columbia and that the board was powerless to seize it. Meighen was sympathetic, but he feared the international repercussions if such an action were taken. "Considerable success" had been attained using the normal surrender procedures to date, and the Indians had not been unreasonable. But he added a warning:

> If the Indians should become recalcitrant, or if there should be anything in the nature of mere obstinacy as against their own interests and the interests of the State, we might consider at a later session the advisability of taking expropriationary power to be applicable in such cases.[39]

Ultimately, extraordinary measures were not required as an adequate supply of reserve land was secured through the surrender process. Frequently, it was the soldiers themselves or veterans' organizations that initiated the procedure by approaching the department when a desirable piece of Indian land came to their attention. Many seemed to believe that the property they coveted could be theirs for the asking. As Commissioner Graham reported to Scott:

> A large number of returned soldiers are under the wrong impression with regard to Indian lands. They are of the opinion that these lands are Government property and can be thrown open for free entry, without consulting or dealing with the Indians. I find this wherever I go.[40]

The department was sometimes disposed to refuse veterans' demands. Scott felt, for instance, that surrenders were unwarranted in Alberta's Peace River area because it was sparsely settled and still contained large tracts of crown land suitable for homesteading.[41] And he rejected a request by residents of Hodgson, Manitoba, to throw open part of the Peguis reserve for soldier settlement. In that instance, he pointed out that the land had been given to the band in lieu of what they had lost in the controversial surrender of St. Peter's Reserve and that the Peguis council had adopted a resolution on 5 May 1919 refusing further surrenders.

The department acted as the defender of Indian lands only in exceptional cases, however. Most of the time it co-operated, willing to meet settler demands. Even in British Columbia, where reserves were generally inadequate, surrenders were eagerly sought. The dispute between the province and the federal government over the former's reversionary interest in Indian lands had not been resolved at the time (see Chapter Eight). Therefore, the department confined its attempts at securing surrenders to those reserves in the railway belt. The natives of British Columbia were reluctant to part with any of their lands, and agents sometimes used intimidation to achieve compliance. This was particularly evident in the case of the Sumass reserve in the New Westminster agency, which was surrendered on 31 October 1919.[42]

Both aspects of the soldier settlement scheme profoundly affected Indian communities across the country. The plan to settle returning Indian veterans on reserves was accompanied by an Indian Act amendment permitting the deputy superintendent to grant location tickets without band consent. It represented a further erosion of band council power. Nonetheless, the plan also brought a new source of investment money to the reserves, and that was undoubtedly desirable. In their adoption of agriculture, the Indian veterans seem to have been at least as successful as their non-Indian counterparts. On the other hand, the plan to make Indian lands available to non-Indian veterans had little to commend it, and it was deeply resented by the native population. As a result of the department's efforts in that regard, more Indian land was sold between March 1919 and March 1920 than during the entire subsequent five year period.[43]

Although Scott was overruled on his proposal to enfranchise veterans, he remained a persistent advocate of facilitating the process of enfranchisement and of extending it to as many Indians as possible. This was consistent with his long-term goal of ending the Indians' special status and their dependency on the federal government. But enfranchisement was a cumbersome process. The candidate needed band approval and was required to make a success of farming as a location ticket holder on reserve land over a lengthy probation period. The regulations outlining this procedure had first been framed in the Canadas in 1857 and were later incorporated into the Indian Act of 1876. They had remained unchanged ever since, and few had taken advantage of them.

Scott was particularly concerned that the legislation made no provision for the enfranchisement of Indians residing off reserves.[44] He also felt that the department ought to be able to initiate the procedure, rather than waiting for Indians to do so. Many who were fully qualified for citizenship were allowed "to cling to the benefits and protection attendant upon their wardship." He stated his case in the following manner: "It is neither just nor reasonable that the state should continue to bear expense and responsibility on behalf of those who are quite capable of conducting their own affairs."[45]

Section 122 of the Indian Act was amended in 1918 to simplify the enfranchisement process in accordance with Scott's wishes. It enabled an Indian who held no land on a reserve and did not follow "the Indian mode of life" to apply to the superintendent general for enfranchisement. In order to be successful, he had to prove that he was self-supporting, accept his share of band funds, and relinquish further claims to band property. Widows and unmarried Indian women over twenty-one were also eligible to apply.[46]

There were some immediate results. Between Confederation and 1918 only 65 families or 102 persons had become enfranchised. But in the two years following the amendment, 97 families, 258 persons, underwent the process.[47] Scott noted this development with satisfaction, but he felt that additional measures were needed:

> I think it would be in the interest of good administration if the provisions with regard to enfranchisement were further extended as to enable the Department to enfranchise individual Indians or a band of Indians without the necessity of obtaining their consent thereto in cases where it was found upon investigation that the continuance of wardship was no longer in the interests of the public or the Indians.[48]

An amendment to the Indian Act incorporating the procedure that Scott envisaged was subsequently drawn up in the department and won Meighen's approval.[49] Introduced into Parliament in March 1920 as Bill 14, it allowed for the enfranchisement of an Indian against his will following a report by a person appointed by the superintendent general on his suitability. The bill also sought to impose school attendance on Indian children between the ages of seven and fifteen (see Chapter Five).

The compulsory enfranchisement was by far the most contentious part of the amendment, and it attracted the most attention. Reaction in the press was mixed. The Toronto *Globe*, for example, wondered if the time was ripe for such a radical departure from traditional policy.[50] But the Ottawa *Journal* welcomed the legislation, noting that the Indians deserved full citizenship immediately, especially after their effort during the war.[51] The Indian response was universally hostile, and the proposed amendment became an immediate rallying cry for those opposed to department policy.

In view of the controversial nature of the measure, the government considered it advisable to submit it for consideration to a special parliamentary committee. The committee, under the chairmanship of W.A. Boys, M.P. for South Simcoe, convened on 31 March. That Indians were invited to make submissions was a source of concern to Scott, who correctly anticipated that they would attempt to wreck the bill. He advised Boys early in April that there was no point in sending out notices to all bands regarding the hearings as the city would be "flooded with Indians." And he explained further:

> Their evidence is really not needed, because we know that those who would come would be opposed to the Bill or any Government measure, unless they saw some immediate profit, financial or otherwise, without any outlay on their part.

He went on to say that the Indians who were already in the city at his invitation would suffice. It was unfortunate that in that group British Columbia was underrepresented, but he felt that as far as that province was concerned, "it would be difficult to get the Indians who [were] favourable to the Bill to make any appearance."[52]

The committee to consider Bill 14 held seventeen meetings in all, during which it heard the evidence of thirty-five Indian witnesses, including legal counsel for the Six Nations and for the Allied Tribes of British Columbia. In spite of Scott's attempts behind the scenes to control the number of negative representations, the overwhelming majority of Indian witnesses were hostile to the amendment.[53] For example, a memorandum drawn up by the Six Nations and by the Iroquois of Tyendinaga, St. Regis, Caughnawaga, and Oka for submission to the committee argued that if an Indian were sufficiently intelligent to be enfranchised, then surely he was intelligent enough to be consulted about it.[54] The Indian witnesses generally argued along similar lines, demanding the continuation of consultation and expressing the fear that the measure would destroy their communities.

Scott was also called as a witness, and he aired his views with his accustomed frankness. He pointed out that the prevailing system required a long probationary period; he favoured making enfranchisement available immediately to those who were ready for it. He admitted that the amendment would introduce compulsion, but there would still be ample room for consultation during the investigation by the department official. Acceleration of the enfranchisement process was vital to the achievement of the department's ultimate aim:

> I want to get rid of the Indian problem. I do not think as a matter of fact, that this country ought to continuously protect a class of people who are able to stand alone. That is my whole point. Our objective is to continue until there is not a single Indian in Canada that has not been absorbed into the body politic, and there is no Indian question, and no Indian Department and that is the whole object of this Bill.[55]

The majority of committee members ultimately favoured the bill, and it was returned to the Commons with one small amendment. Instead of the original proposal to appoint an official to report on the fitness of an Indian to be enfranchised, the bill now required the establishment of a three-person board. The triumvirate was to consist of two department officials and someone nominated by the band to which the candidate for enfranchisement belonged.[56] The compulsory school attendance clause was endorsed in its original form.

When Bill 14 was discussed in Parliament in June, Opposition leader W.L. Mackenzie King attacked it on the grounds that the views of the Indians had been ignored. To illustrate his point, he read a statement which had been submitted to him by the Allied Tribes of British Columbia. The statement claimed that the bill would break up the tribes, destroy Indian status, and undermine native land claims. The Allied Tribes asked why Indians could not obtain the vote and citizenship while retaining their lands and status. The Liberal leader accused the government of trying to find Indians favourable to the bill as witnesses to appear before the committee. The fact that the vast majority who did so were opposed to it was indicative of widespread hostility.

Meighen, who must have known of Scott's manipulations, denied the allegation. He explained that certain Indians had volunteered to come to Ottawa and that they had been helped to do so.

Then King proposed suspending passage of the bill until a representative body of Indians could be consulted. Meighen retorted that the department was already aware of the Indians' views, and, after all, wards could not be given the same considerations as citizens![57] The bill was passed on 25 June and assented to 1 July.

Indian opposition to the amendment continued after its enactment as Section 107 of the act. In fact, so great was the hostility that nobody was enfranchised at the initiative of the department under its provisions. Under a more resolute regime, the mass enfranchisement of Indians might have taken place. But by this time the Union government had lost much of its drive and seemed increasingly less capable of dealing with the country's problems. Nor did the selection of Meighen as Borden's successor in the summer of 1920 help to revive its flagging fortunes. The Indians were only a minor consideration in the overall scheme of things, but there seemed to be little point in antagonizing them unduly and in the process allowing the opposition to score easy political points. Meighen's administration fell towards the end of 1921, paving the way for a repeal of the hated amendment.

Repeal, of course, was not inevitable. Parties in opposition often disparage measures that they retain if they achieve power on the grounds of political expediency. Nonetheless, Mackenzie King's Liberals took steps to rescind the compulsory features of the legislation shortly after their election. In June 1922 Charles Stewart, the new minister of the interior and superintendent general of Indian affairs, introduced an amendment to the act which, while leaving the three person enfranchisement board provision in place, required that the process be initiated "upon the application of an Indian."[58]

Meighen continued to defend compulsory enfranchisement on the grounds that the Indians were reluctant to abandon certain advantages of wardship. He observed: "Experience showed the department—and I know that the deputy minister was firmly convinced of it in my time—that we ourselves had positively to take the first step, or it was not going to be taken." Stewart responded that the Indians had been "up in arms" and argued that the government ought to educate them so that they would desire citizenship of their own free will.[59]

Even though he admitted upon taking office that he knew little of Indian affairs in general, Stewart was cognizant of the growing mood of militancy on the part of some native groups.[60] The Six Nations' council, the Allied Tribes of British Columbia, and the League of Indians of Canada were becoming particularly troublesome, and the question of compulsory enfranchisement had only served to galvanize their militancy. In repealing the measure, the superintendent general was hoping to stem the rising tide of organized opposition and to pave the way for smoother administration. It was a major setback for Scott, but it was one of the few instances in which he was overruled. Stewart soon came to rely heavily on his advice, and the conciliatory approach that characterized the minister's early months in office was superseded by the more draconian and prescriptive tactics of the deputy superintendent.

During Scott's incumbency, a number of important developments took place which tended to clarify the nature and extent of native hunting rights. Hunting, trapping, and fishing were important activities to Indians, not just as means of sustenance but also as integral components of their way of life. The inclusion of clauses guaranteeing the continuation of these rights in the treaties underlines their significance. In fact, the principal difficulty that faced treaty commissioners often lay in convincing the Indians that such rights would not be restricted.

Hunting was equally important to Indians outside of the treaty system, and they claimed the privilege of doing so on the basis of aboriginal rights.

For non-Indians, hunting was a sport. At best, it provided some supplement to an already adequate diet; at worst, it adorned living rooms with specimens of the taxidermist's art. Long before the nineteenth century ended, white sports-men were competing in ever-increasing numbers with Indians in the chase. As settlement advanced and the north was opened up, the competition intensified. In the new century, American tourists began to come north to join in the fray as game was being depleted in their own country.

Provincial game laws attempted to regulate the killing, especially as it became evident that measures were required to prevent the extermination of species. The imposition of licences, closed seasons, and "bag limits" were the usual features of these regulations. In many cases, special exemptions for Indians were written into the laws, but otherwise they were required to abide by the restrictions. The fact that the restrictions violated promises made in the treaties was a source of considerable discontent among the Indians. It also posed a problem for the federal government. It did not want to be accused of having broken its word, yet it favoured conservation measures. The game laws of Ontario provide one example of how Indian Affairs dealt with this dilemma.

Section 32 of the Ontario Game Protection Act, in operation in the 1890s, exempted Indians from its provisions under certain circumstances. They could take game for personal use only on reserves, in unorganized territories, and on land to which their claims had not been surrendered. When Indians were prosecuted for violations of the act, it was usually for the sale of game to non-Indians. Indian Affairs felt that the legislation was somewhat vague and requested an opinion from the federal Department of Justice. The latter body offered the view that Indians could sell the pelt, but not the meat of the animals they killed. When the act was amended and consolidated in 1900, the exemp-tions remained in place. Indians continued to protest against restrictions on their right to hunt and dispose of game. The department advised them that the laws were binding "even if it could be shown" that they violated treaty rights.[61]

The policy of advising Indians to obey game laws continued during Scott's years. The department agreed that such laws superseded the hunting and fishing rights guaranteed in the treaties. And when prosecutions took place, the courts usually concurred with this judgment and found against the Indians. In such instances, the department urged leniency.[62]

The harassment of Indians by Ontario provincial police and game wardens took place with sufficient frequency that the department felt obliged to intervene. In January 1917, Scott wrote to the provincial deputy minister of game and fisheries protesting the action of the warden at Killaloe, who had seized a gun, a tent, blankets, and four deer from a party of Indian hunters. The deputy superintendent suggested that each native family should be allowed one or two deer in the winter. The protest was effective, and the warden was asked to return the confiscated venison and equipment. In fact, in the same month, and again at Scott's request, instructions went out from the provincial Game and Fisheries Department to all officers urging leniency when it came to enforcing the law in the case of Indians.[63]

The department's policy was partly prompted by a gnawing doubt in the minds of its leading officials that treaty obligations were being broken by provincial game laws. Those living under the terms of the Robinson treaties had a particularly interesting case. The agreements entered into in 1850 gave the Indians the explicit right to hunt and fish throughout the surrendered territories with the exception of such portions as might "from time to time be sold or leased to individuals or companies of individuals and occupied by them with the consent of the provincial government." The western numbered treaties, by way of contrast, granted the right to hunt and fish, but subject to government regulation.

In March 1917, the Ft. William band of Ojibway Indians sent a petition to the King asking him to intercede with the Ontario government to secure the hunting privileges outlined in the Robinson Superior Treaty. The fate of this petition was similar to that of all such documents. It was returned by Downing Street to the governor general, and it was referred in due course to Indian Affairs. It was one of many petitions and protests, and Scott, who all along had suspected the strength of the Indians' case, sought advice. He informed E.L. Newcombe, the deputy minister of justice, that the situation was becoming "more and more acute" and proposed testing the question in the courts so that it be clarified for once and for all.[64] This was an unusual move for Scott as he generally abhorred the notion of Indian claims being subjected to judicial procedure with the inevitable bad publicity such a course of action would entail. But the Justice Department responded negatively, and he abandoned the idea. Instead, he continued with the policy of advising Indians to obey the law while urging leniency on the provincial authorities.[65]

The blame for the restriction of Indian hunting rights cannot be laid entirely on the shoulders of provincial governments. A number of federal agencies, with the active collusion of Scott, were also responsible. Nowhere is this more evident than in the case of the Migratory Birds Convention Act.

By the early decades of the twentieth century, the North American game bird population was showing the effects of the systematic slaughter that accompanied its annual migrations. The Eskimo curlew, Labrador duck, passenger pigeon, and great auk were extinct or on the verge of becoming so. These developments alarmed bird-watchers, naturalists, sportsmen, arms manufacturers, and similar interest groups in the United States, and they began to lobby Washington demanding conservation measures. Protective legislation followed, but it was deemed inadequate by itself.[66] The birds spent the summer months in Canada, and without the co-operation of the Canadian government, the slaughter would have continued. Consequently, Washington approached Ottawa in February 1914, and subsequent negotiations led to the signing of the Migratory Birds Convention between the two countries on 16 August 1916.[67] The American Congress ratified the treaty almost immediately, and Canada followed suit in the following year with the Migratory Birds Convention Act.

The convention specified closed seasons on a large number of birds, but a number of exemptions were provided for native peoples. For example, the closed season on migratory game birds was to be between 10 March and 1 September, except in those states and provinces on the Atlantic seaboard north of Chesapeake Bay, where it was to extend from 1 February to 15 August. During those closed seasons, Indians were allowed to take scoters for food but not for sale. The closed season on migratory non-game birds was to extend throughout the year. However, "Eskimos and Indians" were allowed to take at any time "auks, auklets, guillemots, murres, and puffins, and their eggs for food and their skins for clothing," but the birds or their eggs could not be sold. The Canadian legislation ratifying the convention permitted the minister of the interior, under whose authority it was to operate, to appoint game officers with powers of justices of the peace to enforce its provisions.[68]

An interest in conservation had appeared in federal circles before the American initiative. The Conservation Act of 1909 had established the Commission of Conservation to advise the government on conservation and resource development. The commission's membership was drawn from prominent academics and leading federal and provincial politicians. A new body was added after the international agreement. In December 1916, the Advisory Board on Wild Life Protection was established. It was an interdepartmental committee of the federal government whose purpose was to formulate policy and propose legislation in light of the Migratory Birds Convention and also with reference to the northern territories. The commissioner of dominion parks, the dominion entomologist, representatives of the Commission of Conservation and of the Geological Survey, and Duncan Campbell Scott for the Department of Indian Affairs made up the advisory board.[69]

The advisory board and the Commission of Conservation were primarily interested in the protection of wildlife, and there was general agreement regarding the necessary measures. There were some differences of opinion among the various interest groups, however, and the issue which was the source of greatest contention was native hunting. It was not that the concessions granted under the Migratory Birds Act or under some provincial game laws were regarded as excessive, but rather that Indians were frequently accused of abusing those privileges.

Scott did not share the view that was sometimes expressed that Indians should be allowed to endure hardship so that sufficient game would be available for the amusement of white sportsmen. There were several instances during the 1920s in which he defended native hunting rights and rejected allegations of irresponsible behaviour on their part.[70] He insisted at the same time that the Migratory Birds Act be obeyed. When four Indians were prosecuted for the possession of gulls' eggs in Prince Rupert during the summer of 1923, the department refused to intervene on their behalf.[71]

Predictably, protests from the native population against these restrictions on their traditional activities made their way to Ottawa. In July 1927, for example, the chiefs of the Fort Chipewyan band, Alberta, wrote to Scott denouncing the act. They pointed out that their treaty guaranteed hunting rights and that it had been signed prior to the convention with the United States. Wild fowl had long been their staple food during the summer, and they were now allowed to hunt only for a few weeks in the fall. "Are we then to starve during the summer months," they asked, "because the whiteman has broken his word to us?"[72] Protests of this nature generated some discussion within the department. The official position remained, however, that the Migratory Birds Act superseded the treaties and would have to be obeyed.[73]

The federal government was involved in game management in the Northwest Territories as well, and concessions to the native population were also features of the policies that it initiated in those regions. The Northwest Game Act, which became law in September 1917, protected indefinitely such endangered species as buffalo, musk-oxen, elk, and white pelicans. It placed a closed season on a large number of birds and animals whose existence was in no immediate danger and required that licences be purchased by those wishing to hunt, trap, or trade in game. Indians, Eskimos, and half-breeds who were bona fide inhabitants of the north were exempted from the licence requirement and were permitted to take any of the non-endangered species throughout the year "to prevent starvation."[74]

This law had been made necessary by the invasion of the north by white trappers. Well-equipped and eager for quick profits, they plundered the countryside of its wildlife. They posed a danger not only to the animals, but also to the native hunters whose livelihood they were destroying. The law proved inadequate to curb the activities of these intruders, and in September 1923 three game preserves, Yellowknife, Slave River, and Peel River, were established for the exclusive use of the Indians.[75]

The overlapping jurisdiction of Indian Affairs and the Northwest Territories and Yukon Branch of the Interior Department complicated administrative matters during the 1920s. The Indian Department tended to press for further concessions to the native population such as the creation of additional hunting preserves, but to little avail. In fact, at a meeting of the Advisory Board on Wildlife Protection in February 1932, Scott urged that hunting and trapping in the north be confined to natives only and pointed out that Quebec had already made such an arrangement in that part of the province lying north of the transcontinental railway. But nothing came of his proposal.[76]

It might appear that in securing modifications to game laws and in negotiating the establishment of game preserves, the Department of Indian Affairs was championing native hunting, trapping, and fishing rights. But this was not the case. In reality, the department encouraged such traditional pursuits only in those regions in which alternative means of making a living did not exist. As Scott explained:

> In considering this question, it should be understood that the department only desires special hunting privileges for Indians in the outlying districts where other sufficient employment is not available. In the settled and organized localities, the department affords the Indians ample opportunity for agricultural and industrial pursuits, and discourages them from dependence on the chase.[77]

As long as Indians in remote locations could maintain themselves in their traditional manner, they would not require government assistance and become a burden on the public purse.[78] Hunting was not perceived as a desirable mode of existence, but as a means whereby relief expenditure could be kept at a minimum.

The policy of curbing expenditure applied not just in the case of dispensing relief, but also in the provision of medical services, as Scott's circular of October 1913 made clear. This was particularly contentious since the Indians' susceptibility to a number of serious maladies gave them a death rate far in excess of the rest of the populace. Tuberculosis was the major killer, especially among the Indians of the prairie provinces and British Columbia. Influenza epidemics and outbreaks of smallpox were also devastating. In attempting to deal with the problem of the general ill-health of its charges, the department faced a troublesome dilemma. On the one hand, it was necessary to restrain demands on the public coffers; on the other, it was important to show that the native population was benefiting from the paternal care provided. Evidence of an increasing population would have constituted proof of such benefit, but growth of this nature could only be accomplished with a comprehensive system of health care—an expensive proposition. During Scott's incumbency, the department struggled with only minimal success to overcome this administrative dilemma.

The appointment of Dr. P.H. Bryce as the department's first medical officer in 1904 has already been alluded to. It was a positive step to deal with a problem that was receiving increasing public recognition. As Bryce's crusade against tuberculosis focused largely on residential schools, it is dealt with in Chapter Five.

The restraint that characterized the Borden and Meighen administrations resulted in less funding for Indian Affairs and a consequent reduction in the department's provision of health services. Scott's economizing attitude reinforced this tendency. It was an ill-advised course of action, for the department found itself without a medical officer in 1918, the year of the Spanish 'flu.[79] This deadly epidemic swept away over 30,000 people, among whom were close to 4,000 Indians.[80] This latter figure comprised about 4 per cent of the status Indian population. The crisis was of such magnitude that the federal government created a national Department of Health in the following year.[81] Nonetheless, Indian health remained the responsibility of Scott's department.

An improvement in medical services became possible during the 1920s with the more liberal appropriations of the Mackenzie King government. In 1922, four nurses were hired by the department for the prairie provinces. Their responsibilities were to visit Indian schools and communities, giving instruction on hygiene, nutrition, infant care, and other matters. It was at this time also that the department began to build its own hospitals on the larger reserves.[82] Some hospitals maintained by churches became eligible for grants if they catered to a native clientele. In 1927, the department created a medical branch, and Dr. E.L. Stone was placed in charge.[83] By 1929 the number of hospitals owned and operated by the department had risen to seven. It was still policy not to maintain sanitaria for the treatment of tuberculosis but rather to find places in existing facilities for afflicted Indians. The department employed twelve physicians at the time, of whom four combined their medical activities with the duties of Indian agent. The system of travelling nurses had been expanded to all provinces and territories with the exceptions of Prince Edward Island and the Yukon.[84]

These were undeniable improvements, but they were far from adequate. In times of crisis, this became all the more evident. For example, when an influenza epidemic swept down the Mackenzie Valley during the summer of 1928, it killed an estimated 600 Indians. The total Indian population of the Northwest Territories was about 4,000. Several communities were wiped out entirely and many others were reduced to a few straggling survivors.[85]

The ravages of epidemics and the steady toll of tuberculosis and other ailments meant that the native population showed little growth during Scott's years as department head. The total number of status Indians was recorded as 106,490 in 1913. It fell to 103,774 in 1914 and to 103,531 in the following year. A slow increase then ensued, bringing the figure to 108,012 in 1929.[86] The difficulty in acquiring accurate information about those living in the northern forests meant that these figures were not completely reliable. They did indicate, however, that the Indian population had stabilized and was no longer heading for extinction.

Progress in combatting tuberculosis had largely contributed to this state of affairs. The tubercular death rate for Indians had fallen from 8 per 1000 in 1926 to 2.79 per 1000 in 1931. The rate for whites at the latter date was about 0.5 per 1000.[87] The figures indicate that some advances were being made but that the disparity in the health conditions of native and white was still considerable. In fact, tuberculosis remained the principal cause of death among Indians until the early 1950s when the introduction of streptomycin made dramatic improvements possible.

Scott's annual reports invariably sounded a note of optimism. Glowing accounts of progress in agriculture, education, and the adoption of "civilized manners" appeared with predictable regularity. But on the question of Indian health, such optimism was conspicuously absent. In the Deputy Superintendent's Report for 1931 (his last), for example, Scott presented a bleak and discouraging picture. He admitted that the Indians living in the northern forest belts of the provinces were "not showing any satisfactory tendency towards increased resistance to tuberculosis." Their plight was being aggravated by the invasion of their lands by white trappers who were decimating the game. And he concluded, "It may be that an actual decrease in these bands is inevitable, and some of them may be reduced to remnants of their present numbers." The department's inability to deal with this situation was a result of its limited budget. Scott estimated that there were 5,000 Indians in Canada suffering from active tuberculosis and that it cost approximately $1,000 to maintain a patient in a sanatarium for one year. Yet the department's annual expenditure on health was only about $1,000,000, or less than $10 per person. And he could hardly help concluding, "it is obvious that the health service is administered with economy."[88] Undoubtedly, the struggle between providing adequate health care to the native population and keeping expenses at a minimum was decided in the interests of the latter.

The 1920s saw an expansion of the Indian Affairs bureaucracy to the last frontier, the Northwest Territories. In August 1920, oil was discovered at Norman Wells on land to which the aboriginal title had not been surrendered. There could be no question of leaving such valuable property in the hands of its original occupants. The terms of a new treaty were immediately drawn up by the department—Treaty No. 11. H.A. Conroy was appointed treaty commissioner, and he set out for the Mackenzie Valley in the summer of 1921 to negotiate with the native population. The surrenders were duly secured, and what was seen as a minor obstacle to the development of the north was removed. Initially, little changed for the Indians, except that once a year an agent of the department would appear bearing the token payment of five dollars.[89]

As the decade progressed, the federal presence in the north was increasingly felt. In 1924 Eskimos were placed under the jurisdiction of the superintendent general of Indian affairs, but the terms of the Indian Act were not imposed upon them. No Indian agents were appointed in the Arctic regions, however, and the only federal officials with whom Eskimos had any sustained contact were the Mounted Police and employees of the Interior Department. In 1930, control of Eskimo affairs was removed from the superintendent general and transferred to the Northwest Territories Branch of the Department of the Interior.

As Indian administration was extending its boundaries, it was also intensifying its control over its charges. It would be tedious to recount in detail the various amendments to the Indian Act that were instituted between 1920 and Scott's retirement. Like those that had preceded them, they tended to increase the power of the department while concomitantly weakening the autonomy of the Indians. One of these amendments is worthy of some scrutiny nonetheless since it had a direct bearing on a number of issues that will be discussed later.

In April 1924, Scott wrote to the deputy minister of justice proposing a new amendment to the Indian Act which would prevent lawyers and agitators collecting money from Indians for the pursuit of claims against the government without department approval.[90] This proposal was incorporated into the Indian Act as Section 149a in 1927. In the consolidation of the act later that year, it became Section 141. In introducing the amendment in the House of Commons, Charles Stewart observed that lawyers all across the country were taking advantage of Indians by convincing them to pursue legal claims for substantial fees. And he added, "We think it is to the advantage of the Indians that these contracts should be scrutinized by the department in order to protect them from exploitation."[91]

Exploitation was hardly the issue. The real concern of the department was agitation by such groups as the Allied Indian Tribes of British Columbia (see Chapter Eight), the Six Nations' council (see Chapter Seven), and the League of Indians of Canada (see Chapter Six). These groups were proving more and more troublesome during the 1920s. Frequently employing the services of legal counsel, they tended to disrupt efficient administration and hinder the achievement of department aims by advancing claims to land, special status, and other considerations. Section 141 was but another weapon in the hands of the department in its efforts to control these activities. Scott's struggle with native militancy will be discussed in detail in the chapters that follow, along with a number of other aspects of policy.

4

The Treaty Maker

The role played by treaties in the relationship between Indians and whites in Canadian history has been discussed in some detail in Chapter One. By the opening of the twentieth century there were still some parts of the country that were yet to be brought into the treaty system. Among these was that wilderness of rock and muskeg that constituted northern or "new" Ontario—the area north of the height of land that drained into Hudson and James Bay. Several years prior to his promotion to deputy superintendent general, D.C. Scott played a pivotal role in securing the surrender of the Indian title to this land.

The extinction of Indian land title and arrangements for compensation were complicated in the Ontario setting by the overlapping jurisdictions of the federal and provincial governments. Difficulties had first arisen in the 1880s. When Treaty No. 3 was signed in 1873, it secured the surrender of the aboriginal title to tracts of land northwest of Lake Superior which spanned the present-day Manitoba-Ontario border. While this was transpiring, the location of Ontario's northwestern boundary was a matter of dispute between the federal and provincial governments. Ottawa felt that it should follow the height of land (which, coincidentally, was also the boundary of the Robinson-Superior Treaty of 1850) to a point directly north of Fort William. Ontario attempted to claim a more extensive domain, with a boundary along the Albany River, west to Lac Seul and the English River.[1]

The dispute was ultimately settled in Ontario's favour, and when the province expanded in 1889, it took over a large proportion of the Treaty No. 3 area. Ottawa subsequently argued that the province should be responsible for the annuities payable to the Indians under that treaty. This created further difficulties between the two levels of government, and the problem was not solved until 1910 when Ontario was declared free of such obligations.

This dispute showed that responsibility for Indians was a source of contention, if not animosity, between Ottawa and Toronto. Nonetheless, the two governments had agreed in 1894 that should further treaties become necessary in the territories ceded to the province, they would require the concurrence of Toronto. Of course, the extinction of Indian title has only been sought when the land in question acquires economic importance to the dominant society. As the nineteenth century drew to a close, the new territories of northern Ontario were quickly assuming that mantle. Though composed mainly of the Laurentian Shield—a wilderness of forests and lakes long regarded as an obstacle to development—certain innovations were casting a new light on it, and leading to unprecedented exploration and settlement.

Perhaps the foremost harbinger of economic good times was a series of technological achievements making possible the generation of electricity from falling water. By 1900, the hydraulic turbine, the dynamo, the alternator, and distribution systems were all in place, allowing electricity not only to be produced cheaply, but also to be transmitted economically for hundreds of miles over the most difficult of terrains.[2]

These developments were crucial to Canada's industrial growth in the new century, and they were particularly important for Ontario and Quebec. Neither province possessed much coal, upon which the first industrialization had been based, but both were blessed with extensive river networks. The St. Lawrence system was one of the first to be harnessed, but the water-power potential of the Laurentian Shield—in particular that of the rivers that flowed into James Bay—was quickly realized.[3]

The generation of hydro-electricity became a vital factor in the continuing prosperity of one of Canada's great industries: pulp and paper. Here was a manufacturing process that required large amounts of motive power but relatively small amounts of heat. Electrical energy suited it perfectly. The industry had grown steadily since the 1860s when commercial methods for the manufacture of paper from wood pulp had first been developed. The rise of mass-circulation newspapers in the large urban areas of Canada and the United States created an ever-increasing market for the product, and the industry was seeking to satisfy its voracious appetite for wood by advancing into the Laurentian Shield.[4]

The economic exploitation of northern Ontario would not have been practicable without the creation of a transportation infrastructure. At the dawn of the new century, plans were already afoot to traverse the muskeg with lines of steel. In 1902, the Grand Trunk Railway decided to gamble on reviving its slumping fortunes by building a line to the west coast and thereby competing with the CPR in transcontinental trade.[5] Pressured by the federal government, the company adopted a route that commenced in Moncton, passed through Quebec City, and crossed the Hudson Bay drainage basin in northern Ontario on its way to Winnipeg. From there it went on to Edmonton, the Yellowhead Pass, and the Pacific at Prince Rupert. It was hoped that a railway through the Hudson and James Bay basin would stimulate settlement in the area and accelerate economic development.[6] That hope was soon realized as small stations and depots along the way developed into the towns of Cochrane, Kapuskasing, and Hearst.[7]

Of even greater import for the future of the region was the decision to build a railway on a north-south axis with the objective of ultimately reaching James Bay. Colonization of the north was its *raison d'etre*. The idea had first been mooted by groups of Toronto and Montreal businessmen in the 1880s, but none had proven willing to risk their capital on such a venture. However, Premier A.S. Hardy made it one of his promises in the Ontario provincial election of 1898. The first phase was to run from North Bay to New Liskeard. Hardy won the election, and by 1902 work had begun on the Timiskaming and Northern Ontario Railway.

The railway reached New Liskeard at the end of 1904 but before the completion of that initial phase there had been a dramatic change in its importance. Construction crews discovered significant deposits of silver at a place subsequently called Cobalt. Predictably enough, this led to a flurry of mining activity which resulted in further silver finds and, in addition, the discovery of gold, copper, and other minerals.[8]

The invasion of northern Ontario by miners, lumbermen, construction workers, and settlers was thus assured. In a few short years, investors recognized the region's potential value. Vast wealth was sitting in Ontario's backyard just waiting to be gathered up. As D.C. Scott observed when he reflected on the possibilities: "This territory contains much arable land, many million feet of pulpwood, untold wealth of minerals, and unharnessed water-powers sufficient to do the work on half the continent."[9]

But the lands of the Hudson and James Bay basin that were now attracting the covetous attention of speculators and developers constituted the hunting terrain of thousands of Cree and Ojibway Indians. Nor had the aboriginal title to these vast domains ever been extinguished. It quickly became evident to officials in Ottawa that the smooth and uncomplicated development of the area would best be effected by dealing with the question of aboriginal title at the earliest convenience.

In 1899, Scott and Inspector J. Macrae visited New Brunswick House to meet with Robinson Treaty Indians. While there, they also came into contact with Indians whose lands lay north of those ceded in 1850. These non-treaty Indians expressed concern at the erosion of their rights as miners and surveyors invaded their territories in increasing numbers and disrupted their hunting activities. Rumours regarding the construction of railways in the area were causing particular alarm. Scott and his companion assured them that the government would "certainly not fail to properly consider their claims" and that they would be dealt with "in the same spirit of justice" that the department had always manifested towards Indians—a promise with somewhat ominous over-tones whose subtlety was probably lost on its recipients. Macrae reported this meeting to the superintendent general and suggested that the time was ripe for the incorporation of these northern Indians into the treaty system. He pro-posed sending an officer to the major settlements in the James Bay area to collect information upon which to base the technicalities of the projected agreement.[10]

From that point, discussion ensued within the department concerning the most desirable approach to the scheme and the jurisdictional problems a treaty would pose. The wisdom of extending the treaty system itself was not ques-tioned and the necessity of doing so quickly became all the more apparent as petitions from Indians, alarmed at encroachments, arrived in Ottawa.[11] There were also representations from mining and lumber companies who sought assurances that their ventures would not be compromised by the technicality of aboriginal title.[12]

J.A.J. McKenna was of the opinion that the adhesion of the northern Indians to the Robinson Treaty with some modifications would be the approach least fraught with complications.[13] Nor was it necessary for anyone to make a special visit to the area. Agents making annuity payments under the Robinson Treaty could collect any information that was required.[14] McKenna's latter suggestion was adopted, and by December 1902 agents had ascertained that there were 2,140 Indians living in the territories. The possibility of a larger number was admitted, but it would not exceed 3,000.[15]

In his role as chief accountant, Scott translated these figures into a rough budget for the treaty. He estimated the cost of negotiating the agreement at $15,000, while the first annuity payment and the gratuity offered upon signing would come to $24,000. He based his calculations on the assumption that the annuities and gratuities would be paid at the rate of $4 per head.

In August 1903, Deputy Superintendent Frank Pedley passed on Scott's estimates to Superintendent General Sifton and discussed some of the legal complications. The principal difficulty lay in defining the role of the provinces. Even though much of the James Bay basin lay in Quebec, Pedley suggested that the Indians resident in that province be omitted from consideration since the French-Canadian tradition had always been to eschew treaties and the concept of aboriginal title.

The treaty, then, was to be confined to those Indians within the Ontario boundary. Pedley pointed out to Sifton that after Confederation Ontario and Quebec had paid the federal government the sum of $205,000 to represent their all-time contribution to the on-going costs of the Robinson Treaties. This established a precedent for Ontario's proportionate contribution to the treaty.

The deputy superintendent suggested that the province be asked to pay for the annuities and the surveying of reserves while Ottawa assumed the cost of making the treaty and supporting schools. The treaty ought to be a new one, similar to those signed in the west. Treaty No. 9, or the James Bay Treaty, was the proposed title.[16]

The minister accepted these recommendations, and the department proceeded with its arrangements. In May 1904, Pedley sought the advice of S.C. Chipman, commissioner of the Hudson's Bay Company, on the best means of reaching the Indians in question. He also requested the assistance of the company in transporting the treaty party. Chipman was only too willing to help and suggested that if the Indians were notified between Christmas and March, meetings for the signing of the agreement could be organized for the subsequent summer and autumn months.[17] His reply convinced department officials that the entire operation could be conducted in 1905. Much depended, however, on the attitude of Ontario.

In April 1904, Pedley opened negotiations by contacting E.J. Davis, the province's commissioner of crown lands. He informed Davis of Ottawa's intention of conducting the treaty and proposed that Ontario incur the financial responsibility for annuities and reserve surveys. The province would thereby benefit since "the shadow of the Indian title" would be removed from its territories.[18]

The response from Toronto was not encouraging. Aubrey White, the assistant commissioner of crown lands, demanded a clearer indication of Ontario's proposed responsibility and even wondered why a treaty was necessary at all.[19]

Pedley's reply was conciliatory, and he attempted to show what an incredible bargain the proposed treaty was. He pointed out that the terms were the maximum that would be offered the Indians "in any event." In fact, they were identical to those found in the Robinson treaties, and "the Governments interested might be considered fortunate to cancel the Indian title at this time by considerations which were thought adequate in the year 1850."[20] But Premier George Ross's decision to dissolve the provincial legislature and hold an election in the following January temporarily suspended negotiations.

In March 1905, Scott proposed that the federal government proceed with the treaty independently and settle Ontario's liability later.[21] This idea won support as a last resort, but Ottawa continued to seek an agreement. However, an itinerary which required departure for the north in July had been received from the Hudson's Bay Company and Scott and Pedley were determined to adhere to it. As Pedley pointed out to Sir Wilfrid Laurier, there was an urgency to proceed because "the influx of white men naturally causes uneasiness amongst Indians and leads to extravagant demands."[22]

Meanwhile, Scott had drawn up a draft order-in-council which, if approved by the governor general and the lieutenant-governor of Ontario, would permit the treaty to proceed. On 8 May, Pedley forwarded the document to J.J. Foy, the provincial commissioner of crown lands, urging immediate acceptance. In January, J.P. Whitney's Conservatives had swept the Ontario polls, ending thirty-four years of Liberal rule and bringing to power a regime which had avoided the antagonism of federal-provincial relations over the previous decades. Ottawa was therefore more hopeful that a settlement could now be reached.

Ontario's reply, received on 1 June, agreed in principle to the joint orders-in-council. However, the province demanded a number of minor changes. It asked that one of the treaty commissioners be appointed by Toronto and that the reserves be selected, not by the Indians, but by the commissioners. Pedley agreed on the assumption that the Indians would not be excluded completely from the selection process.[23]

A draft of the treaty was then prepared and forwarded for approval to A.J. Matheson, the provincial treasurer, on 12 June. At this late hour, the Ontario government decided that it wished to go beyond the joint orders-in-council and enter into an agreement with Ottawa specifying the province's liabilities prior to the signing of the treaty. This was quickly arranged, and the province accepted responsibility for the gratuities and annuities. In return, it demanded that "no site suitable for the development of water-power exceeding 500 horse power shall be included within the boundaries of any reserve."[24] Pedley conceded that this was a reasonable stipulation since it was "not desirable to have the Indians located near the large centres of population which usually grow up around large falls where the water power can readily be utilized for commercial purposes."[25] The agreement was signed between Interior Minister Frank Oliver and Francis Cochrane, provincial minister of lands and mines on 3 July. A few days before, Ontario had asked for one more concession—that precious minerals on reserves be retained for the province—but it was unacceptable.

Officials in Ottawa worked out the terms of the treaty and submitted them to the Ontario government for approval. There was no suggestion at any time that Indians or their representatives should be involved in these initial deliberations. The terms were similar to those offered in the western treaties of previous decades, but there were some important differences that cleverly protected the economic interests of the dominant society at every turn.

The treaty required the Indians to abandon their proprietary claims to the territories of "New Ontario," stretching from the height of land to James Bay and the Albany River—an area of approximately 90,000 square miles. In return, they would be offered reserves amounting to one square mile per family of five. As noted, at Ontario's insistence these reserves were to be selected by the treaty commissioners and in such a way as to exclude lands of potential value to whites. In the event of an error in that regard, a clause stipulated that

such portions of the reserves and lands above indicated as may at any time be required for public works, buildings, railways, or roads of whatsoever nature may be appropriated for that purpose by His Majesty's government of the Dominion of Canada, due compensation being made to the Indians.[26]

This expropriation clause was a feature of the western treaties with the exception of Nos. 1 and 2.

The Indians of the James Bay basin were hunters, trappers, and fishermen by occupation, and their primary concern in ceding title was that they be permitted to continue in these activities. The authors of the treaty knew this, and they allowed for such pursuits in the surrendered lands, but with certain restrictions:

And His Majesty the King thereby agrees with the said Indians that they shall have the right to pursue their usual vocations of hunting, trapping, and fishing throughout the tract surrendered as heretofore described, subject to such regulations as may from time to time be made by the government of the country, acting under the authority of His Majesty, and saving and excepting such tracts as may be required or taken up from time to time for settlement, mining, lumbering, trading or such purposes.[27]

In other words, the traditional economic activities of the Indians would have to be sacrificed whenever the white man's economic activities required, and, in addition, they could be restricted by the white man's game laws.

The government agreed to pay the salaries of teachers and to construct schoolhouses on the reserves. Presumably, education would prepare the young Indians for employment in the industries that were destined to encroach upon their hunting grounds. This educational clause was also similar to that included in the western treaties.

But the white man's largesse did not end here. The Indians were to be granted a gratuity of $8 upon signing the agreement and an annuity of $4 in perpetuity, courtesy of the Ontario government. These payments were lower than those under the western treaties.

In Treaties Nos. 3 to 8 provision was made for equipment and supplies to enable the Indians either to adopt agriculture or to pursue hunting and fishing with greater success. This clause was conspicuously absent from the terms of Treaty No. 9, and it was to be a source of embarrassment to the commissioners on at least one occasion during the negotiations.

Treaty No. 6 required the Indian agent to keep a "medicine chest" at his house for the benefit of the people—a clause that in recent years has been interpreted as an entitlement to free medical care. No such promise was made in Treaty No. 9.

None of the Indian treaties was remarkable for their generosity, but that scheduled for negotiation in 1905 appeared distinctly parsimonious compared with its predecessors. It is certainly conceivable that Scott's penny-pinching attitude and the need to persuade a reluctant Ontario government to contribute to the anticipated costs resulted in its niggardly provisions.

On 29 June 1905, Scott and Samuel Stewart were appointed as the Dominion's representatives on the treaty commission. A few days later, D.G. MacMartin was confirmed as the Ontario commissioner. The treaty party also included a physician, Dr. A.G. Meindl, whose task was to vaccinate the Indians *en route* and to attend to any other matters of medical concern. Two officers of the North West Mounted Police, James Parkinson and J.L. Vanasse, were brought along to guard the "treasure" of $30,000 in small notes—a potential windfall for some enterprising bandit of the north. It also seems that their presence was designed to intimidate the Indians and make resistance to the treaty less probable. By Scott's own admission: "The glory of their uniforms and the wholesome fear of the white man's law which they inspired spread down the river in advance and reached James Bay before the Commission."[28]

The party travelled west via the CPR early in July, stopping at Dinorwic, a station two hundred miles east of Winnipeg. There they were met by T.C. Rae, an official of the Hudson's Bay Company, who had been instructed to travel with the expedition and arrange for transportation, supplies, and other necessities. He made available three canoes to carry the commissioners and their baggage and engaged the services of a paddling crew headed by Jimmy Swain, a half-breed Albany River guide.[29] Scott was impressed by Swain, who, in spite of his sixty-seven years, could still work with the vigour of a young man. And he was amused by the guide's stories and by the curious renditions of popular tunes which he gave on an old fiddle.[30]

The expedition left Dinorwic on 3 July, and within a few days the canoes were making their way across the waters of Lac Seul. The Indians of that region had long since surrendered their land title under Treaty No. 3, but the commissioners nonetheless found some business to attend to with them. While approaching Lac Seul reserve, the commissioners heard drumming and learned from their crew that a dog feast was being held. Since parts of this ceremony were illegal, they decided to put to shore and stop the proceedings. Upon landing, Scott demanded to see the "conjurer." After much procrastination, he was produced. His name was Neotamaqueb—a man of great influence among his people and supposedly highly skilled in driving out "evil spirits." In the interrogation which followed, the commissioners were surprised by the wisdom and diplomacy with which he defended his work. But they nevertheless lectured and warned them that they would be watched in future. Scott was ill that evening, but he was well enough to travel the next day.[31] Whether the malady was related to the spells of the conjurer or not is beyond speculation.

Scott and his companions crossed the height of land on 10 July via Root River and reached Lake St. Joseph, the first body of water in the Albany River drainage system. They were now in the territory that was to be ceded under Treaty No. 9, and the next day they landed at Osnaburg, the first point at which negotiations were scheduled.

The rituals surrounding the treaty signing followed a similar format at each stop on the itinerary. The procedure commenced with an explanation of the terms offered by the commissioners. These were communicated to the assembled Indians by an interpreter—usually a Hudson's Bay Company official or a missionary. Discussion followed, and it inevitably ended with the Indians agreeing to the terms with varying degrees of enthusiasm. They then elected chiefs and councillors, and the chiefs appended their signatures or marks to the agreement. The gratuity of $8 was distributed, and the chiefs received flags and copies of the treaty as symbols of their authority. Next, the commissioners hosted a feast for the entire community. Tea, bacon, and bannock were the staples at these open-air banquets. The selection of reserves brought the commissioners' responsibilities to a conclusion.

Treaty negotiations were almost always held adjacent to H.B.C. posts, which willingly provided the supplies for the banquets at Ottawa's expense. The gratuities were usually also spent at the post. It is little wonder that the company proved so co-operative in transporting and accommodating the treaty party and in arranging the itinerary.

Native communities did not always welcome the commissioners as the happy bearers of government munificence. In fact, their motives were often viewed with suspicion. At Osnaburg, for instance, the Indians expressed concern that they would be confined to their reserves and have their hunting restricted should they sign the treaty. The commissioners insisted this would not be the case. As Scott put it in his inappropriately titled essay, "The Last of the Indian Treaties":

> So they were assured that they were not expected to give up their hunting-grounds, that they might hunt and fish throughout all the country, but that they were to be good subjects of the King, their great father, whose messengers we were.[32]

The official report of the commissioners recounted the incident in the following terms:

> On being informed that their fears in regard to both these matters were groundless, as their present manner of making their livelihood would in no way be interfered with, the Indians talked the matter over among themselves.[33]

Evidently impressed by these reassurances, the Indians agreed to sign on the following day. Neither Scott's essay nor the report makes it clear that the restrictions on hunting were explained fully. Possibly they were conveniently overlooked to secure concurrence. If the historical record does not prove misrepresentation, it certainly implies it.

Shortly after leaving Osnaburg, the expedition entered the Albany River, which drains Lake St. Joseph, and made its next scheduled stop at Ft. Hope. There the commissioners had to contend with the embarrassing revelations of an Indian dubbed "Yesno" because of his limited English vocabulary. Yesno announced to his assembled friends that they were to receive cattle, tools, and seed-grain as in Treaty No. 3. The commissioners were forced to admit that their terms were less generous and that such materials would not be offered. But the Indians agreed to the treaty nonetheless.[34]

From Ft. Hope the route followed the Albany River to its mouth at Ft. Albany on James Bay. The group made stops along the way to bring the inhabitants of the area into the treaty, and they reached Ft. Albany on 3 August. After a couple of days of negotiations and payment at that settlement, the treaty party left for Moose Factory by sailboat.[35] From that point a difficult journey upstream on the Abitibi River to Lake Abitibi lay before the commissioners. It took three weeks of paddling and portaging around rapids. The coastal Indians who manned the canoes on that portion of the trip impressed Scott with the veneer of Christianity they had acquired from the missionaries. As he noted in his inimitable way:

> The crew that took the Commission from Moose Factory to Abitibi were constant in their vespers and every evening recited a litany, sang a hymn and made a prayer. There was something primitive and touching in their devotion, and it marks an advance, but these Indians are capable of leaving a party of travellers suddenly and returning to Moose Factory in dudgeon if anything displeases them.[36]

Apparently, Scott and his companions experienced some anxiety that they might be abandoned in the wilderness. As they ascended the Abitibi, such fears likely dissipated as "evidences of approaching civilization and of the activity in railway construction and surveying, which had rendered the making of the treaty necessary, were constantly met with."[37]

The expedition entered Lake Abitibi on 29 August and on the following day landed at the H.B.C. post established on its shore. To the disappointment of the commissioners, not many Indians were present, and the treaty work had to be left unfinished. The situation was also complicated by the proximity of Indians whose lands lay in Quebec and who were not to be admitted to the treaty.

The return journey involved another week of travel to the northern reaches of the Temiskaming and Northern Ontario railway. From there a leisurely train ride brought the commissioners back to Ottawa by 9 September.[38]

In their report to the superintendent general of Indian affairs the commissioners recounted their achievements with satisfaction. Ninety thousand square miles had been ceded, and 1,617 Indians had been paid. A return trip would be necessary in the following summer to secure adhesion to the treaty by about 1,000 additional inhabitants of the area. The commissioners were particularly proud of having secured the land surrender at minimum cost to the federal and provincial governments:

> Throughout all the negotiations we carefully guarded against making any promises over and above those written in the treaty which might afterwards cause embarrassment to the governments concerned. No outside promises were made, and the Indians cannot, and we confidently believe do not, expect any other concessions than those set forth in the documents to which they gave their adherence. It was gratifying throughout to be met by these Indians with such a show of cordiality and trust, and to be able fully to satisfy *what they believed to be* their claims upon the governments of this country.[39] (Italics mine)

This passage suggests that the commissioners harboured serious doubts about the very legitimacy of the Indian claims. And when it came to the selection of reserves, they gave the interests of the dominant society first consideration:

> The treatment of the reserve question which in this treaty was most important, will, it is hoped, meet with approval. For the most part the reserves were selected by the commissioners after conference with the Indians. They have been selected in situations which are especially advantageous to their owners, and where they will not in any way interfere with railway development or the future commercial interests of the country. No valuable water-powers are included within the allotments.[40]

Scott undoubtedly felt that he had served his masters well. However, the two months he spent in the north had been far from enjoyable. He complained throughout of the mosquitoes and black flies, which were particularly troublesome at the portages.[41] In a letter to his friend Pelham Edgar a few weeks after his return, he reflected on the expedition as follows:

> my own trip was vastly different—I spent day after day without seeing a living thing—except the Indians and my own party. The landscape for the most part desolate beyond compare, loneliness seven times distilled—a country never to be the glad home of any happy people.[42]

The odyssey by canoe had been arduous and depressing. To compound matters, Scott had to return to the north country the following summer. He surmised that congenial company would render the voyage more enjoyable and applied to have Edgar appointed as the expedition's secretary. Approval came in March 1906, and Scott exulted "You've been appointed. Ain't it bully! All the flies and mosquitoes *en embryo* throughout the interior tremble with anticipation."[43]

Apart from his literary skills, Edgar proved to be a suitable choice because he shared Scott's perception of the nature of the treaty making process. Some years later, he wrote approvingly of the "irresistible northward march" of civilization and boasted that because it offered compensation for the surrender of aboriginal land title, Canada treated its native population "with more equity than other countries have shown." He also observed: "It will be conceded that the Province of Ontario treats its Indian population with a fairness that amounts to generosity."[44]

The treaty party of 1906 was the same as that of the previous year except for the addition of Edgar and the absence of Rae and Parkinson. It was to treat with Indians at Abitibi, Matachewan, Mattagami, Flying Post, New Brunswick House, and Long Lake. These settlements, though isolated, were generally only short paddling distances from the stations of Biscotasing, Chapleau, and Missinaibi on the CPR. The fact that the commissioners could do much of their travel by rail and were never too far from "civilization" meant that the trip was not as tiresome or depressing as before.

These treaty negotiations concluded without difficulty or controversy. The Indians appeared willing to sign—a willingness that signified their belief that the government would assist them in times of need. For instance, the Long Lake chief expressed the hope that provision would be made for the sick and destitute. He pointed out that even in the best of seasons they were barely able to make a living. The commissioners replied that the government was "always ready to assist those actually requiring help, but that the Indians must rely as much as possible upon their own exertions for their support."[45]

The 1906 expedition, which took most of June, July, and August to complete, was a particularly pleasant one for Scott.[46] On the portions of the journey made by canoe, he and Edgar sat side by side and took turns reading from the *Oxford Book of Poetry*. Occasionally, Scott read some of his own compositions and was inspired to create some new verse. "Spring on Mattagami" and a number of other pieces that appeared in *Via Borealis* were written at this time.[47]

Edgar also found the experience exhilarating. In his essay "Travelling with a Poet," he wrote of the "tonic clearness in the air" and the "enchanted waters." The weather, too, was "simply enchanting." He took every opportunity to indulge in his passion for fishing, especially when they were delayed at Chapleau.[48]

The painter Edmund Morris joined Scott and Edgar there and helped make the journey even more agreeable. He served as one of the witnesses to the treaty signing at New Brunswick House on 25 July. When the treaty party turned south for home, Morris stayed on a Long Lake to complete a series of Indian portraits that later graced the walls of the Royal Ontario Museum.[49]

Some of the atmosphere of the trip was conjured up by Edgar:

> the drifting, pungent smoke, the many flies, the cool plunge in the lake or
> river, the Gargantuan meal, the pipe which refreshes; then early to bed with
> the rush of the rapids in our ears, and up again while the dew lies heavy on
> the grass and glistens on the bushes.[50]

In the negotiations of 1905, a number of Indians whose hunting grounds lay
north of the Albany River had been admitted to the treaty. The Dominion
assumed the cost of their annuities since they were residents of what was still
federal territory. With the extension of the Ontario boundary to its present
limits in 1912 and the gradual exploration and settlement of the area north of
the Albany, it was almost inevitable that sooner or later the terms of the treaty
would be extended to all native inhabitants in a process that would once more
require the co-operation of the province.

By the early 1920s, Ottawa began to receive representations from Indians in
the unceded area asking for admission to treaty because white men were
encroaching upon their lands. Consequently, in 1922 Indian Affairs approached
the Ontario government to seek its support for the extension of the agreement.
Toronto, however, proved reticent. In fact, in November of the following year,
Premier G.H. Ferguson stated that all Indian claims in the province had by then
been attended to.[51] This brought a reminder from Scott that the area north of
the Albany River was still not subject to treaty.

When the deputy superintendent approached Ferguson once more on the
question in May 1926, he found the premier more receptive, and they agreed
that preliminary arrangements should proceed.[52] By August of 1927, Scott had
gathered the information he needed regarding the area and its inhabitants in
order to draw up a realistic budget. And by the summer of 1929, the treaty
negotiators were ready to embark on their venture to the north.

On this occasion the entourage consisted of two commissioners—H.N. Awrey
representing Indian Affairs and W.C. Cain representing the Ontario government.
Two floatplanes carried the party northwards, and they visited several of the old
treaty signing spots along the way to distribute annuity payments. Since it was
impossible to arrange for sufficient gasoline caches at the remoter settlements
along Hudson Bay, Trout Lake was the only community at which adhesion to
the treaty was scheduled that summer.

In their report to the superintendent general, the commissioners left a
detailed account of the rituals and negotiations surrounding the signing. What
distinguished this meeting from those of 1905 and 1906 was the pains taken by
the government officials to explain fully the meaning of the terms that were
offered:

> The ground was thoroughly covered, the commissioners entering into explanations with a particularity of detail, realizing that in the past certain claims have been made that the Indians did not fully understand the meaning of their act. Cognizant of their stolid character in certain circumstances and extremely desirous that any suspicions or apprehensions should be removed, the commissioners not only invited and received many questions but prompted the Indians in seeking data on points such as fishing, hunting, trapping, mining, etc., that might hereafter arise.[53]

This statement implies some disatisfaction with the way treaty terms had been explained in the past. Certainly, Scott's accounts of the 1905 expedition indicate that the restrictions on traditional Indian economic activities contained in Treaty No. 9 were either minimized or ignored. This tactic had evidently generated criticism over the years, and Cain and Awrey were anxious to avoid similar misunderstandings. Nevertheless, the Indians proved ready to sign, and a total of 627 members of the Trout Lake band were admitted to the treaty. Another trip north was necessary in the summer of 1930 to secure the adhesion of those resident around Wendigo, Fort Severn, and Winisk.

With the extension of Treaty No. 9 to the shores of Hudson Bay, the treaty signing activities of the Department of Indian Affairs came to an end. Like similar agreements that had preceded it, it constituted little more than "a gentleman's way to take without grabbing."[54] The glaring disparity between what was offered to the Indians and the potential wealth whites hoped to realize from the surrendered land makes it difficult to dispute that fraud of a high order was involved.

Nor were the expectations of the speculators disappointed. The silver mines at Cobalt, which had started all the excitement, produced in excess of $206,000,000 of the precious metal during their first eighteen years of operation.[55] Knowing that the budget for the first round of treaty negotiations was less than $40,000 makes the magnitude of the "bargain" clear. And Cobalt was no exception. The gold-mining operations at Dome, Porcupine, and Kirkland Lake, which all began shortly after the initial land surrender, were soon producing fabulous wealth, and even today can still generate excitement on the Toronto Stock Exchange. The mining activity created the predicted demand for power, and hydro companies obliged with dams on the Mattagami and Abitibi waterways. The anticipated growth of the pulp and paper industry was also realized. For example, the Abitibi Pulp and Paper Company's plant at Iroquois Falls was considered to be the world's largest by the end of the 1920s.[56]

A number of other treaties were also signed during Scott's years of influence in the federal service. Treaty No. 10, which covered a large area of northern Saskatchewan, was concluded in 1906, and Treaty No. 11, which secured the surrender of aboriginal title to the Mackenzie River Valley, was signed in 1921 and 1922. The circumstances surrounding the negotiation of Treaty No. 11 have been analysed in depth by Rene Fumoleau in his *As Long as This Land Shall Last*, but one observation is worth making for purposes of comparison. Just as the discovery of silver at Cobalt in 1904 underlined the urgency of a treaty in new Ontario, so the discovery of oil at Norman Wells in August 1920 spurred Indian Affairs into action to secure the aboriginal title to the Mackenzie Valley. In both instances, the potential profits to be gleaned from land that was hitherto regarded as worthless precipitated moves to extinguish the title of the native occupiers. No consideration was given to inviting the Indians to share in the profits. In fact, the treaty terms offered deliberately ensured that they would be excluded.

Scott's collusion in all of this was complete, and especially so with regard to Treaty No. 9. As chief accountant, he was intimately involved in drawing up the budget and terms, and he served as one of the commissioners. What is most astonishing is that he seems to have regarded the entire process as a charade. He could not accept that the notion of aboriginal title constituted a legitimate claim to the lands. And he believed that the Indians were incapable of understanding the complexity of the issues. Scott's attitude is best illustrated in the following passage from his essay, "The Last of the Indian Treaties":

> To individuals whose transactions have been heretofore limited to compu-
> tation with sticks and skins our errand must indeed have been dark. They
> were to make certain promises and we were to make certain promises but
> our purpose and our reasons were alike unknowable. What could they
> grasp of the pronouncement on the Indian tenure which had been deliv-
> ered by the law lords of the Crown, what of the elaborate negotiations
> between a dominion and a province which had made the treaty possible,
> and what of the sense of traditional policy which brooded over the whole?
> Nothing. So there was no basis for argument. The simpler facts had to be
> stated, and the parental idea developed that the King is the great father of
> the Indians, watchful over their interests, and ever compassionate.[57]

5

Schooling and Civilization

The education of native children in day and residential schools was one of the key elements in Canada's Indian policy from its inception. The destruction of the children's link to their ancestral culture and their assimilation into the dominant society were its main objectives. Although they remained unquestioned during the rise of Duncan Campbell Scott in the Department of Indian Affairs, success continued to elude the policies. When Scott was appointed superintendent of education in 1909 and deputy superintendent general in 1913, he took measures to render the system more efficient.

Because of its peculiar objectives and the division of powers worked out at Confederation, education for Indians operated on different principles from that provided for non-Indians. The BNA Act had declared education a provincial responsibility. Consequently, most children attended schools functioning under the jurisdiction of provincial departments of education and locally elected school boards. At the same time, the act had given the federal government the responsibility of legislating for Indians, which meant, in effect, that Indian children were to attend schools established under the auspices of the federal Indian Department. And the segregation inherent in this provision was further reinforced by clauses in the numbered treaties committing the federal government to the support of schools and teachers on reserves.

In fulfilling its obligations, Indian Affairs relied heavily on the active co-operation of the major Christian denominations. The Roman Catholic, Anglican, Methodist, and Presbyterian churches had all been involved in educational and missionary work among the native population prior to the Confederation. Federal officials quickly realized that building on existing ecclesiastical institutions would result in far greater economy than would creating a new educational infrastructure. They also believed that the dedication and moral suasion of missionaries would be a vital element in the success of the venture.

As a result, the system of Indian schooling that emerged was financed largely by the federal government but managed and manned by ecclesiastics or their nominees. Of course, this arrangement was also agreeable to the churches. Not only would their missionary activities now be established on a more secure financial basis, but in areas experiencing rapid settlement, such as the west, they could build up their organizational structure with the aid of state subsidies.

The co-operation between church and state resulted in the establishment of both day and residential schools for Indians. The department generally favoured the latter category, and a significantly higher proportion of the its educational budget was allocated to its support both before and during Scott's incumbency as deputy superintendent. Lay and ecclesiastical authorities tended to agree that the residential experience accelerated the process of becoming "civilized." As Frank Pedley, Scott's predecessor, observed, residential schools secured "the removal of the pupils from the retrogressive influence of home life," and they also ensured regular attendance.[1]

Residential schools were divided into two distinct categories: boarding and industrial. Industrial schools were first established in Upper Canada in the 1840s, and in the 1880s, the system was extended to the west. By the opening of the twentieth century, these institutions had proven disappointing in their results. Scott, ever mindful of budgetary considerations, seriously questioned their continued existence when decision-making powers passed into his hands. In many ways, the story of the industrial schools illustrates the dilemmas of Indian education policy, and it shall therefore be considered here in some detail.

In January 1879 Nicholas Flood Davin[2] was sent by the federal government to investigate and to prepare a report on the system of Indian industrial schools operating in the United States. These schools were the principal feature of the policy of "aggressive civilization" which had been inaugurated by President Ulysses S. Grant in 1869. Davin discovered that they were administered either directly by the Indian agencies or through contracts with church bodies. In the latter instances, per capita grants ranging from $100 to $125 were paid by the Bureau of Indian Affairs. In addition to the academic program of the schools, boys were instructed in cattle-raising and agriculture and in a number of trades such as carpentry, blacksmithing, and shoe-making; girls were instructed in household skills.

Davin was impressed by what he saw. As part of his mandate, he visited Winnipeg and consulted with leading church and state officials regarding the possibility of instituting a similar system in the Canadian west. His report, which was submitted to Lawrence Vankoughnet in April 1879, proposed the initial establishment of four denominational industrial schools. In Davin's opinion, the first step in civilizing the native population was "to take away their simple Indian mythology." And the active involvement of the churches would ensure a teaching body of superior moral calibre—men and women fired by zeal and dedication.[3]

Davin's recommendations were eventually acted upon.[4] The supplementary estimates of 1883-84 allocated \$44,000 for the establishment of industrial schools in the west.[5] There were to be three to begin with: at Qu'Appelle and High River under Roman Catholic management, and at Battleford under the Anglican Church.

The new industrial schools differed from boarding schools in a number of important respects. Boarding schools were usually located on reserves and catered to students of a younger age group—students between the ages of eight and fourteen approximately. Selected graduates of these institutions could go on to the industrial schools until they reached eighteen.[6] In a sense, they were to function as high schools. They were deliberately located at a distance from reserves and close to centres of white settlement. Both types of schools aimed "to give a plain English education, adapted to the needs of the working farmer and mechanic." However, boys in industrial schools had training in a greater number of trades open to them. The girls' programs emphasized domestic skills in both cases. In recognition of the more elaborate offerings of the industrial schools, their per capita grants ranged from \$110 to \$145 in the early years of operation. The rate was fixed at \$72 for boarding schools until Scott became superintendent of Indian education.[7]

The industrial schools were administered through arrangements worked out between the department and the various church authorities that took on the task of management. The department provided the land—usually on lease from the Interior Department—and the initial fencing. It also constructed the building. Repairs, however, were a joint responsibility; the department supplying the materials, the management, and the labour. The department paid for all school equipment such as books and globes and the travel expenses of pupils. It also undertook to pay for the services of medical doctors when they were obliged to visit the schools. All other operating costs, such as teachers' salaries and food, clothing, and heating bills, were to come from the per capita grant.[8]

These arrangements were not binding contractual agreements, and the element of ambiguity that they harboured was to be the cause of considerable difficulty when large deficits were run up. Nor was the per capita system always instituted. In its initial enthusiasm for the scheme, the department sometimes agreed to pay for all costs directly. This proved to be a much more expensive *modus operandi* from the government's perspective, and for the same reason it was much preferred by the churches. Regardless of the financial arrangements entered into, management was obliged to maintain exact accounts at all times. And even though the schools were to be showpiece institutions, measures of "the strictest economy" were encouraged.[9] And they were to be open to inspection by department officials upon demand.

Education was not compulsory for Indians when the industrial schools were first established, and securing a regular supply of pupils remained a persistent difficulty. Indian agents played a role in the selection of prospective candidates, and they were permitted to employ pressure, such as withholding rations, on recalcitrant parents to persuade them to part with their children.[10]

The industrial schools were intended to be the culmination of an education deliberately designed to sever young Indians' connections with their ancestral culture. Locating the institutions at a distance from reserves was part of this plan. As Indian Commissioner Hayter Reed explained in 1889:

> every effort should be directed against anything calculated to keep fresh in the memories of children habits and associations which it is one of the main objects of industrial institutions to obliterate.[11]

Reed was adamant that graduates of the schools should not be permitted to return to their reserves. He hoped instead that they would be hired out to the white settlers who were entering the Territories in increasing numbers.

During the 1880s and 1890s, the system of industrial schools expanded rapidly. New schools were usually created at the instigation of church authorities, who saw the system's advantages. Expansion did not always entail the construction of new buildings; sometimes existing boarding schools were upgraded. By 1896 there were twenty schools classified as industrial in Manitoba, the Northwest Territories, and British Columbia. The Roman Catholics administered eight; the Church of England six; the Methodists four; and the Presbyterians one (at Regina). The school at Metlakahtla was designated undenominational.[12] In addition to these, a number of schools in Ontario, such as the Mohawk Institute near Brantford, operated in a similar manner.

However, the Indians failed to share the enthusiasm of church and state for the experiment. In fact, one of its foremost problems was the persistence of Indian hostility, which stemmed from a number of concerns. One was the policy of holidays for the students. In the early years, the department tended to discourage any leave because it involved the expense of transportation over long distances and brought the young Indians into contact with "undesirable influences" at home. When parents realized that they might not see their children for several years, they were naturally reluctant to part with them.[13]

Reports of the mistreatment of children in industrial schools also did little to encourage the adults. In September 1886 the *Montreal Gazette* contended that parents were opposed to sending their children to Battleford Industrial School because of the physical abuse one boy, "Charlie No. 20," had received there. Indian Affairs denied the allegation, but it was not an isolated occurrence.[14]

In March 1899, Indian Commissioner David Laird was obliged to investigate complaints laid by the chief and councillors of St. Peter's Reserve against J.H. Fairlie, principal of Rupert's Land Industrial School (near Selkirk, Manitoba). The Reverend Fairlie, an Anglican clergyman, admitted to feeding bad butter to the children and to entering the dormitories at night to kiss some of the girls. He was also accused of administering harsh punishment; some young girls (around eight or nine years old) showed marks on their bodies several weeks after being strapped.[15]

The health problems of the children and the attendant death rate in the institutions was an additional source of worry.[16] And, of course, the Indians were hardly enamoured of the deliberate policy of cultural transformation.[17]

The first of the industrial schools, Qu'Appelle, Battleford, and High River, were originally administered through a system in which the department paid the entire cost. By 1890 the government wanted to change the method, mainly because of escalating expenditure. Between 1888 and 1889, for instance, the cost per pupil had risen at Battleford from $329 to $400, and at Qu'Appelle from $155 to $202. Deputy Superintendent Vankoughnet described these figures as "most excessive" and proposed that all new schools (several were planned) be operated on a fixed per capita grant.[18]

Changes in administrative arrangements always involved delicate, and sometimes tempestuous, negotiations with the churches, and while Vankoughnet's proposal was generally adopted in 1893–94, it was never made an absolute rule.[19] At two of the schools under Anglican management—Calgary and Elkhorn, Manitoba—it was not applied, and they continued to be significantly more demanding on the public purse. For example, in 1899–1900 the operating costs per pupil at Calgary were $204.88 and at Elkhorn, $252.65. In comparison, the average per capita cost in seven Roman Catholic industrial schools in the west at the same time was $119.56.[20]

The concern with financial considerations and measures of economy that increasingly circumscribed Indian policy as the 1890s progressed had much to do with Scott's influence as chief accountant. But it was also a reflection of the attitude of Clifford Sifton, who had become minister of the interior and superintendent general in 1896. In the following year, Sifton announced that expenditure on Indian education had reached "a high water mark" and that it was time for retrenchment. Moreover, he felt that industrial school education was probably a waste of time since Indians did not have "the physical, mental or moral get-up" of the white man and could never compete with him on equal terms.[21]

Sifton's harsh judgment may have been influenced by the undeniably bleak results. In July 1897, he asked for a full report on the industrial schools with regard to students' ages and academic attainments. The following return from the Regina school is illustrative:[22]

AGE GROUP	NUMBER OF STUDENTS
Over 20	2
Between 18 and 20	32
Between 14 and 17	51
Between 10 and 13	45
Between 6 and 9	21
Under 6	2

Of the 34 students who were eighteen or older, the following academic levels had been attained:

    7 were in standard 6
    8 were in standard 5
    12 were in standard 4
    5 were in standard 3

Since students were supposed to attend industrial schools between the ages of fourteen and eighteen, the large numbers outside this age group indicates one of the major managerial dilemmas—how to maintain enrolment at a level that would ensure an adequate per capita grant.

By the end of the 1890s, the department had placed a moratorium on the construction of new industrial schools. And it was rumoured that some existing ones might be reduced in status to boarding schools or even closed down completely. The following memo from Martin Benson, the head of the department's schools branch, in 1902 clearly shows the growing disillusionment:

> Returns from the industrial schools show that up to the 30 June last there had been 2752 pupils admitted and of these 1700 had been discharged. Of the latter number 506 are known to be dead; 249 lost sight of; 139 in bad health; 86 transferred to other schools; 121 turned out badly and 599 said to be doing well.[23]

A combination of disappointing results and escalating costs led to the gradual phasing out of the industrial schools. A brief case study of the Presbyterian-managed Regina Industrial School will illustrate both some of the difficulties attendant upon administering the system and Scott's emerging role as decision-maker.

The Regina school opened in April 1891 and was run economically by its first principal until his death in 1901. His successor, J.A. Sinclair, evidently found it impossible to manage on the per capita grant and began to run up large operating deficits. The debt stood at $5,941.62 by the summer of 1903 and was continuing to rise, and neither church nor state officials wished to incur responsibility for it. The two parties agreed on an investigation; J.A. Menzies, a Winnipeg accountant, J.A.J. McKenna, assistant Indian commissioner, and the Rev. R.P. MacKay, a representative of the Presbyterian church, were appointed to conduct it. They submitted their report in March 1904.

The investigators noted that Regina had experienced a steady decline in enrolment from 106 students in 1900, to 72 in 1904. Consequently, per capita grants fell, and operating expenses per pupil rose. Rising fuel costs aggravated the difficulties, and the deficit amounted to $9,201.56 by January 1904. But the unfortunate set of circumstances were not the entire reason. There also appeared to be evidence of financial mismanagement. The school had had three different bookkeepers during the previous year, for instance, and the accounts were in disarray. And, apparently, departmental guidelines regarding expenditure on food, clothing, and other necessities had not been strictly adhered to.

In spite of the large sums spent, the school building was in a state of poor repair. A number of ceilings and floors were in "wretched condition," while some stairs were "really dangerous." The structure itself had been badly planned, with only two exits, which made it extremely hazardous in case of fire.

The investigators advised that the department pick up the deficit since the school's creditors were pressing for payment. They also recommended that the per capita grant be increased. On the other hand, management needed to display greater financial responsibility, and they suggested that monthly accounts be submitted to the department.

As a result of their findings at Regina, the investigators concluded that it was time for a complete re-examination of Indian education policy to ascertain the relative merits of industrial, boarding, and day schools. One of the on-going problems with the industrial schools was the fact that the principals had to scour the countryside annually in the hunt for new recruits. As the number of schools grew, the competition between churches became all the more intense. Many agents and missionaries were coming to the conclusion that the distance of the institutions from the reserves was a distinct disadvantage. And all the more so as it became evident that their graduates would likely return to them. Few had made the hoped-for transition into white society.[24]

In commenting on the report to Frank Pedley, Martin Benson rejected the idea that the department ought to pick up the Regina deficit. Apart from creating a dangerous precedent, the deficit was largely caused by the incompetence of the principal, although McKenna and his companions had failed to blame him specifically.[25] Pedley was less than satisfied with this advice and asked Scott for his opinion on the matter.[26] Scott examined the school accounts before making his judgment, and he concluded that, in spite of adverse conditions, the principal's inability as an administrator was the main cause of the debts. He had spent money carelessly and without proper authorization. However, according to Scott, it did not logically follow that the department could refuse to pay up since there was a regrettable "lack of definiteness" in the arrangements surrounding the administration of industrial schools. The agreements with the churches were "loose and indeterminate." In the past when the churches had appealed to the department to pay outstanding debts, the department had complied. In doing so, it had accepted financial responsibility, and it would have to shoulder this latest burden.

But Scott believed that the department could seize the prevailing opportunity to "reconstruct the whole school system." The Regina deficit might be paid, but only on condition that the school be closed down in June. The students could be transferred to the Elkhorn Industrial School, which would make that institution more viable. The whole question of Indian education, he said, should be opened for discussion.[27]

Pedley endorsed Scott's suggestions and forwarded them to Clifford Sifton.[28] Officials of the Presbyterian church were duly informed of the plans to close the Regina school. When the General Assembly of the church met in June 1904, it passed a resolution condemning the proposed loss of its only facility of that kind, and Principal Sinclair invoked the aid of Walter Scott, M.P. for Regina. These representations changed Sifton's mind, and he granted the school a stay of execution.[29]

In allowing the Regina institution to continue, the department came forward with terms that were generous indeed. It agreed to pay the deficit, to raise the per capita grant to $145, and to repair the buildings. The church, for its part, was required to secure competent staff.[30]

The ecclesiastics appear to have taken their part of the bargain rather lightly. When the school reopened in the autumn of 1904, Sinclair was retained as principal. And by December, department officials became concerned that the old pattern of irresponsibility had appeared once more. They were presented with evidence that suggested flagrant extravagance. Apparently, the principal was running up bills for large quantities of such luxury items as oysters, pineapples, dates, honey, peaches, figs, kippered herrings, salmon, chocolate, and tobacco.[31] An audit of the school's accounts was called for immediately, but before it could be undertaken, Sinclair died in January 1905.

When Inspector W.M. Graham visited the school in February, he discovered that a further deficit of $2,851.72 had been accumulated since the previous June. Of even greater concern, the buildings were still in a "most unsatisfactory and unsanitary state" and constituted a "menace to the lives of the inmates."[32] In spite of this new evidence of managerial incompetence, the Regina Industrial School was allowed to continue for a number of years. Evidently, department officials hoped that a new principal would make a difference. But efficiency and economy, the two great hallmarks of Indian administration, continued to elude the institution, and it was closed in March 1910.[33]

The decline and fall of the Regina school shows that the department was increasingly unwilling to allocate substantial portions of its educational budget to such institutions. The industrial schools had lost their lustre, and unless they could be managed with the utmost economy, their days were numbered. Many of them became victims of the rethinking of educational policy that took place within the department during the first two decades of the twentieth century. The Rupert's Land School was destroyed by fire in 1906 and was not re-opened. The schools at Calgary and St. Boniface closed in 1907; Metlakahtla was phased out in 1906 and 1907; Battleford closed in 1914; Elkhorn in 1918; Red Deer in 1919; and High River in 1922.[34]

Scott's appointment as superintendent of education early in 1909 clearly marked an identifiable new policy direction. Under his guidance, it was decided to phase out the inefficient industrial schools and to concentrate instead on improving boarding and day schools. Scott's initiative was to a large degree forced by the persistent problems of the ill health and high mortality rate of the children in residential schools. It had been present since the inception of these institutions, but owing to the activities of Dr. P.H. Bryce, it began to receive increased attention.

In October 1903, Bryce, who was secretary of the Ontario Provincial Board of Health wrote to James Smart, deputy minister of the interior, expressing concern at outbreaks of contagious diseases on Indian reserves. He suggested that the Indian Department needed a better organized medical service, not only to control and suppress disease, but also to study new methods of combatting it. In commenting to Pedley, Scott noted that Bryce's proposal would mean an extra parliamentary appropriation of between $10,000 and $15,000 per annum for the provinces of Ontario and Quebec. And he added:

> When the peculiar conditions are taken into consideration, the Department is doing as well as can be expected for the Indians, and to do anything further would entail a very heavy expenditure, which, at present, I am not able to recommend.[35]

But Bryce was soon in a much stronger position from which to advance his plans. In February 1904, Clifford Sifton appointed him medical inspector to the Department of the Interior. After a brief spell of working with immigrants, the health of the native population became his principal responsibility. He quickly came to view his mandate as a personal crusade against tuberculosis, the primary cause of Indian mortality and debilitation. Almost inevitably, his proposals came into conflict with Scott's preoccupation with minimizing expenditure.

Early in 1907, Pedley asked Bryce to investigate the health of children in industrial and boarding schools in the prairie provinces.[36] Consequently, during the months of March, April and May the physician visited most of the institutions. He discovered a large number of instances in which students with infectious diseases had been admitted to schools, where diseases spread in the "defective sanitary condition" of many of the buildings. Bryce was particularly appalled at the ventilation he found at the schools. With only two or three exceptions, the windows in the dormitories were kept sealed during the seven colder months to save on heating costs. As a result, the air became progressively more foul, especially when infected students were present. Nor did it appear that provision was made for regular physical exercise. It was almost as if the prime conditions for the outbreak of epidemics had been deliberately created. The medical officer noted that principals and teachers were inclined to minimize the dangers, and they proved remarkably reticent in providing statistical information regarding the fate of their ex-pupils.[37]

Bryce's report was widely distributed to politicians and to church officials, and it found its way into the press, which gloated, predictably enough, over the more sensational aspects.[38] Martin Benson described it as "damnatory" and suggested to Pedley that agents and principals be asked to confirm or deny the findings. Church officials and principals responded defensively, while Indian agents were generally prepared to substantiate Bryce's allegations. Commissioner David Laird accused the medical officer of exaggeration, but he admitted that Indian ill-health was a problem and that poor ventilation was likely at fault. However, he rejected the implication of wrongdoing by pointing out that the sanitary arrangements of the schools were as good as in most buildings in the west.[39]

In 1909 Bryce was again on the investigative trail examining conditions at seven boarding schools in southern Alberta, an area where health problems were of particular concern. Tuberculosis was the great scourge of the Blackfoot in those days, and Bryce discovered it in school children of all ages. He postulated that many children were infected by their parents, among whom it was widespread, and that conditions in the boarding schools facilitated its development and diffusion. Its ravages had led to a decline in the area's school age population, and some shocking statistics were brought to light. Of all the students who attended the Sarcee Boarding School between 1894 and 1908, 28 per cent had died, mostly from tuberculosis.

In reporting his discoveries, Bryce drew up a comprehensive plan to overcome the problem. He claimed that special sanitaria should not be necessary in most cases if existing school buildings were properly modified. Each school should appoint a nurse or sanitary director trained in the new methods for treating tuberculosis. Their activities should be supervised by district medical officers allocated to that task on a full-time, permanent basis. Apart from the actual treatment of infection by medical personnel, Bryce had a number of preventative measures that he wished to see implemented, including better nutrition, more fresh air and exercise, and a general improvement in cleanliness.

In one school, for example, he had observed swarms of flies in the dining room. Such conditions would have to go.

Bryce probably knew that his plan would entail increased expenditure and that the department's budget would not permit its wholesale adoption. Therefore, he proposed that it be tried out on an experimental basis at first, perhaps in the schools of one province, to see if the results warranted universal application. He was adamant, however, that church authorities should not be allowed to interfere with its implementation.[40]

These recommendations stood little chance of adoption without Scott's endorsement. But his response was unenthusiastic. In a commentary on Bryce's report prepared for his superiors, he observed that much of it was unrealistic under prevailing conditions. The churches, for instance, would not co-operate with a scheme in which their authority was undermined. In fact, Bryce's revelations had caused "considerable irritation" in ecclesiastical circles and had brought "protests from the Roman Catholic authorities who have the larger number of pupils under their charge."

Nevertheless, Scott was prepared to admit that a problem existed and that some remedial measures would be necessary:

> If the schools are to be conducted at all we must face the fact that a large number of the pupils will suffer from tuberculosis in some of its various forms. The admission indiscriminately of such pupils into the schools in the past, and the failure to recognize any special treatment which could be accorded to them has no doubt led to the high death rate which has rendered ineffectual to a large degree the past expenditure on Indian education in Boarding and Industrial schools. More stringent regulations as to the admission of pupils will doubtless have a beneficial effect, and it is only necessary to carry out some common sense reforms to remove the imputation that the Department is careless of the interests of these children.

Citing the authority of Dr. William Osler, an expert on tuberculosis, he proposed a number of changes which he felt would be adequate to deal with the problem. They involved more specific regulations regarding ventilation, exercise, and diet in the schools and an increase in the per capita grants to offset the additional expenses.[41] Scott objected to Bryce's grand plan not only because of the difficulties which it was likely to cause with the churches, but also, as he admitted later to Pedley, because it would "add considerably to the appropriations."[42]

Bryce blamed Scott personally for sabotaging his proposals, and in 1922, many years after the event, he published a scathing pamphlet, *The Story of a National Crime*, in which he denounced the deputy superintendent for his vanity and his indifference to the health problems of the native population.[43]

Unfortunately, it was not taken very seriously, since Bryce was known to be bitterly disillusioned at the time. He had hoped to become deputy minister when the federal Department of Health was created in 1919, and he had been profoundly disappointed when the promotion did not materialize. To make matters worse, he had been forced to retire from the public service in 1921.

It might be tempting to conclude that Scott was more interested in countering allegations of carelessness on the part of his department than in making a wholehearted effort to combat death and disease among the Indians. Certainly, there is little doubt that questions of economy played a major role in all of his deliberations on the issue. Nevertheless, when it came to working out the details of his new education policy initiative, he did not omit health considerations.

On 8 November 1910, a conference was arranged in Ottawa between Scott and representatives of the Anglican, Methodist, Presbyterian and Roman Catholic churches to discuss means of improving the boarding schools. They had been built on reserve lands at the expense of the religious bodies, and they were given an annual per capital grant of $72 to cover operating costs. By the twentieth century, they had surpassed industrial schools in number and significance, and there were corresponding increases in the churches' financial responsibilities. However, the department was often called upon to pay for repairs, enlargements and improvements, and it generally complied. Such *ad hoc* arrangements were not satisfactory to either the churches or the government. Scott felt that a substantial increase in the per capita grant should enable the managerial authorities to make repairs and improvements from their operating funds and obviate unanticipated demands upon the public purse.

Scott advised the church officials that he was prepared to increase per capita grants for boarding schools to between $100 and $125. Certain conditions would have to be met. Buildings ought to be sanitary and in a good state of repair. Hospital accommodation should be provided for the isolation of pupils with infectious diseases—rooms that were well-lit and ventilated and with southern exposure if possible. Guidelines regarding air space in dormitories and classrooms were also specified. These were Scott's less expensive alternatives to the comprehensive system of medical supervision that Bryce had proposed.

The differences in the proposed per capita grant schedule were designed to compensate for differences in operating costs in various parts of the country. Officials assumed that they would be lowest in the east, somewhat more in the west, and highest in the north. Variations in the grant could also exist within a particular region to reflect the difference between a first rate building and one that was minimally acceptable. The scheme was designed to encourage the churches to build and maintain schools of a high standard. Any additional government expenditure on education would, however, be accompanied by an increase in government supervision. Grants would only be forthcoming after inspection by the department's officials.[44]

When the churches accepted Scott's proposal, the department entered into a more active role in the provision of education. The larger per capita grants, the greater supervisory role for Indian agents and inspectors, and the increasing willingness of the department to contribute to the capital costs of boarding schools, soon blurred the distinction that existed between them and their industrial counterparts. In fact, the "industrial" component of the latter institutions had never been a great success, and most had attempted to impart only ranching and agricultural skills to their male charges. Therefore the curricular differences between the two types of school had not been significant either. In recognition of this reality, the terms "boarding" and "industrial" were phased out of administrative terminology and were replaced by the all-encompassing "residential" by 1923. In fact, under Mackenzie King's Liberal administration the appropriations for Indian Affairs, and particularly for education, increased substantially. The department began to take on the entire capital costs of new residential institutions and to purchase existing facilities; the role of the denominations was being transformed into one in which they provided personnel only.

The elimination of the worst of the industrial schools and the new regulations introduced by Scott in 1910 did not entirely eradicate the hazards of residential education. Ill-health, for instance, persisted at unacceptably high rates in places. While some of the blame may lie with the haphazard system of medical supervision, the diligence of the managerial bodies was of equal significance. Insofar as it is possible to generalize, it seems that the Roman Catholics, who managed the greatest number of residential institutions, were more successful than their Protestant counterparts in dealing with health problems. A few examples will illustrate this.

Having dispensed with the services of the troublesome Dr. Bryce in 1913, Scott appointed Dr. O.I. Grain of Selkirk, Manitoba, as medical inspector for agencies and residential schools in the west.[45] In the following year, Grain visited the boarding and industrial schools in his domain and reported a generally satisfactory situation. However, he noted the particular success of the Catholics as administrators: "I cannot see how it is but the R.C. people have the C of E people beaten forty ways in the management of their institutions. Order and cleanliness appear lacking in Anglican schools."[46]

Grain's impact on the course of events appears to have been negligible. He recommended a number of minor changes at individual institutions, but he saw no necessity to go beyond that. He soon became involved in the inspection of military recruits, with the department's concurrence, and neglected his Indian work. In 1918 Scott decided to abolish the position of medical inspector "for reasons of economy."[47] This was in the year of the Spanish 'flu!

Regular and systematic medical inspection of the schools was deemed an unwarranted extravagance. But when any inspection took place, it invariably brought problems to light. While visiting the west in the summer of 1920, Scott arranged that Regina physician F.A. Corbett should inspect a number of boarding schools in Alberta. Conditions at the three Roman Catholic schools visited, Hobbema, St. Albert, and Crowfoot (Blackfoot reserve), were satisfactory. The children were reported to be clean, well-fed, and healthy.

But Corbett found quite the opposite at two Anglican institutions. At Old Sun's school on the Blackfoot reserve the children were reported to be "below par." Tuberculosis and eye disease were present, and scrofula and scabies were widespread. The dormitories were overcrowded, there was no infirmary, and the ventilation was poor throughout. At the Sarcee boarding school, things were even worse. The building was unsanitary and twenty-nine out of thirty-three students suffered from tuberculosis. The physician discovered one child whose neck and chest were covered with "foul ulcers," lying in a "filthy, dilapidated infirmary." He proposed that the school be closed and turned into a hospital to treat the entire reserve.[48] Scott agreed to Corbett's suggestion regarding this school, and he brought the "regrettable" comparison between Roman Catholic and Anglican school administration to the attention of his minister, Sir James Lougheed.[49]

In June 1922, Corbett was engaged again to carry out an inspection of the same institutions. Once more, the Roman Catholic schools were highly commended, and conditions at Old Sun's were almost as bad as before. But at the Sarcee reserve, where the school had been transformed into a hospital, the health of both young and old Indians had improved considerably.

Although medical inspections were carried out irregularly, some improvements resulted. Nevertheless, there is evidence of cynicism in official attitudes to the entire exercise. The department was as much concerned with deflecting public criticism of its policies as it was with improving the health of its charges. When Commissioner Graham forwarded Corbett's second report to Scott in June 1922, he noted that investigations of that sort were useful because, as a result, "we cannot be accused of neglecting the Indian children who are in our schools."[50]

The rudimentary and haphazard reform of residential institutions was accompanied by a new interest in day schools, which had long been the poor orphans of Indian education. Located on smaller and more remote reserves, they were neglected and maligned during the heyday of their industrial counterparts.[51] Irregularity of attendance and the inability to find and keep competent teachers were the two principal difficulties which they faced. But when educational policy came under serious reconsideration in the department during the first decade of the twentieth century, day schools were found to have one great advantage that outweighed these problems: they were eminently cheap to operate.

In his annual report for the year ended 31 March 1909, Frank Pedley indicated the change in departmental thinking that was taking place. He noted that the "pronounced favour for industrial and boarding schools" that had hitherto prevailed was being questioned. With improving home conditions on reserves, it was no longer quite as necessary to separate children from their parents. There was renewed interest in day schools, which would require hiring better teachers to make the educational experience "interesting and agreeable to Indian children." Salaries would have to be increased, but the money thus invested would prove an economy in the long run. Pedley also anticipated the provision of mid-day meals and transportation for the children in order to combat poor attendance.[52]

The new favour shown to day schools had been announced by the department in April 1908 in a circular to the various churches involved in Indian education. The response was mixed. The Roman Catholics were decidedly unenthusiastic, but the Anglicans had generally been favourable. Their Advisory Board on Indian Education, a body that formulated policy, proved remarkably compliant. S.H. Blake, a Toronto lawyer who served as chairman of the board, had long been critical of the excessive spending on industrial schools, and he strongly endorsed the new emphasis on day schools.[53]

The advisory board met in Toronto on 8 February 1909, and Scott, who evidently impressed board members, attended in his capacity as superintendent of education. He explained that budgetary considerations were the primary reason for the greater interest in day schools. Some ecclesiastics were reluctant to lose residential facilities in their jurisdictions, but the board in general was prepared to accept the closure of inefficient institutions provided that the savings were used to improve day schools.

Securing a body of competent teachers was a principal challenge. Day school teachers were employees of the department, and their work was subject to inspection by local Indian agents. But, at the same time, they were nominated for their position by the churches. This curious arrangement arose out of a clause in the Indian Act that permitted the chief and councillors of a band to determine the religion of the teacher.[54] In practice, a church that claimed a reserve as its terrain based on a record of missionary activity in the area assumed the right of nomination. In return, the church was supposed to contribute a portion of the teacher's salary, although this rarely happened. Instead, the church usually paid for the teacher's accommodation and transportation to the reserve.

Indian day schools did not attract the elite of the teaching profession. In 1903, Indian Commissioner Laird noted that those institutions were manned by "a good number" of indifferent teachers and that it was often impossible to secure anyone to take on the job.[55] Probably many a young pedagogue was deterred by the apparently inhospitable surroundings, but the paltry salaries offered were undoubtedly the main reason why the day schools were obliged to rely on the services of the marginally competent members of the profession. Church and state officials quickly realized that unless salaries were improved, the schools would never come to serve the new, vital role that was being carved out for them in Indian education.

Bishop Newnham of Saskatchewan wrote to the department in October 1907 complaining that he could not find reliable teachers for the prevailing salary of $300 per annum. He urged that the remuneration be raised to $400.[56] In passing on the letter to Deputy Superintendent Pedley, Martin Benson expressed his agreement. He pointed out that public school teachers in the west earned between $500 and $650 and that anyone who accepted $300 was probably worthless. He suggested that the department should not only raise salaries, but also take on responsibility for the provision of transportation and accommodation. Scott's opinion was solicited, and he concurred: "I am in sympathy with any movement to increase the efficiency of these Day Schools, and we cannot obtain qualified teachers now for less than $400 a year."[57]

But no action was taken until Scott became superintendent of education. In a memo to department officials in the field in June 1909, he announced that salaries of day school teachers would be raised to $400 for the following year.[58] In some cases, certified teachers might be given $500. It was a modest improvement, but it still left the teachers financially disadvantaged when compared to their public school colleagues.

Scott had a number of other ideas for the improvement of the day schools. He arranged for footwear and clothing to be distributed to deserving children and for a "plain, warm meal" to be provided during the day. Games and "simple calisthenics" were introduced to add variety to the program of instruction. All these measures were designed to improve attendance and to counter the "apathy if not active hostility" of parents.[59]

Such enticements were soon supplemented by greater powers of coercion. Because of Hayter Reed's entreaties over a number of years, a school attendance clause had been inserted into the Indian Act in 1894.[60] Reed had been particularly concerned at the inability of the industrial schools to maintain adequate enrolment, and the measure was designed primarily to deal with that problem. It had not proven satisfactory as a general means of compulsion, and Scott was soon seeking more comprehensive powers. He arranged for a compulsory school attendance clause to be included in the controversial Bill 14, the amendment to the Indian Act introduced in 1920 which enabled the department to enfranchise Indians against their will. At the beginning of April that year, he sent urgent messages to major ecclesiastics involved in Indian missionary work in the west requesting their support for the attendance clause. They all responded promptly and positively, and Scott forwarded their letters and telegrams to the parliamentary committee on the amendment chaired by W.A. Boys. With the adoption of the legislation in June, the superintendent general was empowered by means of truant officers and penalties to compel the attendance at school of all Indian children between the ages of seven and fifteen years.[61]

With compulsory attendance and general improvements to both the day and residential school programs, the department looked forward to an era of steady progress in its educational activities. Like all government departments, Indian Affairs was accountable to the public. But Indian administration was always rife with potential controversy and tended to attract the attention of politicians and journalists who sought to embarrass the government. It was therefore necessary, not just to cover up scandal, but to offer tangible evidence that something was being achieved. Such evidence was particularly vital with regard to education— perhaps the key element in Indian administration and certainly its most expensive component.

The department's annual report was its principal vehicle for disseminating the statistics of progress. Occasionally this exercise took on the tone of smug self-congratulation. This was increasingly apparent in the final years of Scott's incumbency as deputy superintendent, and he may have been summing up for posterity the educational accomplishments of his era. In his report for the year ended 31 March 1929, for example, Scott drew attention to the academic progress of Indian students during the previous ten years. In 1918-19 there had been only 878 children studying at the grade five level and higher. By 1928-29 the number had reached 2,228.[62]

Statistics on total school enrolment also showed a gratifying improvement by the time of Scott's retirement. The number of Indian students rose steadily from 11,303 in 1912 to 17,163 in 1932—an increase of 51 per cent. During the same period, the increase for day students was from 7,399 to 8,775 (an 18 per cent increase), and for residential students from 3,904 to 8,213 (a 110 per cent increase).[63] Enrolment at day schools fluctuated considerably, indicating the persistent problems of staffing schools and securing attendance. On the other hand, enrolment at residential schools increased steadily, underlining the central role these institutions played in Indian education.

In his final report as deputy superintendent (for the year ending 31 March 1931), Scott noted with satisfaction that school attendance of Indian children (as a percentage of enrolment) had risen from 64.29 per cent in 1920 to 74.51 in 1930. He acknowledged, of course, that attendance had never been a great problem in residential institutions for reasons that are self-evident. The improvement, therefore, had largely taken place in day schools. The compulsory education legislation had contributed to this happy state of affairs, he surmised, but he also discerned an attitudinal change that had played an even more important role:

However, the main reason for improvement in attendance at Indian schools is a growing conviction on the part of our wards that their children must be better fitted for the future. Fewer and fewer natives are finding it possible to live by the chase and they are turning towards education to prepare themselves for encroaching civilization.[64]

It is difficult to say for certain whether this change in attitude had taken place. It is not even clear if Scott really believed that it had. In April 1930 Section 10 of the Indian Act had been amended to strengthen and expand the department's power to enforce school attendance. As the deputy superintendent observed:

> It is now possible to compel the attendance of every physically fit Indian child between the full ages of 7 and 16 years, and, in very special cases, the Superintendent General may direct that a pupil be kept in school until he has reached the full age of 18 years. The usual practice at Indian residential schools is to encourage pupils to remain until they are 17 or 18.[65]

These were far-reaching powers, considerably in excess of those existing to enforce school attendance among non-Indians. They were part of Scott's legacy to his successors, reflecting the central role of education in his grand plan to "civilize" the native population.

Some of the more critical reinterpretations of Canadian educational history suggest that universal schooling made its appearance, not so much as an adjunct of onward marching democracy, but rather as an instrument of social control. Dominant groups perceived the school as an effective mechanism for fostering loyalty to the prevailing political, economic, and social order among less advantaged groups. In addition, the culture of the classroom deliberately promoted the virtues of punctuality, obedience, frugality, and other components of the work ethic in order to prepare the young for productive lives on the factory floor. In the late nineteenth and early twentieth centuries, the Canadian public school was confronted by a further challenge: the need to assimilate large numbers of non-English-speaking immigrants into the Anglo-Saxon cultural milieu.[66]

There are some obvious similarities between the *raison d'etre* of the public school system and that provided for the native population. The working classes, immigrants, and Indians exercised no control over the aims, content, or methods of schooling prescribed for their children. Effective control remained in the hands of the political and economic elite. But here the similarities end. The Indians were regarded as an exceptional case. The fact that a federal, rather than a provincial, department directed the process underlined its unique characteristics. And the preponderant role accorded to organized religion and to the residential experience provided further evidence that this was no ordinary educational enterprise.

What singled out the Indians for special treatment was the vast cultural distance that separated them from their Anglo-Canadian masters. They could only bridge that distance by intense and prolonged application of schooling to the younger generations. In that way, a cultural wedge would be driven between younger and older Indians, and the former would gradually be absorbed into the dominant society. In the process, they would abandon their native languages for English, their "pagan superstitions" for Christianity, and their primitive economic activities for the steady labour of agriculture or industrial employment. Education was to be nothing less than an instrument of cultural annihilation, which would at once transform the Indians into an unskilled or semi-skilled workforce while forcing them into the mold of Anglo-Canadian identity.

These objectives of native education policy had been well established before Scott rose to prominence in the Department of Indian Affairs. They remained operative during the years of his ascendancy and continued after his departure. Scott's contribution was to render the school system more effective so that its objectives would be better realized. When he became superintendent of education, he inherited a situation that was generally acknowledged to be unsatisfactory. He moved quickly to eliminate some of the more glaring abuses of the system and continued in this reformist vein after his elevation to deputy superintendent general.

On the eve of his retirement, Scott could point to impressive statistical evidence of the success of his educational policies. The number of Indian children enrolled in school, the length of their stay, and the regularity of their attendance had all made substantial gains under his guidance. In his opinion, Indians were increasingly embracing education in a conscious effort to become "civilized."[67]

However, numbers in school did not automatically translate into numbers being assimilated. Undoubtedly, the school experience profoundly affected the outlook of young Indians. But it did not result in their absorption *en masse* into the dominant culture. The vast majority remained distinctly Indian and only marginally in the workforce, if indeed at all. In terms of its objectives, then, the policy of educating Indian children in segregated day and residential schools failed. Its failure was openly acknowledged by the joint parliamentary committee that examined the Indian Act between 1946 and 1948 when it rejected that policy and proposed instead the integration of young Indians into public schools.

6

Indian Political Organizations

Early in the twentieth century, native organizations which attempted to oppose
the policies emanating from Indian Affairs made their appearance. In doing so,
they were often prepared to employ the white man's own political and legal
system. Initially, these organizations tended to be tribal or regional in composition and focused on grievances of a local nature, such as land claims and treaty
rights. But by the time that D.C. Scott became deputy superintendent general,
the notion of expanding these activities beyond such boundaries was already
taking root.

The Grand General Indian Council of Ontario was one of the first native
political organizations to make its appearance in the post-Confederation era. It
drew its support largely from the Ojibway tribes of the Great Lakes region,
although initially it also attracted some adherents from the Six Nations. In the
1870s, councils began to be held at two-year intervals. They provided a forum
for the discussion of relevant contemporary issues and resolutions arising out of
the deliberations were forwarded to the department for consideration.

The department's attitude to the council can best be described as one of
reluctant acceptance. It generally permitted payment out of band funds (if
available) for delegates travelling to meetings of the council, but it insisted that
grants be requested beforehand and that receipts be furnished afterwards. It
often also demanded a reduction in the number of delegates that bands
proposed to send. These restrictions became particularly noticeable when Scott
took charge of the department's financial affairs in the 1890s.

The council usually invited the department to send one of its high-ranking
officers to attend its meetings in the hope of seeking greater recognition from
the government. Though it often sent a representative, the department was
hesitant to commit itself to anything resembling official recognition. For instance,

in 1896, when Scott was acting as deputy superintendent, he asked Inspector J.A. Macrae to attend the meeting to be held at Cape Croker in June. But he warned Macrae to make sure that the Indians understood that he was there only as a visitor and would not take part in the proceedings. Should he make any remarks, they ought to be carefully guarded so as not to bind the department to anything.[1]

The absence of department hostility to the council is probably best explained by the innocuous tone of the resolutions it adopted. Loyalty to the government was a dominant theme, and criticism of Indian administration only rarely made its appearance. At the Grand Council meeting held at Saugeen in June 1904, for instance, a resolution was passed endorsing Section 114 of the Indian Act, which forbade the celebration of "pagan and other gambling and indecent dances."[2] At this time, a vigorous campaign was being waged by the British Columbia and prairie Indians against this very restriction.

Occasionally, the resolutions of the council took on an unusual character, such as that adopted in 1906:

> That the Department of Indian Affairs be asked to insert a new section in the Indian Act, providing that any Indian who marries a negro woman should cease to be an Indian, as it was unjust and out of keeping with Indian usages to bring negro women on the various Reserves, and unless restricted will cause the Indian race an injury, by the infusion of negro blood into the veins of the Indian race.[3]

As the twentieth century progressed, the compliant tone was occasionally interrupted by tinges of radicalism. In 1906, the department's management of Indian monies came under criticism, and the council demanded that the power of hiring teachers for reserve schools be granted to the band. In 1912, a council resolution condemned the Oliver Act of the previous year, the amendment to Section 49A of the Indian Act that permitted the expropriation of reserve lands adjacent to towns of eight thousand or more inhabitants.

The incipient radicalism of the movement became even more evident when Henry Jackson was elected president of the Grand Council in 1918. Thirty-four years old, he was the youngest president in its history. At a special meeting at Parry Sound in May 1919, he asked what had happened to the liberties for which Indians had fought in the recent war. He argued that hunting and fishing rights, guaranteed in the treaties, were being trampled on by provincial laws. He attacked the amendment to Section 90 of the Indian Act in 1918 which permitted "unused" Indian lands to be leased without a surrender. And, of course, the Oliver Act received its share of abuse.[4]

Still, the Grand Council failed to establish itself as the voice of Ontario Indians. It continued to value the tenuous sanction it received from Ottawa, which proved a mixed blessing in the long run. By the early 1920s, its members were deserting for F.O. Loft's League of Indians of Canada.

The department was quite prepared to grant unofficial support to the Grand Council as long as it confined itself to holding meetings. This seemed to dissipate latent discontent and perhaps served to discourage Indians from joining more troublesome groups such as the Council of the Tribes or the League of Indians of Canada. However, when the council attempted to make more substantive challenges to government policy, it was chastised sharply.

An incident which illustrates this took place as a result of a decision made at a meeting of the Grand Council at Sarnia in September 1924. On that occasion, a committee was formed to investigate "Treaties and rights of Indians that have been violated by the Government at any time." This committee engaged the services of J. Carlyle Moore, a lawyer of Wiarton, Ontario to conduct the investigation on its behalf. The lawyer wrote to the department in January 1926 seeking its co-operation and also to determine if his fees would be reimbursed from Indian monies. In response, J.D. McLean explained that the department considered such an undertaking unnecessary since the council could purchase the book *Indian Treaties and Surrenders* for $15, and it contained all relevant information. Therefore, no payment could be guaranteed for legal fees.[5] Upon receipt of this information, the Grand Council dropped the issue.

The council seems to have lost its appetite for radicalism in any form after that. Its resolutions increasingly dealt with minor matters affecting individual bands rather than general policy. Its willingness to co-operate closely with the department was especially evident at the meeting held at Garden River in September 1928. The following resolution, addressed to Scott, said it all:

> The Grand General Indian Council of Ontario assembled in session at Garden River do herein wish to express our humble and heartfelt gratitude to the kind and magnificent manner in which the Government of the Dominion of Canada has responded to the call of the educational needs of the natives of this Grand Dominion of Canada of which we your humble servants are representatives at this Grand General Indian Council of Ontario. We can but feebly express our thanks to you and to the Government of the Dominion of Canada.

This was the sort of resolution that Scott loved, and he communicated his delight to the council.[6]

But the Grand Council's subservience to the government meant that it continued to lose support on the reserves. A few years after Scott's retirement, the department forbade the use of band funds for any organizational activities, and the council disintegrated.[7]

Yet, the Grand General Indian Council of Ontario was in many respects not representative of Indian organizations at this time. Though it spoke out occasionally against government policy, it did so reticently and never to an extent that would have jeopardized its good relations with the department. Other organizations did not share this concern and viewed conflict with Ottawa almost as an inevitable prerequisite to the achievement of native rights. The department, in turn, perceived these organizations as a threat and was prepared to combat them by any means, fair or foul.

Among the organizations perceived as most problematic by Indian Affairs was the Council of the Tribes, a body established by Chief Thunderwater, a resident of Cleveland, Ohio, around the time that Scott succeeded to the deputy superintendency. The *Constitution and By Laws of the Council of the Tribes* set out in detail its structure and objectives. Thunderwater, who was also known as Oghema Niagara, argued that the white man had demoralized and defrauded the Indians. The Indians could only fight back by acquiring better education, medical aid, and scientific knowledge, but a united and vigorous organization was needed above all. With knowledge and political and legal action, the white man could be fought with his own weapons.[8]

On each reserve where Thunderwater secured a sufficient following, the characteristic structure of the council was put into place. There was an Inner Council of Grand Councillors, a Second Circle of Councillors and firekeepers, and a number of committees responsible for education, funerals, medical attention, and entertainment. Members were required to observe a strict moral code involving belief in the Great Spirit, abstention from alcohol, and dedication to the fight for Indian rights.[9] In spite of the democratic image of the circles and the stated commitment to "unanimous agreement," Thunderwater ran the council on autocratic lines. All officers were his personal appointees, and he retained absolute control over the funds raised either as contributions or as membership fees.

The cultural revitalization aspect of the movement was evident in its employment of a kind of pan-Indian terminology. Time, for instance, was calculated in what was said to be the traditional manner. Accordingly, months became "moons," years became "great suns," and so forth. And the calendar was reorganized so that "All time shall date from the Great Sun of Entry of the White Man into our territory in 1492 A.D."[10] Further elements of strange ritual and peculiar passwords gave the movement an aura of secrecy and mystery which tended to strengthen loyalty and commitment.

In its early years Thunderwater's movement attracted favourable media attention. The *Utica Observer*, for instance, noted approvingly that the council aimed to achieve a better way of life for Indians and that it was vigorously opposed to the sale of reserve lands. The newspaper suggested that the agitation would likely be effective since "the organization appears to be established upon business principles and to have strong backing." The council was said to have a membership of 26,000, mainly concentrated in the American mid-west states. It was also securing a following in the western states and in Canada.[11]

Thunderwater and his activities first came to the attention of the Department of Indian Affairs in November 1914. In that month, the chief held a large rally on the St. Regis reserve which spanned the international boundary, and many Indians from the Canadian side crossed over to hear him speak. F.E. Taillon, Ottawa's agent at St. Regis, informed headquarters of this development. He claimed that the Indians were "flocking" to Thunderwater with tales of injustice and lists of grievances for which the department was largely to blame. The chief was promising to investigate these complaints even if it meant taking them to the highest court in the land. In Taillon's opinion, the agitation was a source of potential inconvenience and embarrassment for the government, and he sought instructions on what to do.[12] J.D. McLean's response was that the department did not recognize Thunderwater or his "so-called society" and that the Indians should be advised to have nothing to do with him.

The chief did take up the cause of Indian grievances by protesting to Ottawa about the behaviour of government agents. Scott, however, adopted a policy of ignoring him and refused to answer his letters. Nonetheless, the deputy superintendent felt obliged to learn more about this charismatic leader who was increasingly making a nuisance of himself. In April 1915 he was in communication with the Society of American Indians, an organization that co-operated closely with Washington's Bureau of Indian Affairs. Arthur C. Parker, the society's secretary-treasurer, informed Scott that Thunderwater was probably an imposter.[13] Further enquiries brought the revelation that the Bureau of Indian Affairs had no record of the chief's Indian status, and Scott readily gave credence to these suspicions.

In spite of the conspiracy to discredit him, Thunderwater continued to find success. For much of 1916, he was actively recruiting adherents to the council at Caughnawaga, and more than half the population rallied to his call. Postal has argued that he found acceptance because he arrived at a crucial time in the cultural transformation of the reserve. In their three hundred years of contact with white society, the Caughnawaga Mohawks had experienced substantial acculturation, particularly since their conversion to Catholicism and removal to the banks of the St. Lawrence had cut them off from the traditions of the Six Nations and revitalization movements such as that of Handsome Lake. However, the Iroquois language had remained their lingua franca and still served, if tenuously, as a symbol of identity. Thunderwater's movement provided the essential institutional framework and therefore won widespread support.[14]

The Council of the Tribes also made headway on other reserves in Quebec and Ontario. However, as at Caughnawaga, the "circles" tended to have a divisive effect. Several elected band councils began to complain to Ottawa that Thunderwater's activities were undermining their authority. The evident success of the movement convinced Scott that his policy of ignoring the chief was no longer adequate. In 1916 he began to explore the possibility of preventing the Indian leader from entering Canada, but immigration authorities could see no substantial grounds on which to do so.

In October 1917, the *Ottawa Citizen* reported that a legation of eight Indians led by Thunderwater had arrived in the capital in order to inform Indian Affairs of the work of the council. Scott refused to see them, thereby avoiding a personal confrontation with the chief. Instead, he advised them through an intermediary that he believed the Council of the Tribes was designed to rob the Indians. This was not sufficient to deter Thunderwater, and he told a *Citizen* reporter that he would seek incorporation for his organization through a special act of Parliament and would force the department to recognize him.[15]

The chief was not a man of idle threats, and on 3 April 1918, Bill 30, an Act to Incorporate a Council for the Indian Tribes of Canada, received its first reading in the House of Commons. It was a private member's bill that had arisen from a petition signed by 176 Indians from all the major reserves in southern Ontario and Quebec: Mohawks Bay of Quinte, St. Regis, Caughnawaga, Oka, New Credit, Onondagas Six Nations, Cayugas Six Nations, and Mohawks Six Nations. In itself, the petition showed how the Council of the Tribes had been expanding.

Scott was acutely aware of the problems the success of this measure would cause, and he was determined to prevent the bill from going any further. In a memo to Arthur Meighen on 23 April, he impressed upon the superintendent general that Thunderwater was supported only by "unprogressive, shiftless and complaining" Indians. On the other hand, the "better class of Indians" were opposed to him. The department had given some thought to prosecuting him for obtaining money under false pretences. However, such action had been reconsidered since it might have been interpreted as persecution. Scott claimed that the chief had collected hundreds of dollars in membership fees and that his object in seeking incorporation was to increase membership and thereby contributions. An equally reprehensible aim of the council was to seek for Indians "the recovery of their alleged lost privileges and rights rather than to take their places in civilized communities; to conduct their own affairs in their aboriginal way, absolutely independent of and in defiance of the Government."[16] Here was the key to Scott's opposition. It was not so much his growing conviction that Thunderwater was an imposter, but rather the realization that the success of the Council of the Tribes would weaken, if not destroy, Indian subservience to officialdom.

As a consequence of Scott's overtures, Meighen and Prime Minister Borden cajoled E. Guss Porter, who was responsible for private member's bills, to withdraw the incorporation bill after first reading.[17] This was a major setback for Thunderwater. He was soon to experience further misfortune, but as much as a consequence of his own conduct as that of Scott's subversion. In the autumn of 1916, the chief had adopted the son of Mary Ann George, a widow of the St. Regis reserve, and took him to live in Cleveland. On a subsequent visit by his mother, the boy, Mitchell Benedict, complained of physical and sexual abuse and insisted on returning to Canada. Reports of this incident came to Scott's attention early in 1919, and he felt that it might be used to stop Thunderwater. He ordered an immediate investigation and passed on the results to Immigration Superintendent W.D. Scott, suggesting that it might constitute grounds to keep the chief out of Canada.[18]

Immigration officials still refused to act, and Thunderwater continued to operate in the country for another year. But even he must have realized that time was running out. Ottawa received reports from Cleveland that he was indeed an imposter whose real name was "Mr. Palmer" and that he was of black ancestry. With this information and the news of the adoption scandal circulating among Indian agents and opponents of the council, Thunderwater's credibility was soon undermined. His principal base of operations was now Caughnawaga. In 1920 he was busily raising money—or "filling his canoe" as he put it—to pursue a land claim against the United States' government. Contributors were promised a return on their investment when the claim was settled. But at a meeting in the town hall, he was openly accused of fraud. A melee ensued which required police intervention, and Thunderwater fled to the United States, never to return.[19] According to some estimates, he had collected in the region of $20,000 from his followers in Canada over the years.[20]

It appeared that this strange comic-opera had stumbled to its conclusion. But there was one scene left to be played after an interim of several years. In March 1927, Thunderwater turned up in Louisville, Kentucky, on a visit sponsored by one of the local newspapers, the *Herald Post*. The 10 March edition of the paper featured a major story on the chief, in which he was shown attired in plains Indian regalia visiting schools and meeting thousands of school children. The editor of the rival *Louisville Times* was evidently irked at the success of this publicity stunt. He wired Scott on the following day inquiring if Thunderwater was a Canadian Indian.[21] Scott replied in the negative, adding that the chief was an imposter and was most likely a black. A similar enquiry also arrived shortly afterwards from another Louisville newspaper, the *Courier Journal*.

The *Louisville Times* did some further investigation, and on 15 March it carried a major expose on Thunderwater. The story claimed that neither the American or Canadian governments had any record of his Indian status. Thunderwater had duped state, city, and school officials by posing as a chief. According to the Cleveland police, he was really a furniture polish salesman who ran the Preservative Cleaning Co. in that city. The police also had a record on him as a peddler of worthless herbs such as Jee-Wan-Ga (dog-grass tea) in the "black belt" for many years. The story featured a photograph of Thunderwater's house—an unimposing wooden structure in the black district of Cleveland. Here was the fabled headquarters of the Council of the Tribes! Another photograph showed the "chief" standing in the rain in the streets of Louisville, *sans* war bonnet. The point of this item was that he was bald—an affliction rarely visited upon the Amerindian race.[22]

It was a devastating expose. Thunderwater responded by suing the *Times* and the *Courier Journal*, which had run a similar story. A legal firm representing the Louisville newspapers requested Scott's assistance. The deputy superintendent was unable to go to Kentucky in person, but he sent the department legal clerk, A.S. Williams, in his stead, as well as the files on Thunderwater. At the 1928 trial, the jury could not agree and no verdict was rendered.

Thus, the curious saga of Chief Thunderwater came to an end. In retrospect, Scott's opposition to the imposter seems justified. Yet, his opposition was not based on the supposition of fraud alone. In fact, it manifested itself long before the question of fraud arose. The Council of the Tribes purported to improve the health, education, and living conditions of Indians. These were aims that could hardly be objected to and even reflected those of the department. But the council also sought greater autonomy for the Indians and a concomitant weakening of department control of their lives. In addition, it fostered cultural revitalization, although the Indian symbolism it invoked was of the cigar-store or movie industry genre. The objectives of autonomy and aboriginal cultural revival were unacceptable to Scott because they hindered the achievement of assimilation—the department's ultimate aim.

The disappearance of Thunderwater's council, however, coincided with the creation of a genuine Indian movement which aimed to unite all the native people of Canada and which also posed one of the most serious threats to the smooth and efficient administration of Indian Affairs—the League of Indians of Canada.

The First World War was an event of great significance for Canada's native population. Indians served overseas in the armed forces in numbers exceeding their proportion in the population, evidence of patriotism often noted with satisfaction by Scott. The granting of the federal franchise to Indian veterans without loss of their status was one reward for their contribution. The land grant and loan system established under the Soldier Settlement Act was another.

But these concessions did not blind all returning veterans to the restrictions and disabilities under which their people continued to live. The war had brought Indians from many parts of Canada into contact with one another for the first time and sowed the seeds of pan-Indian consciousness. It created an awareness of common grievances, which led naturally to a perceived need for political action on a national scale. Grievances which affected most Indians included the gradual alienation of reserve lands, restrictions on traditional hunting and fishing rights, the suppression of native customs, the debilitating effects of boarding school education, the inadequacy of health services, lack of economic opportunities, and the paternalistic overlordship of Indian Affairs. An organization of Indians that transcended tribal boundaries was deemed essential to combat this interrelated collage of injustices.

A returning veteran, F.O. Loft, seized upon the potential for a national Indian movement and provided the leadership factor so essential in such ventures. Loft was born in 1862 on the Six Nations' reserve and was a member of the Upper Mohawk band. Unlike most Indians of his day, he received a secondary education. He left the reserve and spent most of his adult life as a clerk in the insane asylum in Toronto. In 1898 he married Affa Northcote Geary of Chicago, a cousin of Sir Stafford Northcote, later Lord Iddesleigh.[23] When the First World War broke out, Loft was commissioned as a lieutenant in the Canadian Forestry Corps. He spent seven months in France, but he was not permitted to engage in combat because of his age. He was a charismatic speaker and an effective writer, although his prose was somewhat unorthodox and colourful. Given these skills, his status as a veteran, and his striking physical appearance, he was well suited to the leadership mantle which he eagerly donned when destiny beckoned.

The initial organizational moves took place on 20 December 1918 when a grand council of Ontario Indians was held on the Six Nations' reserve. It resolved to form a "League of Indians of Canada" which would eventually embrace native people in all parts of the country, and Loft was elected president.

Press reaction was favourable. The *Edmonton Journal* speculated that a new phase in the history of Canada's Indians was at hand; the principles for which they had fought overseas could not now be denied to them at home. It saw the organization as a protest against the loss of Indian lands and the denial of treaty rights.[24]

One of Loft's tactics in fostering support for his league was to hold large meetings or "congresses" on reserves at which he could ply his oratorical skills. These events were publicized well in advance, ensuring both satisfactory levels of attendance and adequate press coverage. The first congress of the league was scheduled for 2-4 September 1919 at the Garden Hill reserve near Sault Ste. Marie. The venue was well chosen because it meant that delegates from Manitoba and Saskatchewan did not have to travel unreasonable distances to attend. The presence of these delegates showed that the league was already moving outside its Ontario origins.

To judge from press reports, the first congress augured well for the organization's future. The *London Free Press* noted that the Indians were

> all deeply interested and enthusiastic in the new movement to see what the Indian can do towards formulating higher planes of social, moral, political and industrial economies, also to advance the cause of better and higher educational facilities for the native race in general. The delegates are composed of men who speak splendid English and are fully qualified to understand the needs of their people.[25]

While this optimism was not without foundation, it overlooked the enormous practical difficulties entailed in creating a national Indian body. There was no widespread consensus among the native population regarding either the need for such an organization or its putative objectives. Equally formidable was the fact that communication between Indian bands was difficult, if not impossible. Even where networks of roads, railways, and rivers permitted the exchange of ideas and information, travel was time-consuming and expensive. Indians usually had some funds at their disposal which might have been employed to travel to organizational meetings, but these funds were held in trust for them by Indian Affairs and could only be spent with the department's approval. Much, then, would depend on the attitude of government officials, and that turned out to be the greatest obstacle of all.

Ottawa's attitude became apparent even as arrangements were underway for the congress of 1919. The Indian agent at Sault Ste. Marie received a request from the Garden Hill band for $100 to defray the cost of hosting the event. The agent forwarded the request to headquarters, warning that the congress would probably lead to trouble.[26] His superiors agreed, and the request was turned down. A number of Indians applied to have their travel expenses paid out of band funds and were also refused. The department explained that it had not approved of the congress and could not therefore acquiesce in the expenditure of band monies for such a purpose.

Undeterred by Ottawa's lack of co-operation, Loft pressed forward with his organizational activities after the Garden Hill gathering. In November he sought to increase league membership by circulating a letter among a number of bands. Bands were urged to join the organization by paying a $5 registration fee. Five cents per head would subsequently be charged annually. The letter stressed the importance of united action, citing the example of trade unions and farmers' organizations, which had recently formed a government in Ontario.

> We as Indians, from one end of the Dominion to the other, are sadly strangers to each other; we have not learned what it is to co-operate and work for each other as we should; the pity of it is greater because our needs, drawbacks, handicaps and troubles are all similar. It is for us to do something to get out of these sad conditions. The day is past when one band or a few bands can successfully—if at all—free themselves from the domination of officialdom and from being ever the prey and victims of unscrupulous means of depriving us of our lands and homes and even deny us of the rights we are entitled to as free men under the British flag.

The circular went on to say that the league would fight specifically for "absolute control" of reserve lands. It would insist that all matters affecting Indians be decided through consultation with their representatives, the band councils.

After all, they too had fought for freedom during the recent war.[27]

It was an impassioned and articulate appeal for autonomy—a call to arms calculated to sway the undecided. So that his circular might reach the eyes of potential adherents, Loft wrote to C.P. Schmidt, Indian agent at Duck Lake, Saskatchewan, requesting a list of the most educated Indians in the local bands with whom he could then correspond. Schmidt first submitted the request to Ottawa and was directed not to supply the information.[28]

D.C. Scott initially greeted the existence of the league with annoyance and irritation. Here was another unwelcome impediment to efficient administration. What Loft and his organization were proposing was often in direct opposition to established department policy. Scott felt that the problem might disappear of its own accord if the department refused to co-operate, and this was the advice he transmitted to the department's agents as they began to complain of the organization's activities. For example, when J.P. Wright, the agent at Fort Frances, forwarded a copy of Loft's circular to Scott, warning of the League's "Balshevick [sic]" nature, he was told to advise his Indians "to have nothing to do with it." And Scott's irritation with Loft was clear when he added: "I took a particular interest in this fellow's daughter and we strained ourselves to give the girl advantages at Toronto University and this is the sort of thanks one gets for it."[29]

The League of Indians was also attracting attention in other quarters. Copies of Loft's circular fell into the hands of the commissioner of the North West Mounted Police at Regina late in 1919. The police feared that the league was either a scheme to defraud the Indians or to embarrass the government by stirring up discontent. An investigation into Loft's background was ordered, but it revealed nothing that would suggest criminal intent or adherence to revolutionary political ideology. Nonetheless, the information was transmitted to Scott with the warning that "considerable unrest" was being caused.[30]

This seems to have convinced the deputy superintendent that ignoring the league would ultimately prove inadequate. Greater vigilance by his agents would at least be required. When he was informed that a "convocation" of the league was planned for Elphinstone, Manitoba, on 22 June 1920, he wrote to Indian Commissioner W.M. Graham at Regina instructing him to have someone in attendance as "it would seem essential that the Department should as far as possible curb or at least keep informed as to Loft's activities."[31] Unfortunately for Scott, his letter arrived in Regina after the gathering had been held, and no report on the event could be compiled.

Shortly after this episode, Bill 14, which permitted the department to enfranchise Indians without their consent, became law. The amendment had been Scott's brainchild, and it now occurred to him that it could be applied with great effect in the case of Loft. Once deprived of his status, the Indian leader would lose all credibility as a spokesman, and his movement would crumble. In a letter to Major Gordon J. Smith, Indian superintendent at Brantford, Scott told of his inspiration and requested information regarding Loft's livelihood and other matters of relevance where enfranchisement was under consideration.[32] Smith's opinion was that since the Indian leader had been employed in the Ontario Civil Service for some years and had shown his ability to support himself and his family, he was "fully qualified for enfranchisement."[33]

Early in 1921, Loft was informed by J.D. McLean that the department was contemplating his enfranchisement. He reacted by writing a lengthy letter of protest to the superintendent general, Sir James Lougheed. He equated enfranchisement with "denationalization." This was something that he could never accept; he was proud to belong to a race that had always contributed its "share in manhood" to the country "in times of stress and war." Scott, who read this letter first, passed it on with memorandum in which he remarked:

> I fail to see wherein the sentimental and racial considerations upon which he lays so much stress, constitute a reason why he should remain a ward of the Crown, if it is clearly established that his qualifications for citizenship are such that he no longer requires that protection.[34]

A few days later, Scott attempted to discredit Loft in Lougheed's eyes in a more systematic way, thereby removing any potential difficulties in proceeding with the enfranchisement:

> He has some education, has rather an attractive personal appearance, but he is a shallow, talkative individual. He is one of the few Indians who are endeavouring to live off their brethren by organizing an Indian society, and collecting fees from them. He is employed by the Ontario government, and I have proposed to him that he should be enfranchised, which, I think, accounts for this sudden activity on his part. What he ought to get is a good snub. He volunteered for the war and looked very well in a uniform, but he was cunning enough to evade any active service, and I do not think his record in that regard is a very good one.[35]

This passage was a deliberate attempt to mislead the minister. Scott's belittling remark regarding Loft's education was hardly warranted since the Indian leader had achieved the same level of schooling as he had himself. Nor was there much truth in the suggestion that Loft's "activity" had been prompted by his proposed enfranchisement. The League of Indians had been founded almost two years prior to the passage of Bill 14. Moreover, Scott was well aware that Loft had not been allowed in combat because of his age. In fact, he had been fifty-five years when he had enlisted in 1917, the same age as Scott, who had not volunteered at all!

Whether Lougheed was impressed or not, it mattered little. Compulsory enfranchisement became a dead issue with the fall of the Meighen administration in 1921; the hated amendment to the Indian Act was repealed by the Liberals the following year. This fortuitous turn of events saved Loft from the fate of enfranchisement.

It did not, however, prevent Scott from attempting to discredit his adversary in the eyes of the new superintendent general, Charles Stewart. Early in 1922, he explained the situation:

> Mr. Loft is physically a good specimen of an Indian, but he is gifted with a smooth tongue, and a couple of years ago, being incited by the example of other Indian agitators, he set out to organize a society for the supposed benefit of the Indians of Canada. The collection of fees is to my mind the important part of his function.

Scott added that Loft had given evidence before the parliamentary committee on the Indian Act in 1920 and had impressed the members "with his physical vigour and also with the emptiness of his mind."[36]

While Scott was thus trying to undermine Loft, the League of Indians was confidently expanding the horizons of its support, especially in the west. Western bands increasingly took their grievances to the league, which then acted on their behalf in confronting Indian Affairs. Commissioner Graham was reluctant to recognize Loft as a native spokesman, and Scott concurred. Loft was informed bluntly that the department would not acknowledge him as an intermediary or representative of the western Indians.[37]

The deputy superintendent's earlier suggestion that a close watch be maintained on Loft's activities was carried out systematically by his subordinates. A vast network of spies, which included missionaries, police, and subservient Indians, kept the department's agents informed of the agitator's every move. For example, Father Moulin of the Hobbema Mission informed the local agent, C.W. Kirby, that Loft was planning a large meeting of Alberta Indians for the Samson reserve on 21 June 1922. When Kirby transmitted this disturbing news to Ottawa, he proposed that a patrol of Royal Canadian Mounted Police be in attendance. Scott agreed and made the appropriate arrangements through his police connections.[38]

The Samson rally clearly demonstrated the growing support for the League of Indians. Some fifteen hundred Indians from all over Alberta attended, including Blackfoot, Bloods, Piegans, Stonies, and Crees.[39] In accordance with Scott's wishes, two Mounted Police were also present. In their report, the police noted that the conference ended on the evening of 23 June with a "big tom-tom dance." One of the officers remained "in the inner circle of the dance as a check to the Indians getting out of hand and committing any foolishness," while the other patrolled the outer circle "to see that nobody was in a state of intoxication."

But they discovered no trouble of any sort.[40]

Commissioner Graham was particularly disturbed at the growth of the league in his western domain. He was concerned not only because of the political implications of the movement, but also because the large rallies distracted Indians from essential farm work during the summer months. The commissioner was obsessed with leading the native population to agriculture and, therefore, opposed any activities that tended to hinder the achievement of that end. He made frequent representations to headquarters demanding that steps be taken to put an end to the rallies.[41] Ottawa continued to insist, however, that while it strongly disapproved, these events could not legally be prevented from taking place as long as they retained their peaceful and law-abiding character.

Why was Loft treated like a subversive whose activities required constant police vigilance? There is no evidence that he ever advocated violence or subscribed to revolutionary ideology. The answer probably lies in his persistent claim that the principal difficulty facing the native population was its subservience to the federal Indian Department. This was a source of constant embarrassment to the government, especially insofar as the press tended to sympathize with Loft's view. Newspapers frequently portrayed him as a champion of his people locked in combat with a heartless bureaucracy. In June 1920, for example, the *Toronto Sunday World* featured a major story on Loft and reported that he was "putting up a determined fight against the disintegration of Indian lands under the plea of enfranchisement and soldier settlement."[42]

A few months later, the *Toronto Star Weekly* portrayed Loft in an equally favourable light. In fact, it quoted him on what he perceived as the major predicament of the Indian:

> if anything is responsible for the backwardness of the Indians today, it is the domineering, dictating, vetoing method of the Indian Department. The position and treatment of the Indian today is as if he were an imbecile.[43]

In July 1922, Loft was invited to address the Regina Rotarians. His assertion that Indians ought to pull themselves up from their degraded state through education and hard work undoubtedly found a ready audience. But he went on to lay much of the blame for prevailing conditions on Indian Affairs, the administration of which kept the native population in a state of tutelage and prevented the development of self-reliance. He was also critical of provincial game laws which restricted access to the Indians' traditional source of food, rendering them weak and subject to disease. The *Regina Leader* noted that while wild animals ought to be protected, it made little sense to do so at the expense "of the race which owned the land before the whiteman came." The newspaper proposed that these laws be modified to prevent cases of hardship to Indians.[44]

It is hardly surprising, in view of this kind of publicity, that the department viewed Loft as a nuisance, if not a dangerous menace, whose activities threatened the implementation of its policies. As he continued his speaking engagements in the early 1920s, the department's network of espionage remained ever vigilant lest he use "seditious language" and thereby render himself liable to prosecution.

At this stage, Loft was evidently planning to expand the base of his operations to those parts of the country in which the league had not yet been organized. However, his wife became ill and he took her to live in her home town, Chicago, for a number of years. In his absence the league declined perceptibly. It survived best in the prairie provinces, where a vibrant "western branch" had been established in 1920. When Loft eventually returned to active politicking, it was only in the west that he could pick up the pieces of his disintegrating organization. In the late 1920s he still attracted large audiences at a number of conventions on the prairies—events that continued to be carefully monitored by the police and department officials.[45] By this time Loft was in declining health and hampered by absence of funds and the unceasing opposition of Indian Affairs, he was unable to resurrect the league as a national body. Nevertheless, he resolved to pursue at least one issue that had remained prominent on the list of Indian grievances: provincial game laws which restricted hunting and fishing rights. In a circular dated 31 March 1931, Loft suggested that this question could only be settled in a "legal test" by the Judicial Committee of the Privy Council in England. A judgment by that court would clarify finally the nature of treaty rights. He urged his supporters for contributions in order to raise the sum of $4,000 to finance a trip to London for himself and a lawyer.[46]

A copy of this circular came into the possession of Father J. Brachet at Camperville, Manitoba. He presented it to the local Indian agent, and it soon made its way to Scott's office. The deputy superintendent passed it on to Superintendent General Thomas G. Murphy, explaining that Loft was an agitator who made a living by exploiting Indians. He suggested that the circular offered a long-awaited opportunity to prosecute the Indian leader either under the Criminal Code for fraud or under Section 141 of the Indian Act. Prosecution would be facilitated, in Scott's opinion, if further copies of the circular could be obtained. He proposed to invoke the aid of the RCMP for that purpose.[47]

Murphy, who was new to the job and generally unfamiliar with the protocols of Indian administration, gave Scott a free hand. When he was contacted, the commissioner of the RCMP agreed to conduct an investigation, and Indian agents in Ontario were warned to be on the lookout for copies of the circular and evidence of contributions. During the first few weeks of May, agents and police officers, through their connections with post office personnel, missionaries, and co-operative Indians, succeeded in garnering a modest collection of the circulars. They also discovered that there appeared to be little support on the reserves for Loft's proposed trip and that contributions had reflected this indifference.

The Indian leader was undoubtedly discouraged by this lack of response. Conceivably he was informed of the ongoing police investigation and the possibility of prosecution. For whatever combination of reasons, he abandoned his political activities about this time. He was scheduled to speak at a convention of the League of Indians at Saddle Lake reserve, Alberta on 15-17 July, but failed to appear. He was by then almost seventy years old and died within a few years.

Though his career ended somewhat ignominiously, Loft's achievements were considerable. The western branch of the league continued in existence even after his demise. It held major conventions in 1931 and 1932. By 1933 it had split into two groups representing the Indians of Alberta and Saskatchewan. The league itself eventually vanished but it formed the organizational foundation upon which Indian associations were built in those two provinces.

Loft's vision of a nationwide organization of Indians may have been premature. Without a well-established infrastructure at the provincial or tribal level, it was difficult to keep the league's far-flung components in active existence. And his own absence during the critical mid-1920s caused a loss of momentum. These factors, combined with the unrelenting opposition of Indian Affairs, made success impossible.

The government's attitude to Indian political activity must be seen in the context of the time. During the 1920s the authorities had an inordinate fear of subversion. The Winnipeg Strike of 1919 had cast an ominous shadow across the land. One response had been the enactment of the notorious Section 98 of the Criminal Code, which forbade attendance at meetings of organizations considered revolutionary. Movements such as the League of Indians of Canada were sometimes viewed in this light, and many reports from Indian agents accusing Loft and his followers of "Bolshevism" arrived in Ottawa. Though no Indians were actually arrested for espousing revolution, a close police vigilance was maintained on all those who engaged in politics.

Scott's attempts to crush Indian political activity were by no means a resounding success. As individual organizations collapsed, others rose from their ashes. By the time of his retirement, Indians were not significantly better organized than they had been at his debut. Nonetheless, the idea of political action, including the manipulation of a sympathetic media, was well established as the best prospect for future progress.

7

The Six Nations' Status Case

When Indian political organizations attempted to oppose the policies of the federal government, measures were taken to disrupt or destroy them. Yet their agitation proved far less troublesome than that which was instigated during the 1920s by the the Six Nations. The largest and wealthiest native group in the country, they put forward claims to special status that went far beyond those sought by other native peoples, and they proved particularly resourceful and persistent in advancing those claims. As a result, the response from Indian Affairs was all the more draconian.

The history of the Iroquois Confederacy or Six Nations, especially in its relationship with the European settlers, was unique in many respects. Unlike most of their fellow Indians, the Iroquois did not experience military subjuga-tion and removal from their homelands upon initial contact with the invaders. The explanation has much to do with their prowess in warfare, their sophisti-cated social and political structures, and their skill in diplomacy. The British soon recognized the value of a military alliance with these formidable warriors and entered an arrangement with them. It proved a devastating combination in the struggle for control of the continent between the British and the French.

After this conflict ended on the Plains of Abraham, the loyalty of the Six Nations to the Crown continued to be useful. When the American Revolution-ary War broke out, the Iroquois maintained a precarious neutrality, but some openly took the side of their traditional allies. Those who did found themselves on the losing side, and to compound matters their lands were incorporated into the emergent republic. In compensation, and in recognition of their military contribution, the British offered them alternative lands in the northern territo-ries still under crown control.

A large number of the Six Nations Indians under their leader, Joseph Brant, chose to move to Canada. With a certain touch of irony, their new home was secured by the Mississauga surrender of their lands along the Grand River in what is now southern Ontario. In 1784 this property was granted to the Six Nations by Sir Frederick Haldimand, governor of Quebec and commander in chief of the British forces in North America. The Indians were subsequently confirmed in their ownership of that land by Lieutenant-Governor John Graves Simcoe of Upper Canada in 1793.[1] The terms of what became known as the Haldimand Grant and the Simcoe Deed were to play a pivotal role in the arguments for special political status that were later advanced by the Six Nations.

The confederacy was ruled by what was known as the hereditary council, a body comprising the chiefs of the six tribes, although the number of representatives from each one was not the same. The women of certain clans selected the chiefs, making the positions hereditary in a certain sense. This form of government had served the Six Nations well for centuries, and it continued to function effectively in Canada.

The military defeat and the loss of their traditional homelands were certainly traumatic for the Iroquois, and it has been argued that some social disorganization with consequent increases in drunkeness and promiscuity accompanied settlement in Canada.[2] Nevertheless, these tendencies were soon counteracted by a religious revival. The prophet of this movement was Handsome Lake, who claimed to have experienced a series of visions beginning in 1799. While thus in communication with the creator, he received a set of instructions designed to revitalize Iroquois religion and culture.

Handsome Lake's religion required a strict moral code. Witchcraft, drinking, abortion, adultery, and similar practices were unequivocally condemned. In fact, much of what the prophet preached bore great resemblance to the Christian code of ethics. And his theology featured equivalents of the Christian notions of heaven and hell—a post mortem system of rewards and punishments as a deterrent to inappropriate behaviour. Elisabeth Tooker has claimed that this code of behaviour was more than a means of social stability. The values inherent in the new religion were precisely those required in an agricultural community, and they therefore fitted the economic activity which the Iroquois were now obliged to adopt.[3]

While the longhouse religion, as it became known, thus featured elements that facilitated adaptation to changing conditions, it also accommodated ancient customs which the white man found less acceptable. Prominent among these was the white dog sacrifice, traditionally the most important aspect of the Iroquois mid-winter ceremonies. After ritualistic strangulation, a pure white dog was decorated, hung on a long pole for a few days, and afterwards burned. It was believed that in being burned the dog was sent as a messenger to the creator. This neglected practice was revived among the Iroquois about the time of

Handsome Lake's visions. Though the prophet condemned the sacrifice, his followers evidently ignored his admonitions, and it became part of the long-house rituals.[4]

The work of Protestant missionaries among the Six Nations during the nineteenth century failed to eradicate the new beliefs, and the reserve became divided along religious lines between pagans—as the adherents of the long-house were derisively labelled—and Christians. This division eventually became an important factor in the controversies surrounding the political status of the Six Nations and the nature of their form of government which came to a head when Scott was deputy superintendent.

Because of their peculiar historical relationship with the British, the Six Nations put forward a claim to special political status after their settlement in Canada. They argued for autonomy in the conduct of their own affairs on the grounds that they had never been conquered by the British, but had been their allies, first against the French and later in the American wars. They contended that they continued to be allies, not subjects of the Crown. The Haldimand Grant of 1784 was the document most frequently cited in support of this assertion. Haldimand had referred to the Indians as "His Majesty's allies," and the lands were granted "which them and their posterity [were] to enjoy forever" under the king's "protection."[5]

During the War of 1812, the Iroquois again played the role of allies when they took up arms on the British side. However, this was to be the last venture of this sort on their part. No longer useful militarily, they soon saw their political claims rejected. When they demanded to be governed according to their own laws in 1839, the authorities of Upper Canada refused to entertain such a possibility.[6]

The restrictive features of the federal Indian Act of 1876 and subsequent amendments increased bureaucratic control over the lives of Indians, and the activities of the Department of Indian Affairs were deeply resented by the Six Nations council. The hereditary chiefs saw their jealously-guarded independence threatened by the presence on the reserve of a departmental official known as a superintendent.[7] In a petition to Ottawa in 1890, the chiefs demanded recognition of their autonomy and exemption from the provisions of the Indian Act. The government's respose was almost predictable: "The Superintendent-General of Indian Affairs is unable to concur in the view put forward in this petition, and he is of opinion that there is no ground on which the same can be supported."[8] This rebuff did not close the issue, and there was to be further and more far reaching agitation for special status in the new century. In the meantime, the hereditary chiefs, the most persistent advocates of autonomy, were to have the very basis of their own authority challenged from within the reserve.

Part of the council's difficulty arose from its inability to cope with changing circumstances. In the closing decades of the nineteenth century, it was obliged to deal with an expanding complexity of issues ranging from alcohol abuse to the management of timber resources. The traditional method of conducting business—which required arriving at unanimous decisions—proved increasingly cumbersome for a gathering of approximately seventy individuals.[9] Frustration over this inherent inefficiency led to the first demands for reform.

The reformers argued that the replacement of the hereditary council by an elective one would provide an administration more suited to the times, which would also create the level of autonomy operative under the municipal form of government. The fact that Indians in eastern Canada were granted the federal franchise by John A. Macdonald in 1885 gave further impetus to the movement for democratic reform.[10] The Liberals, however, continued to oppose this measure as a cynical attempt to win the Indian vote, and they rescinded the privilege in 1898 during Laurier's term of office.[11] In the interim, the Six Nations Indians had experienced the electoral process, even though the chiefs attempted to discourage the practice of voting as out of harmony with Iroquois traditions.

The prospect of changing the council from an hereditary to an elective one was improved in 1890 when an amendment to the Indian Act permitted Indian Affairs to institute such a change without band consent. And the movement for reform had gathered enough momentum in 1894 that a petition, signed by 212 Six Nations men, was sent to Ottawa demanding an elective council. But, Indian Affairs was reluctant to act since a majority clearly did not support the change.[12]

The opponents of the hereditary system were generally known as the Dehorners, although they were also called the Warriors Association, the Six Nations' Rights Association, and the Indian Rights Association.[13] The composition of this group is difficult to identify on purely tribal grounds; apparently, supporters and opponents of the chiefs were found in all six groups making up the confederacy. If any division is discernable, it was along religious lines. The council attracted most of its following among the adherents of the longhouse religion, while the reformers tended to be Christians.[14]

This difference led Indian Affairs officials to distinguish between traditional and progressive elements on the reserve. In fact, when the Dehorners stepped up their agitation against the hereditary system in the early years of the new century, they were apt to accuse the chiefs of being "uneducated" and "wedded to traditional ways."[15] Allegations of bribery, mismanagement and partiality were also made.

Nonetheless, a Dehorner petition to Ottawa in 1907 could only muster three hundred signatures—only one quarter of the adult male population. In spite of the persistent campaign, the reformers failed to demonstrate convincingly that their views reflected majority opinion at Grand River, and Ottawa refused to move against the hereditary government.

The Dehorner campaign, then, ultimately faded for lack of substantial local support. Nonetheless, the chiefs still felt that their position was being gradually undermined by the burgeoning regulations and meddlesome officials of Indian Affairs. They resolved to reassert their authority by advancing once more the historical claims to special political status.

The chiefs were by no means united on this question. A radical group, which comprised about half the council members, proposed to settle for nothing less than total sovereignty. Levi General, also known as Chief Deskeheh, was the acknowledged leader of this group. Approximately one-third of the remainder of the council aimed at a more moderate political objective—the status quo with a greater degree of local autonomy and co-operation with Indian Affairs. These chiefs felt that independence was impractical and insisted on loyalty to the Dominion and the Empire. A third element hoped to see the old form of government replaced by an elective council.[16]

The moderate forces suffered from disorganization and lack of effective leadership. They could not compete with the oratorical skills of Deskeheh and his followers, who soon dominated local politics. In fact, before the second decade of the century commenced, the moderates had either been silenced or expelled from the council.[17]

This turn of events paved the way for what became known as the Six Nations' status case. A status committee was established by the council early in 1919 to plan the campaign for sovereignty. In subsequent discussions with the federal Department of Justice, the Indians were advised to seek legal assistance if their case was to have any prospect of success. They hired lawyer A.G. Chisholm, who proceeded to compile historical evidence in support of the claim.[18]

In the spring of 1920, while Chisholm was still engaged in his research, Bill 14 was being pushed through Parliament. Indians were invited to make representations regarding the bill to a committee of the House of Commons set up to consider it. The Six Nations sent Chisholm to Ottawa, and he raised the sovereignty question before this committee. But he failed to impress its members with his arguments. In fact, the committee went on to recommend the abolition of the hereditary system of government whenever a majority of adult males should so approve.[19]

The controversy surrounding Bill 14, which became law on 1 July 1920, clearly illustrated the deterioration of relations between the council and the department which characterized those years. The compulsory enfranchisement amendment was deeply resented on the Six Nations' reserve and tended to rally support for Deskeheh and his sovereignty campaign.

In the meantime, a petition prepared with Chisholm's assistance was submitted to the governor general over the signature of the six head chiefs on 12 March 1920. The document reiterated the argument that the Six Nations had always been allies and not subjects of the Crown, and it demanded a judgment from the Supreme Court on the question of their sovereignty.[20]

Scott's initial reaction to what he termed the "so-called status claim" was one of scepticism. He felt that the committee on Bill 14 had adequately dealt with the issue, and he advised Superintendent General Arthur Meighen that it should not be considered by the Supreme Court.[21] A few weeks later, however, Scott evidently changed his mind, and he informed the Six Nations Council in June that he was recommending favourable consideration of its petition. He also promised that the compulsory enfranchisement provisions of Bill 14 would not be applied to Grand River until a decision had been reached.[22] He explained his change of heart to the new superintendent general, Sir James Lougheed. Scott had now concluded that the obsession of the Six Nations with the question of their status was disrupting the smooth administration of the reserve, and if it "could be finally disposed of, it would tend towards harmony." He therefore proposed that Lougheed take appropriate measures to have issue decided in the courts.[23]

Lougheed was not keen to adopt this course of action and insisted that the Department of Justice be consulted first. In September, the deputy minister of justice, E.L. Newcombe, advised Scott that the petition was "a hopeless case."[24] This judgment convinced both Scott and Lougheed that there was no point in proceeding further. On 27 November 1920, the Privy Council handed down an order-in-council rejecting the Six Nations' demand that the Supreme Court consider their status.

Deskeheh and his followers were not deterred. At a meeting on 8 March 1921, they resolved to draw up another petition, on this occasion with the assistance of Montreal lawyer W.D. Lighthall. They had been prompted to action a week earlier when Scott informed them that the provisions of Bill 14 would now be extended to their reserve. The petition, which was sent to the governor general in May, complained bitterly of the compulsory enfranchisement amendment and the Soldier Settlement Act which threatened to disperse the tribe. The governor general was urged to "stay this aggression practice by the Ministry."[25]

The petition, like so many other such documents, was referred to Indian Affairs, and Scott undertook the task of composing the official response. He first attacked the claim for special status, pointing out that there was no tradition of Indian exemption from the laws of the land and referring to the recent order-in-council which had rejected such a notion. And to dispel lingering hopes that government intransigence might wane, he quoted approvingly John B. Robinson, attorney general for Upper Canada, who had said in 1824:

> To talk of treaties with the Mohawk Indians residing in the heart of one of the most populous Districts of Upper Canada upon lands purchased for them and given to them by the British Government is much the same in my humble opinion as to talk of making a treaty of alliance with the Jews in

Duke Street or with the French Emigrants who have settled in England.[26]

Scott went on to explain that the Six Nations' anxiety regarding the Soldier Settlement Act was unwarranted. While the act empowered the department to locate Indian veterans on parcels of reserve land, the land could not be alienated from the reserve even if the veteran defaulted on his loan repayments. He also defended the compulsory enfranchisement amendment as essential to the achievement of the ultimate goals of Indian policy:

> With reference to enfranchisement I may say that the policy of the Government is to carefully protect and educate the Indians and to thus contribute towards their civilization in order that they may eventually be merged in the general body of citizenship. If this in any way conflicts with the aspirations of Indians whose faces are set against ultimate destiny, it can only be regretted.[27]

There appears to have been little public sympathy for the Six Nations' claim to special status. However, their opposition to the compulsory enfranchisement clause was another matter. On this issue they were able to generate considerable publicity, most of it supportive. In the spring of 1921 newspapers such as the *Montreal Daily Star* and the *Globe* condemned compulsory enfranchisement, and the Brantford chapter of the IODE adopted a resolution to the same effect. On 29 March the *Brantford Expositor* published a statement by Chisholm blaming Scott personally for the growing discontent among the Six Nations. In Chisholm's opinion the Department of Indian Affairs had become more autocratic since 1913, as the recent amendments to the Indian Act showed. He was convinced that the deputy superintendent's objective was "avowedly to smash up the Six Nations Confederacy."[28]

Scott was annoyed at the bad publicity. He wrote to a friend of his at the *Globe* complaining of the stand adopted by that newspaper, and in "a strong letter" to the head of the IODE, he protested the action of its Brantford chapter.[29] In addition, he distributed a statement defending government policy to a number of newspapers.

The publicity which the Six Nations had generated was largely the work of their lawyers. Scott was painfully aware of this, and he was adamantly opposed to legal assistance being provided to Indians for such purposes. In fact, he described the bills submitted by Chisholm and Lighthall for their services in 1920 and 1921 as "extortionate." His first impulse was to refuse payment out of Six Nations' funds for these bills, and he only agreed to do so at the insistence of the Justice Department.

Chisholm and Lighthall were unable to produce results satisfactory to the chiefs, and their services were dispensed with in April 1921. Scott was relieved, but his satisfaction was short-lived. Almost immediately, Deskeheh moved to hire American lawyers instead. The most prominent was George T. Decker, a Rochester resident who had been successfully involved in Indian cases south of the border. This turn of events infuriated Scott, who showed his determination to prevent a new round of agitation in a dispatch to Superintendent Gordon J. Smith at Brantford. The deputy superintendent's administrative correspondence was generally terse and prosaic, exhibiting none of the imaginative flourishes which one might have expected from one so prominent in the world of letters. However, this appears to have been an occasion of special concern, prompting an uncharacteristic outburst of sarcasm:

> I was much interested in the resolutions passed at the last meeting of the Six Nations Council with reference to the Status Case. The present situation is highly amusing. I am awaiting your report, but I want to take some reasonably quick action, so do not delay. Try and find out the addresses of these American gentlemen who are to carry on the great work and become in their turn the Saviours of the Six Nations,—Dr. Bates and George Decker. There was a man called Bates whose alias was the Artful Dodger, and the name Decker is naturally associated with a game of Euchre. What I want to do is to squelch these gentlemen at the start. Who is George Nash, the Indian who appears so suddenly like a sort of meteor? I do not remember having heard of him before.[30]

Scott's anticipation of difficulty with the new team of legal advisers was well founded. It was at Decker's suggestion that Deskeheh decided to take the status case directly to the King of England during the summer of 1921. The chief arrived in London in August and presented a petition to the Colonial Office. It outlined the historical grievances of the Six Nations and urged the British government to intervene. The outcome of this entreaty was almost predictable. The secretary of state for the colonies, Winston Churchill, forwarded the document to the governor general in Ottawa, noting that the matter was within the exclusive jurisdiction of the Canadian government.[31] This information was subsequently transmitted to the Six Nations' council through the Indian Affairs network.

It might have been a completely futile exercise but for the publicity it spawned for the Iroquois cause and the inconvenience and embarrassment it caused Scott. The romance of the North American Indian had long intrigued the European public. Indians who arrived on that continent in their colourful regalia invariably attracted considerable attention and a sympathetic hearing from the media.

Deskeheh's visit to England was no exception. *Canada*, a weekly illustrated magazine published in London, featured an article on the chief and his petition which presented the Iroquois claim to special status in a favourable light.[32] By an interesting coincidence Scott happened to be in the city at the time and he was invited by the editor of the magazine to submit his department's views. Scott refused, but his silence did not go unnoticed.[33] The London correspondent of the *Montreal Gazette* cabled a message home that was labelled "Silence Harmful to Canada's Name." He criticized Scott for refusing to defend government policy and then noted, "Canadians over here regret this apathy of officialdom to the good name of the Dominion."[34] By the time this story appeared, the deputy superintendent was back in Canada, and he felt obliged to explain his actions to Sir James Lougheed. He insisted that the Six Nations' case was exclusively a domestic concern and that there was therefore no need either to explain or defend government actions abroad.[35] Lougheed agreed, but such stonewalling soon proved inadequate to protect "the good name of the Dominion" when Deskeheh's campaign to discredit government policy reached a larger international audience.

In the meantime, however, a change of regime in Ottawa raised the spectre of a negotiated agreement between the Indians and their overlords. The advent of the Mackenzie King administration in 1921 brought a less intransigent minister to the interior portfolio in the person of Charles Stewart. His conciliatory approach was evident in his first year in office when he repealed the much-hated compulsory enfranchisement provisions over Scott's protests. The new superintendent general was anxious to avoid international involvement in the Six Nations' status case and believed that some form of agreement could be worked out through an impartial jury.

Consequently, in June 1922 Stewart proposed the establishment of a royal commission to settle the status question for good. It would be composed of three judges of the Supreme Court of Ontario—one chosen by Ottawa, one by the Six Nations council, and the third by the first two appointees. The government and the Indians would agree beforehand to be bound by the decision of the commission.[36]

At a meeting on 7 July, the chiefs rejected this proposal on Decker's advice. Stewart, however, kept the offer open. Scott, on the other hand, felt that compromise would be interpreted as weakness and that only firm measures could now bring results. As he explained to Stewart in September:

> I am convinced that the agitation on the Six Nations Reserve is fanatical, and that there is no foundation for any real grievance. If the Government fails to take the fullest measures consistent with justice and fairness to suppress this agitation, it will weaken our administration of Indian affairs in Canada.[37]

Scott suggested that in dealing with Indians their "vanity and general ignorance" should be taken into account and that they should be "sharply checked in making unwarranted claims and foolish assumptions of all kinds."[38]

But Stewart retained his faith in a mutual agreement throughout the autumn, and in a meeting with Deskeheh on 4 December, some progress appears to have been made. The superintendent general was willing to be more flexible with regard to the composition of the proposed royal commission. Its membership would no longer be confined to Ontario judges, and the Indians could freely choose their own representative, as long as he was a British subject.[39] This was less than the magnanimous concession it might first appear, since Stewart had already discovered that all the Ontario judges were either too sick or too busy to serve. Restricting the Indian appointee to British subjects was obviously a ruse to prevent the selection of Decker.

The superintendent general's search for a compromise was short-lived. While the council was discussing his latest offer, an incident occurred on the reserve which polarized the situation and led the antagonists to resolve the issue through confrontation. A few days after the 4 December meeting, a number of police officers appeared at Grand River to investigate reports of liquor manufacturing. They were evidently opposed by a group of armed Indians. Shots were fired, although the exact details of the incident are unclear. The presence of this "armed force" on their land convinced the chiefs that the government was not sincere in its negotiations with them, and they resolved upon a course of action that Decker had been proposing for some time.

The American lawyer believed that Ottawa's intransigence posed an insurmountable obstacle to the settlement of the status question and that the Six Nations would only receive an impartial hearing before an international tribunal. The recently formed League of Nations seemed to provide the perfect forum. On Decker's advice, the Dutch *chargé d'affaires* in Washington was approached with a view to presenting the claims of the Six Nations to the League.

When Scott heard of this he was furious, and all the more so because of the recent shooting incident at Grand River. On 21 December he attempted to persuade Stewart that the time for compromise had passed and that only "firm action" could now prevent anarchy on the reserve. The solution, in his opinion, was the location of a permanent detachment of RCMP at Ohsweken—a move supported by Major Duffis, commissioner of the Mounted Police, and by Superintendent Gordon Smith.[40]

Stewart agreed, and the Mounties arrived to take up duty in January 1923. The superintendent general still hoped for an agreement on the royal commission, and he kept the lines of communication with Deskeheh open. But the police presence was an ill omen. When the Dutch government responded positively to the Indians' overtures and it looked as if the case would indeed be brought before the League of Nations, Deskeheh broke off negotiations with Stewart. The breakdown was accompanied by the exchange of some sharply worded letters between the chief and Scott.

   Membership in the League of Nations was one of Canada's first steps towards independence, and yet the situation was by no means simple since the country was still very much tied to the imperial umbilical cord.[41] The Dominion's contribution to the First World War effort strengthened its claim to greater autonomy within the empire, and Prime Minister Borden was able to insist that Canada become a fully-fledged member of the League. It became eligible in its own right for election to the League Council and to the Governing Body of the International Labour Organization.[42]

   Beginning in 1920 Canada was represented regularly at the League Assembly, although it did not have a permanent delegate until 1925, which showed that Robert Borden's enthusiasm for the organization was not shared by his successors. Many saw the League as having merit in promoting the Dominion's international standing. Yet there was a reluctance on the part of Canadian delegates to make commitments to other countries, and interference in the Dominion's internal affairs was deeply resented.[43] There was even a tendency on the part of the country's delegates to adopt a posture of self-righteous moral superiority. On occasion, European countries were chastised because their errant ways had led to frequent wars. The amicable relationship between Canada and the United States, on the other hand, was held up as a model to be emulated.[44] This posturing took on a hollow ring when the Dominion found itself the object of international criticism in the Six Nations' case.

   The principal difficulty in bringing their case to the attention of the League was that the Indians themselves were not members. It was therefore necessary to find a sympathetic member country to act on their behalf. The Dutch were approached because they had been allies of the Iroquois during the seventeenth century in what later became the state of New York. In their petition, the Indians suggested that their extinction was being planned by their "British neighbours," who had recently invaded their lands with "armed forces." All attempts to negotiate the question of their status with the British and Canadian governments had failed. Their last resort, apart from an armed uprising, lay in an appeal to the League of Nations.[45]

   In April 1923, the Dutch representative in Geneva, J. Van Panhuys, presented the petition to the secretary general, Sir Eric Drummond. He was careful to point out that his government held no opinion on the question and that the petition was being submitted only for discussion by League members. Drummond, a former official of the British Foreign Office, was prepared to circulate the petition, but he first invited Ottawa to draw up a response to be circulated simultaneously.[46]

   The task of formulating the Canadian response fell to Scott. In a terse statement, the deputy superintendent pointed out that the status of the Six Nations as British subjects was the same as that of any other natives or aborigines born within the Empire. He insisted that there had been no recent change in government policy and that the armed force mentioned by the Indians merely referred to the stationing of an RCMP post on the reserve to maintain law and order. Evidence of the government's determination to resolve outstanding issues was the appointment of a commissioner under the Enquiries Act to investigate conditions at Grand River. As for the on-going agitation, it was "carefully formented by a few reactionaries" and was "sedulously kept alive by interested parties."[47] Scott's statement was submitted to Sir Joseph Pope, under-secretary of state for external affairs, who arranged for its transmission to Geneva. Scott and Pope worked closely together during this controversy. Both government officials and politicians relied heavily on the deputy superintendent's expertise, and he was kept informed of developments.

The government was not content with a mere public repudiation of the allegations being made by Deskeheh. In fact, Ottawa and London both resented the actions of the Dutch government and argued forcibly that the issue was outside of League jurisdiction. The Netherlands' ambassador to London was told bluntly by the Foreign Office that British sovereignty over the Six Nations' land was not in question and that under Article 15, paragraph 8 of the Covenant, the League Council was debarred from interference. And the Dutch were reminded that they too had colonized peoples who could raise a similar protest.[48]

Sir Joseph Pope wrote to Drummond in May expressing the hope that the League would judge the matter beyond its competence. He also strongly protested of the Dutch action in bringing an issue "entirely of domestic concern" to the attention of the international body.[49] The Dutch, however, continued to insist that they had no wish to take sides, and they pursued the matter with a marked lack of enthusiasm.[50] Their minister for foreign affairs, H.A. van Karnebeek, argued that his government was only delivering the Indian petition to its address, seeing that the Indians themselves were technically not permitted to do so. Consequently, on 7 August the Six Nations' petition and Ottawa's response to it were circulated among the ten members of the League Council. None of the members requested that it be placed on the council agenda for discussion, which brought the matter to a temporary conclusion. It also ended the involvement of the Netherlands.[51]

In the meantime, Deskeheh had decided that his own presence in Europe was necessary to generate maximum sympathy and publicity. Accompanied by Decker, he arrived in London in August, on his way to Geneva. While in the British capital, he issued a pamphlet entitled "The Redman's Appeal for Justice," which was addressed to the secretary-general of the League of Nations. This document outlined the historical basis of the Six Nations' claims and urged that the League secure for them the following:

1.   recognition of their right to home rule;

2. an accounting by the British and Canadian governments of their trust
    funds;
3. freedom of transit across Canadian territory to and from international
    waters.

The British press, always avid for sensation, responded positively to the
chief's activities. Headlines such as "Red Indian Wrongs" generated far more
excitement than the terse statement issued by the Canadian High Commissioner's
Office in London in a vain attempt to discredit Deskeheh and his campaign.[52]

The chief also found many sympathetic ears among the delegates to the
League, and he succeeded in presenting his statement "The Redman's Appeal
for Justice" to the president of the assembly on 4 September. However, the
president informed him that for procedural reasons no action could be taken
on the case in that session.[53] Undeterred, Deskeheh remained in Europe
convinced that the League still offered the best forum in which to do battle with
the Canadian government.

George P. Graham, Canada's delegate, was aware of the chief's intentions, and
he warned Stewart in a letter of 6 October that a future petition might be more
successful. He was of the opinion that Deskeheh had made an impression in
Geneva. On the other hand, Ottawa's official statement on the Six Nations' case
was somewhat abrupt and had been less than convincing. He suggested that a
more detailed reply be prepared and forwarded to the League Secretariate.[54]

Scott volunteered to prepare the proposed statement. It was completed by 27
December and was entitled "Statement Respecting the Six Nations' Appeal to
the League of Nations." In this document the deputy superintendent attempted
to dispose systematically of the arguments advanced by Deskeheh. His central
proposition was that the Six Nations' claim to special political status was
inadmissible. This question had been dealt with on several occasions by the
dominion government with the same result, and Scott included extensive
quotations from the rulings of 1890 and 1920 as evidence.

He also unearthed instances in which the Indians had referred to the King as
"Our Sovereign Lord." Here was proof of their historical allegiance to the
Crown. He argued that in the gradual transfer of autonomy to Canada—the
Constitutional Act of 1791, the Act of Union of 1840, the BNA Act of 1867—no
special allowance had been made for the Six Nations. Therefore, sovereignty
over them had effectively been transferred to Ottawa.

Scott vigorously defended his department's policies, denying the accusations
of armed aggression and misappropriation of funds. He offered a detailed
explanation of the operations of the Indian Act, adding that its ultimate aim was
full citizenship. As for "treaties"—a word he placed in quotation marks—Scott
claimed that they merely constituted grants or surrenders of land and had never
entailed the recognition of the Six Nations, or any other group of Indians, as

having sovereign status. Without such status, the Six Nations could simply not have their case considered by the League of Nations.[55] Stewart, Newcombe and Graham all enthusiastically endorsed Scott's "Statement" and it was forwarded to Sir Joseph Pope in January 1924 for transmission to the League of Nations.[56]

It was just in time, it seems. In December 1923, Sir Herbert Ames, financial director of the League and the only Canadian to hold a top Secretariate position, had written to Prime Minister Mackenzie King informing him that Deskeheh's activities in Geneva were beginning to show results. Some weeks earlier the chief Persian delegate at the Fourth Assembly, Prince Arfa ed Dowleh, had asked that the Six Nations' case be considered by the council. His request was refused on the grounds that there had been insufficient time to notify Ottawa. But the possibility existed that the Persians would insist on placing the matter on the agenda for the meeting of the council scheduled for March 1924. The delegates of Estonia, Ireland, and Panama evidently supported Persia in its championing of the Indian cause.[57]

The governments of these countries had no particular animosity for Canada. People who had only recently cast off the yoke of imperialism themselves, which was the case with the Estonians and the Irish, naturally tended to sympathize with the sovereignty claims of small nations. However, when they attempted to pursue the issue once more in the spring of 1924, they were to find that it could prove an expensive exercise.

At this stage, the British government decided to intervene. The Foreign Office informed the offending governments that their efforts to re-open the Iroquois case were resented as "impertinent interference" in the internal affairs of the Empire by "minor powers."[58] This sabre-rattling produced the desired effect, and by May London had been assured that the "minor powers" had abandoned the case.[59]

In spite of his failure to make headway, Deskeheh stayed in Europe for the remainder of 1924. On 22 October, writing from Geneva, he made a direct appeal to King George V in which he deplored the inadequacy of the League in dealing with the plight of small nations. The chief was highly critical of a recent attempt by the Canadian government to depose the Six Nations council by force. He naively appealed for what he called "British justice" and seemed to believe that the King could somehow come to the aid of his people to protect them from the Canadian authorities.[60]

Nothing came of this petition. Like similar documents before it, it was forwarded to Ottawa where it fell into Scott's hands. He transmitted it to Col. C.E. Morgan, the Indian superintendent at Brantford, with the comment, "He must have had somebody assist him in preparing it."[61]

Deskeheh's petition to the King had complained of Ottawa's attempt to abolish the hereditary form of government at Grand River. This was a reference to one of a series of momentous events that had taken place on the reserve in his absence. The government was not content merely with preventing a hearing for the status case in Geneva; it had also been busy at home working to undermine the legitimacy of Deskeheh's credentials as a spokesman for his people. The surest way to accomplish that end was to abolish the hereditary council from which he derived his authority.

The first steps had been taken in the early months of 1923 when negotiations between the chiefs and the superintendent general regarding the composition of the proposed royal commission had broken down. With the rejection of a mutually agreed on arbitration body, Scott decided that a partisan investigation into the Six Nations' affairs would serve the government's purpose. On 1 March 1923, he proposed that Col. Andrew Thompson be appointed to conduct an independent inquiry and Stewart agreed.[62]

Thompson, an Ottawa lawyer and former military officer, commenced his investigations at Ohsweken on 18 September. Notices were posted around the reserve indicating that evidence would be taken from those who wished to give it. Deskeheh's supporters generally boycotted the hearings. They were convinced that there was nothing impartial about the proceedings; the colonel was known personally to many of the Indian veterans on the reserve, who invariably opposed the hereditary council.[63] And the inquiry lost further credibility when the majority of those who did testify were offered "witness fees" in the region of $2 each. This was loudly criticized as evidence of government bribery.[64]

Thompson's report was ready by 22 November, but it was not immediately made available to the public for reasons which shall soon be clear. It dealt with a wide range of topics including education, health, soldier settlement, and the administration of justice and made some sensible suggestions for the elimination of abuses in these less contentious areas.

Interestingly enough, Thompson investigated one of the major complaints that the Indians had made against Ottawa—a complaint that had been frequently dismissed by department spokesmen such as Scott as unsubstantiated. It seems that between 1834 and 1842 almost $160,000 of Six Nations' funds had been invested in the stock of the Grand River Navigation Company without consultation with the Indians. All of it had been lost. Ottawa refused compensation because the incident had occurred prior to the granting of responsible government. The British government, on the other hand, insisted that the matter was a purely Canadian affair. Thompson acknowledged that this was a real grievance which undermined Indian confidence in "British justice" and that it should be redressed.

However, the central concern of the report was the system of tribal government composed of hereditary chiefs. Thompson could see no virtue in this system, in spite of its ancient lineage. Its principal fault, in his opinion, was that "the vast majority of the people [had] nothing whatever to say in the choice of their public servants." He urged that an elective council "be inaugurated at the earliest possible date."[65]

The colonel's zeal for democratic principles was less than forthright. In the elective system he was proposing, women would be deprived of the vote. That some women had always played a role in the selection of the hereditary council was ignored. Nor was Thompson prepared to advocate a referendum on the reserve to enable the people to choose freely the form of government they preferred.

Scott was fully in sympathy with Thompson's principal recommendation. In fact, he had been convinced of the necessity of replacing the hereditary council with an elective one as early as the spring of 1920. Nevertheless, he had refrained from imposing such a change because the majority did not support it. But the rise of militant opposition to the department's policies at Grand River between 1920 and 1923 left him less sensitive to such democratic considerations. The hereditary chiefs, the major source of the agitation, would have to be deposed regardless of popular feeling. Thompson's report would serve to legitimize the change. Should political controversy follow, Scott could point to this apparently impartial inquiry as the evidence upon which the department acted. He kept the report secret initially, waiting for the opportune moment to strike.

The appointment of Col. C.E. Morgan as Indian superintendent at Brantford in October 1923 caused a further deterioration in relations between the department and the hereditary chiefs and precipitated the move against the council that Scott was planning. Morgan was a Boer War veteran who had worked as a colonial administrator in South Africa. He evidently regarded his job with the Six Nations in a similar light. His arrogant manner, military bearing (he frequently wore a pistol), and English accent did little to endear him to the local populace. In his opinion, trouble could only be avoided on the reserve by firm action and constant police vigilance.[66]

Morgan's relations with the Six Nations' council were soon openly antagonistic. He also came into conflict with the Mohawk Workers—a club or society of chiefs and warriors that had been formed in September 1922 to support the hereditary council and the status case.[67] One of the Workers' principal activities was raising money to finance Deskeheh's petitions. At this they were quite successful, especially through the organization of lacrosse games. These well-attended events were usually held on a Sunday, which doubly infuriated the puritanical Morgan.

Early in August 1924, Morgan prepared a special report on reserve conditions for Scott. He stressed the urgency of deposing the hereditary council before rebellious activities got completely out of hand. But he cautioned that a smooth transition could only be effected with the support of a strong police presence.[68] Scott was evidently impressed, and shortly afterwards, on 20 August, Col. Thompson's report was released to the public. The deputy superintendent then moved quickly to secure an order-in-council authorizing the change to an elective form of government for the Six Nations.[69]

Meanwhile, Morgan was making secret preparations for the first election under the new system. His greatest fear was that the Mohawk Workers would contest it and succeed in controlling the new council. He suggested to Scott that perhaps new councillors should be obliged to swear allegiance to the Crown. He also suggested that certain troublemakers be disqualified from voting. But Scott found both of these proposals unacceptable.[70]

7 October 1924 was the day of reckoning for the hereditary council. On that morning, Col. Morgan arrived at a council meeting accompanied by a number of RCMP. The order-in-council abolishing the ancient system of government of the Iroquois was read, and the chiefs were then expelled unceremoniously from the hall. Details of the election for a new council were also announced.[71]

The transition was effected without the violence that had been anticipated by Morgan. But government high-handedness was nonetheless deeply resented, and it antagonized many who might otherwise have welcomed the change.

A few days later, supporters of the hereditary chiefs held a mass meeting at which they proclaimed a boycott of the coming election. The boycott was widely adhered to, and, as a result, the first election to select a new council drew the participation of only 16 to 30 per cent of the voting population. The electorate was confined to males over twenty-one.[72]

The twelve members in the elective council were to hold office for one year. The new body was primarily Christian in composition. It comprised men who had been active in the Dehorner agitation of earlier decades.[73] Its support on the reserve remained minimal. It was viewed with suspicion as the loyal handmaiden of the Department of Indian Affairs, and this impression was reinforced by the fact that Col. Morgan presided at its meetings and approved the minutes.

Scott's action in deposing the hereditary council did not win universal approval off the reserve either. There were many who noted that the council had had a long and honourable history and that its demise would mean a regrettable severing with the past. These sentiments were perhaps best expressed by the *Toronto Star Weekly*:

> But, aside from the objective of the Deskeheh movement, those who have pride in the history and traditions of the Six Nations, much as they desire to see progress among the living descendants of the great confederacy of the Six Nations, mourn the official passing of the oldest continued parliamentary body on the American continent, a body which brought peace among five nations at a time when every man's hand was against the other, and a body which because of its decisions did much to bring about the supremacy of the Anglo Saxon on the North American continent, since Iroquois aid for the British against the French and their Huron allies was effective in preventing the expansion of French influence.[74]

Chief Deskeheh remained in Europe during the momentous events of October 1924. However, his failing health and his frustration with the indifference to his cause in official circles prompted him to return to North America early the following year. He stayed in Rochester with his friend Decker, where he received frequent delegations from the deposed hereditary council, most notably in the persons of Chauncey Garlow and David Hill.[75]

O.D. Skelton, who had become under secretary of state for external affairs upon the retirement of Sir Joseph Pope in 1925, was still apprehensive that the Iroquois case would be raised once more at the League of Nations Assembly. He had been warned of this possibility by Walter A. Riddell, the permanent Canadian advisory officer at Geneva, who believed that Deskeheh had aroused "a good deal of sympathy" among Europeans. Scott did not share this anxiety, and he assured Skelton that in any event the Canadian representatives were well equipped to fight the "absurd claim."[76]

The nervousness of officialdom was unwarranted, however, for fate dictated otherwise. The Six Nations' campaign for special status was dealt a major setback by Deskeheh's untimely death on 27 June 1925 near Niagara, New York. He had been the acknowledged leader of his people and the major force behind their independence movement. To his followers and admirers in both North America and Europe, his passing was an unmitigated tragedy, rendered all the more so by the Canadian government's efforts to undermine his authority in his final days. La Commission des Iroquois, a group of Europeans who had supported the Six Nations' cause as a consequence of their meetings with the chief, noted his death with regret in a communique to *La Tribune de Genève*. The communique observed that in spite of the considerable public support Deskeheh had generated in Europe, the cause of the weak against the strong could not prevail. And it suggested that his illness and death were related to the rebuffs he had received: "Il n'y a pas de doute pour nous que les peines morales qu'il a subies ne soient pour beaucoup dans ce triste denouement." But the struggle would continue.[77]

Scott certainly believed that it would, and he showed no regret at the demise of his adversary. In fact, the moment seemed opportune to crush the independence movement once and for all. The decision to locate a detachment of RCMP at Ohsweken had originally been made with this objective in mind, and police activities on the reserve were noticably stepped up. Two policemen were present at the burial of Deskeheh at the Cayuga Longhouse Cemetery on 30 June. The speeches made on that occasion were given in Iroquois, and the police were only able to get a rough translation by interrogating some of the participants afterwards. Apparently those present had been urged to carry on with the work of Deskeheh and to "trust in the Great Spirit." The police report, subsequently passed on to Scott, noted that unless capable new leaders appeared, the agitation would die a natural death.[78]

This prediction seemed reasonable under the circumstances. The debacle with the League of Nations seemed to leave few options open to the crusaders for special political status. But they did not abandon their cause even though it involved the unpalatable recourse of returning to the bargaining table with Indian Affairs.

In March 1927 the hereditary chiefs engaged the services of Heyd, Heyd, Shorey and Newman, a Toronto law firm, to approach the department on their behalf, and a meeting was arranged between Scott and L.F. Heyd early in April to discuss reopening the status negotiations. Scott was initially receptive and offered the opening gambit of an investigation by a tribunal of three Ontario Supreme Court judges. This was precisely Charles Stewart's in 1922; the Indians had then objected to the restrictions imposed on membership of the tribunal. And now in 1927, when Chauncey Garlow, the leader of the chiefs, voiced similar objections, the offer was quickly revealed as non-negotiable. Scott informed Heyd that compromise was out of the question and that the matter was now closed as far as he was concerned.[79]

The deputy superintendent's determination was unwavering. In February 1928 he received a letter from W.D. Lighthall, the Montreal lawyer who had represented the Six Nations in 1921 on one of their petitions. Lighthall's concern was the fate of the hereditary council. He expressed his regret that "its honourable history and striking origin should altogether disappear." He felt that it could be maintained with advisory functions, as a kind of senate. And its influence might even be positive.[80] Lighthall had more than a passing interest in the subject. A literary figure in his own right, he had written a fictionalized account of the establishment of the Iroquois confederacy—*The Master of Life: A Romance of the Five Nations and of Prehistoric Montreal* (1908).[81] He had also served as a president of the Royal Society of Canada and knew Scott personally as a result of their activities in that organization.

But his friend's appeal did not move Scott. He told Lighthall that he could conceive of no valid reason for maintaining the hereditary council: "It is, I think, entirely in the interests of reasonable administration that the present situation should be perpetuated."[82] The poetic imagination had been dulled by the exigencies of administrative convenience.

Bureaucratic stonewalling could not, however, quell the Indian agitation. Trouble next appeared in the person of John Robert Ockleshaw-Johnson, an English lawyer who claimed to have known Deskeheh during the chief's European soujourn. The Englishman turned up at the Six Nations' reserve on 10 February 1928 and was shown around by a reluctant Col. Morgan. Morgan suspected that his uninvited guest was either employed by the Mohawk Workers or by some "crank society," and he described him to Scott as "shifty, uncomfortable and antagonistic." When Ockleshaw-Johnson returned some months later "preaching the usual stuff," Morgan urged that he be deported. Scott, who tended to be cooler in the face of adversity, felt it would be best to ignore the Englishman.[83]

Unfortunately for "the interests of reasonable administration," this proved impossible. On 1 July 1928 the *Detroit Free Press* carried a full-page story headlined "Ontario Indians Assert Six Nations Independence." The story referred to a declaration of independence that had been adopted by the hereditary chiefs on 19 June. It had been signed by Chauncey Garlow, speaker of the Grand Council of the Six Nations. Ockleshaw-Johnson was described as "Minister of Justice and Intelligence." The declaration, which borrowed much of the rhetoric of its American counterpart of 1776, renounced allegiance to Canada and to the British Crown.[84]

This development, though not taken very seriously, attracted considerable international press coverage which reflected poorly on Canada's image. And this was probably the effect for which its perpetrators had hoped. The Montreal-based *Family Herald and Weekly Star*, for instance, while dismissing the declaration as "a bit of mid-summer madness," suggested that it was symptomatic of something more serious. Evidently all was not well in the country's Indian administration:

> During the past few years an uneasy feeling has been growing among close observers, that the Indian Department at Ottawa has not been as successful in conciliating, and in its general dealing with the Indians as was formerly the case.
>
> It was not, for instance, the wisest thing in the world to allow the impression to get abroad among the wards of our nation, that their Great Father was no longer the King-Emperor, but a departmental Jack-in-office at Ottawa.
>
> Appeals to the Crown were by skillful jockeying sidetracked, so that powerful chiefs whose predecessors had been privileged to stand and plead before kings, found themselves compelled to wait, hat in hand, upon the leisurely convenience of bumptious officials, who displayed far less zeal for Indian rights, than for their own convenience, and the political interests of their party.[85]

This revealing statement encapsulated in a few brief sentences the frustrating experiences that Indian spokesmen had been encountering in dealing with Scott and his associates.

Publicly, Scott dismissed the entire business as "a piece of folly" and informed the press that his department would pay no attention to the "ridiculous" declaration of independence.[86] Privately, however, he realized that some countermeasures would have to be taken. On 5 July he was informed by Morgan that Ockleshaw-Johnson had appeared once more on the reserve to stir up trouble.

This was the signal Scott had been waiting for. He immediately wrote to Col. A.W. Duffus, assistant commissioner of the RCMP, describing the English lawyer as a "mischief maker" likely to incite the Indians against the government. He requested an investigation to determine the possibility of criminal prosecution. At the same time, he inquired of W.J. Egan, deputy minister of immigration and colonization, to see if there were grounds for having his adversary deported.[87]

Scott's requests were acceded to. The police investigation, which was carried out by Inspector C.D. La Nauze, proved barren. La Nauze discovered that Ockleshaw-Johnson had not left himself open to prosecution under the Criminal Code. Nor did it seem that Section 141 of the Indian Act would be applicable since he had not openly solicited money from Indians.

The investigation by the Immigration Department was more promising. It discovered that the Englishman had entered the country illegally and could therefore be arrested and deported. A warrant was issued, but Ockleshaw-Johnson's whereabouts were unknown. He was spotted briefly on the reserve on 19 July by Cpl. E.S. Covell, an RCMP officer stationed at Ohsweken, but he managed to elude his pursuers. By the end of the month, the fugitive was still at large, and the police believed that he had avoided arrest by slipping south of the border.[88]

As it turned out, Ockleshaw-Johnson was well versed in the art of evading the law. The RCMP had called on the British police in their investigations and discovered that they were dealing with a man of dubious reputation. Ockleshaw-Johnson had been born in England in 1871 and had been trained as a lawyer. Following accusations of fraud and blackmail, he had frequently changed address. As a result of these activities and certain outstanding debts, he had been suspended by the British Law Society and was likely to be struck permanently from the rolls. The police report passed on to Scott concluded with the following warning: "this man is an unscrupulous individual whose one object is getting money and his association with any movement is purely for monetary gain."[89] This notion was soon to dawn upon the hapless Mohawk Workers.

The RCMP detachment at Ohsweken was proving indispensible in monitoring the latest round of agitation on the reserve. Aware of the presence of this Trojan horse in their midst, the Mohawk Workers attempted to avoid surveillance by conducting their meetings in private houses. Unknown to them, however, this tactic was undermined because the police had engaged one of the Indians as an informer. This individual, referred to obliquely in police reports as a "special agent," apprised his employers of the all deliberations, and Scott was subsequently informed of what had transpired by the RCMP.

It was through this network of subterfuge that Scott first learned of the Mohawk Workers' disenchantment with Ockleshaw-Johnson. Dissention appeared at their meeting on 5 August 1928. The Englishman had evidently asked for $500 to take the Six Nations' case either to London or to the League of Nations.

He had been given $200 before his hasty departure for the United States some weeks before, and the balance was to be forwarded as soon as the Workers were informed of his whereabouts. The $300 had been raised in the interim, but there had been no word from Ockleshaw-Johnson. Some of the Workers began to wonder if they had been duped. If good lawyers were rich, they reasoned, why was this man in constant need of more money? They decided to take no further action until they heard from him.[90]

By October, Chauncey Garlow had received two letters from Ockleshaw-Johnson proposing meetings with him south of the border. This was insufficient to allay the mounting scepticism. Nonetheless, Jacob Lewis was sent to meet the lawyer in Rochester in January of the following year, which paved the way for another round of agitation abroad. In May 1929 the police reported that Lewis and Ockleshaw-Johnson had left for Geneva and that $1,300 had been raised to finance the venture.[91]

Scott informed O.D. Skelton of this development and a warning was sent to W.A. Riddell.[92] In July Riddell reported that Lewis and Ockleshaw-Johnson had approached the League Secretariate with a view to reopening the Six Nations' case but to no avail. He felt that they might linger in Geneva until the September Assembly and attempt to embarrass the government. Lewis appeared reasonable and eager for a settlement while the Englishman seemed only intent on causing trouble.[93]

To counteract these activities Scott suggested to Col. Morgan that the elective council should pass a resolution condemning the agitation and proclaiming its loyalty to the government. A meeting for this purpose was called on 6 August, and Morgan noted later that he had to use some persuasion to get the council to co-operate. The script of the resolution was obviously supplied by Ottawa, and it praised the government's lavish spending on education and medical services on the reserve.[94] A copy was sent to the Canadian delegation at Geneva to aid in discrediting the agitators.

These measures proved to be unnecessary. While the elected council was proclaiming, albeit reluctantly, its role as a subservient vassal of Indian Affairs, Lewis dispensed with the services of Ockleshaw-Johnson on account of his drunkenness. And when his overtures regarding the possibility of a royal commission were rejected by Ottawa, Lewis decided to return to Canada.[95]

It would be reasonable to assume that at this stage the futility of international appeals should have been evident to all. Yet this was not the case. The supporters of the hereditary council were determined to try once more, and in the spring of 1930, funds were raised for a final sortie onto the international stage.

Towards the end of May, Morgan informed Scott that a delegation of seven men and two women led by Chauncey Garlow had left for London.[96] The Indians remained in the British capital during June and July and received a sympathetic hearing from the press and from M.P.s of all major parties. And

Ockleshaw-Johnson appeared once more, writing letters on behalf of the deputation.

But as time passed, the hopelessness of their cause began to dawn upon the Indians. By August they had failed to breach the intransigence of the government. To compound matters funds had been so depleted that they were unable to pay their return fares. An appeal to Ottawa for financial assistance was rejected at Scott's instigation.[97] The stranded delegates were obliged to borrow money from the Salvation Army to extricate themselves the humiliating anticlimax.

As for Ockleshaw-Johnson, he continued to write letters to the British prime minister concerning the grievances of the Six Nations. In April 1933 a London Metropolitan Police Report noted that he was resident in the Isle of Wight and writing a book on the Iroquois case for eventual submission to the League of Nations. Some months later, he was reported to be attempting to form a holding company based in France with the object of acquiring rights to the property of the Six Nations, including the $600,000 held in trust by the Canadian government. Whether anything came of these schemes is beyond speculation. The enigmatic Englishman had by then ceased to be a factor in Canadian Indian politics.

The European ventures of Jacob Lewis and Chauncey Garlow failed to capture the public imagination to the same extent as those of Deskeheh had some years earlier. But they did make some impact and Scott was forced once more into the role of apologist for Canada's Indian policy.

When Lewis was in Geneva in the summer of 1929, he had made much of Indian Affairs' highhandedness in deposing the hereditary council. This argument had won the sympathetic ear of Henri A. Junod, president of le Bureau International pour la Defense des Indigenes (Races de Couleur), a League of Nations body. Junod was particularly interested in Lewis's assertion that only about 5 per cent of the reserve inhabitants supported the elective system and that most of those were Delawares and not even members of the Six Nations proper.

The misgivings of the president of le Bureau International were transmitted to the Canadian delegation at the League. Walter Riddell wrote to Ottawa on 29 August 1929 warning that problems could arise unless evidence was produced showing that a majority supported the elective council.[98] When O.D. Skelton communicated this request to Indian Affairs, Scott informed him bluntly that the information would not be made available. Of course, the deputy superintendent was only too aware that such evidence did not exist, and he defended his recalcitrance with characteristic bureaucratic bluster—"any interference or meddling with our internal administrative problems on the part of anyone should not be tolerated."[99]

Skelton understandably felt that this was a little abrupt and suggested to Scott that if the information were supplied and a strong case made, it would prevent "any recurrence of this annoyance."[100] Scott remained adamant, and instead of the evidence he had requested, Riddell was supplied with a bland statement to the effect that the Six Nations' council had been elected on 22 October 1928 and that all male Indians twenty-one years and over had been eligible to vote. Riddell later reported to Skelton that le Bureau International had not seemed completely satisfied with this explanation.[101]

Junod then took up the question with Senator Raoul Dandurand, a man he knew and respected. Dandurand was a minister without portfolio and Leader of the Senate in the Mackenzie King administration, and he had acquired special expertise in the affairs of the League of Nations. For much of the 1920s, he had been a member of the Canadian delegation to the League Assembly and had served as president of that body in 1925.[102] Dandurand was receptive to Junod's contention that the imposed change in their system of government violated the guarantees made to the Six Nations in the Haldimand Grant and the Simcoe Deed. And Junod wondered why a plebiscite had never been held at Grand River to determine the extent of support for the hereditary council.[103]

As a result Junod's representation, Dandurand wrote to Scott in June 1930 demanding a full explanation.[104] The deputy superintendent's reply dealt in detail with the two concerns raised by Junod. He pointed out that the Haldimand document simply granted the Grand River lands to the Indians "to enjoy forever." The Simcoe Deed, however, was somewhat more complex. It granted

> the full and entire possession, use, benefit and advantage of the said district or territory to be held and enjoyed by them in the most free and ample manner, and according to the several customs and usages of them the said chiefs, warriors, women, and people of the said Six Nations.

According to Scott's interpretation, this passage referred to aboriginal customs of land tenure and transfer of property only. He claimed that under the Indian Act these were allowed, but they could not be viewed as a carte blanche for the perpetuation of native customs in any form. In fact, he defended cultural changes imposed on the Six Nations on the grounds that the Indians were, after all, British subjects and needed to be brought "under the influence of laws which have been found civilizing and protective under all circumstances." On the question of a plebiscite, Scott's response displayed the same compelling logic. He explained that

> under the provisions of the Indian Act whenever the Governor-in-Council deems it advisable for the good government of a band to introduce the elective system of chiefs and councillors or headmen, he may provide for such election. There is no provision of the Act requiring a vote of the majority of the band for the change to the elective system.[105]

What he failed to point out was that a plebiscite was not expressly forbidden either and had, in fact, been employed in the past. It is doubtful if Henri Junod was entirely satisfied with these responses, but it was the end of the matter as far as Scott was concerned. No further explanation was necessary; nor would it be forthcoming.

The Six Nations' status case was one of the most intractable difficulties which plagued Indian administration during the 1920s. Its underlying assumptions posed a direct challenge to the very foundations of federal policy. The Department of Indian Affairs operated on the premise that it knew what was best for the native population. Its policies were therefore formulated and implemented without real consultation with its charges. The Six Nations Indians not only opposed specific federal regulations, but actually rejected the authority of the department and of the act it administered.

Of course, Scott and other government officials viewed such claims as akin to rebellion and dismissed the historical basis on which they were made as absurd. The deputy superintendent was unwilling to differentiate between the Six Nations and any other group of Indians. While he was prepared to admit that they were more "civilized" or "advanced" than their western and northern brethren, he was not prepared to concede that their ultimate destiny—assimilation— would be in any way different.

What was particularly irritating about this case was the aggressive and persistent manner in which the Six Nations' hereditary chiefs advanced their claims to special status. Scott's initial complacency regarding the agitation was transformed into a ruthless determination to crush it when the chiefs took the question to London and Geneva. The adverse publicity resulting from these international ventures reflected poorly on the department and its policies and threatened to undermine efficiency of administration. Draconian measures were therefore called for. A permanent police presence at Grand River, the replacement of the hereditary council by a compliant elective one, and the use of informers all ensured a degree of official control at the reserve level. On the international front, the services of the British diplomatic corps were effectively employed to intimidate governments sympathetic to the Indians.

In this complex network of intrigue Scott's role was pivotal. Since he was the chief apologist for Canada's Indian policy, few decisions were made without his approval. When criticism of that policy made its appearance, he penned the response. On such occasions his initial impulse was to reject criticism as unwarranted "meddling." If this proved insufficient, he was generally willing to prepare more comprehensive defences. But even in these instances, his arguments relied on one assumption: the ultimate wisdom of government policy and of the men who formulated it.

8

Land Claims in British Columbia

The refusal of the government of British Columbia to recognize aboriginal title to the lands of that province, both in the colonial and post-Confederation eras, was the source of considerable discontent among the native population. And the discontent was further aggravated by Victoria's parsimonious approach to making crown lands available for reserves. In spite of almost constant agitation by Indian leaders over the years, these related grievances remained unresolved. The agitation became particularly persistent between 1910 and 1927 and provided D.C. Scott with a major impediment to efficient administration. This controversy has already been discussed by a number of writers,[1] but Scott's central role in attempting to resolve the dispute, and especially his negotiations with the provincial government, have been largely ignored.

British Columbia was the only western province to enter Confederation with control of its crown lands. Under the Terms of Union, therefore, it became necessary to make special arrangements whereby certain lands would be placed under federal control for Indian reserve purposes. Clause 13 specified these arrangements:

> The charge of the Indians, and the trusteeship and management of the lands reserved for their use and benefit, shall be assumed by the Dominion Government, and a policy as liberal as that hitherto pursued by the British Columbia Government shall be continued by the Dominion Government after the union.

The clause also required the province to convey to the Dominion "tracts of land of such an extent as it has hitherto been the practice of the British Columbia Government to appropriate for that purpose" for the use of the Indians. In the event of disagreement between the two governments, the secretary of state for the colonies would act as arbitrator.[2]

This phraseology was curious, to say the least. Considering the activities of Joseph Trutch in "adjusting" reserves during the 1860s, the British Columbia policy could hardly be termed "liberal" in any meaningful sense. And it seems that Trutch himself had been responsible for the wording of Clause 13. In accepting these terms, federal officials were likely ignorant of the paltry reserve allotments that had been made in the Pacific colony. As Indian unrest grew in the 1870s, they became aware that they had unwittingly acquiesced in a grave injustice.

The Indians themselves were excluded from the deliberations surrounding the union. And they were denied the provincial franchise, making it impossible for them to exert political pressure on Victoria. They hoped for better treatment as wards of the federal government, and all the more so as they learned of the numbered treaties and their comparatively generous land allotments.

In the years immediately following Confederation, Indian complaints to federal and provincial officials about the inadequacy of their reserves and about the encroachment of whites on their traditional domains became more frequent. Upon investigation, Indian Superintendent I.W. Powell came to believe that many of the complaints were justified. But the provincial government remained unmoved and refused to deviate from the policies that had been in effect prior to the union. Many reserves were still to be laid out, and the acreage per family soon became a question of dispute between the two governments.

In 1873 Ottawa suggested an allocation of eighty acres per family. Victoria was only prepared to grant ten. A compromise was arrived at in 1875. The disputants agreed to establish a joint commission empowered to allot and survey reserves. It was to examine individual cases without determining a fixed acreage beforehand. And it was agreed that any lands alienated from a reserve for whatever reason would revert to the province. Thus began the contentious "reversionary interest," which was to cause major difficulties in Indian land administration in subsequent years.

The three-man commission commenced its work in 1876, but it was hampered from the outset by the unco-operative attitude of the provincial government. Pressure from Victoria resulted in its dissolution after two years. One of its members, Gilbert M. Sproat, was allowed to continue with the work until 1880, when he resigned in frustration. Sproat was generally sympathetic to the Indians, and he believed that they ought to have sufficient land for their needs—an idea that found little acceptance in Victoria.[3]

Peter O'Reilly, Sproat's successor, had been involved in reserve allocation under Trutch in colonial days and shared his former superior's prejudices. In addition to laying out new reserves, he reduced some of those granted by Sproat. In the process, the Indians were barely consulted, if at all. They remained dissatisfied, but the danger of an uprising, so real in the 1870s, began to fade as the province filled with settlers. Sometime during the 1880s, the rapidly expanding white population surpassed the declining native one, and the imbalance between the two continued to grow at an accelerating pace, especially after the completion of the Canadian Pacific Railway in 1885.[4]

By 1897 the majority of the reserves in the province had been granted. In that year total reserve area amounted to 718,568 acres, a substantial increase from the 28,437 acres that had been allocated by 1871. With an Indian population of 23,620, the acreage per capita amounted to 30.42.[5] But not all of this land was suitable for agriculture or grazing, and its distribution among the Indians was extremely uneven. It is also worth observing that the native population had declined to about half of what it had been estimated at in 1871.

O'Reilly retired in 1898, and the task of continuing with reserve allocation fell to A.W. Vowell, who had been appointed superintendent of Indian affairs for the province upon Powell's resignation in 1890. Vowell carried on in this thankless role until 1908 when the government of Richard McBride refused all further co-operation.

Throughout this period federal officials had been eager that the Indians be granted adequate reserves as an essential prerequisite to economic self-sufficiency. But Ottawa also believed that if the Indians were satisfied with their lands and with the services provided them, they would be less likely to raise the problematic issue of aboriginal title, which, after all, had never been extinguished. In this expectation they were frustrated by the obstructionist tactics of successive British Columbia governments, whose concern for Indian needs, if it existed at all, was negligible at best.

Before examining the course of events in the twentieth century, when the cry for aboriginal rights forced itself on public attention, it is necessary to consider one development that continued to complicate relations between the two levels of government during these years: the creation of the Railway Belt. British Columbia was in some ways a reluctant bride for the Dominion. In fact, there had been substantial sentiment in the colony against Confederation prior to 1871. Perhaps the deciding factor which tilted the balance in favour of union was Ottawa's offer to build a railway to the coast within ten years. To assist with this project, British Columbia was asked to grant to the Dominion a twenty mile wide belt of land along the route of the proposed line. The costs of construction were to be defrayed, at least in part, by disposing of the lands in this belt. And Ottawa agreed to pay the province $100,000 per annum while it controlled those lands.[6]

After some initial complications caused by changing the Canadian Pacific route from the Yellowhead to the Kicking Horse Pass, the lands of the Railway Belt (10,976,000 acres) were conveyed to the Dominion by the Settlement Act of 1884. But 900,000 acres of the belt had already been alienated by the province, and it was necessary to find compensatory lands for the Dominion elsewhere. It was therefore granted 3,500,000 additional acres in the Peace River area creating what became known as the Peace River Block.[7] Soon enough the status of Indian reserves in the Railway Belt became a matter of dispute.

With the Settlement Act, Ottawa became the owner of some of the choicest lands in British Columbia, and Victoria grew increasingly impatient with the arrangement. Provincial politicians accused the the federal government of dragging its feet on the disposal of the lands and thereby retarding settlement, as one of a large catalogue of complaints they habitually made to Ottawa. British Columbians realized that their province was in a strategic location and that they could demand improvements to the conditions of union from a position of strength. The constant appeals for "better terms" led to the observation that British Columbia was "the spoilt child of confederation."[8] Ottawa's cautious approach on the Indian question must be seen in this light.

The constant bickering between Ottawa and Victoria over the allocation of reserve lands intensified during the premiership of Richard McBride (1903-15). A striking figure with a penchant for grandiose schemes, McBride presided over an era of unprecedented prosperity and economic expansion. He was an enthusiastic supporter of railway construction, which he saw as the key to the development of the north. European and American investors shared his confidence, and foreign capital poured into the province. As the railways expanded, so too did the lumber, fish canning, mining, and fruit-growing industries. Land values soared in places, and there was much speculation and shady real estate deals, sometimes with the approval or involvement of government members.[9]

In this heady atmosphere of growth, Indian reserves were perceived as a nuisance—a hindrance to development. They were too large for their owners, occupied some of the best agricultural land, and were rarely utilized to advantage. This attitude was shared almost universally by politicians and government officials in Victoria, and it was not unknown in Ottawa. Superintendent General Frank Oliver told the House of Commons in 1907 that the Indians had "taken their pick" of the limited agricultural land available in British Columbia. As a result, the development of the province had been "undoubtedly very seriously retarded."[10]

If there was some agreement on general principles between the two levels of government on the Indian land question, there were still areas of contention. Perhaps the greatest difficulty was that surrounding the reversionary claim of the province to reserve lands. As a result of a clause in the agreement of 1875, Victoria automatically claimed title to any lands that ceased to be part of a reserve. Consequently, if a band surrendered part of its property, it would receive no benefit; the land could not be sold at public auction in the usual manner. Indian Affairs was therefore finding it impossible to secure surrenders or to dispose of "surplus" reserve lands. And the difficulty was underlined in

1905-06 when the Grand Trunk Pacific Railway sought to purchase part of the Tsimshian reserve near Prince Rupert for its western terminus. When British Columbia refused to abandon or sell its reversionary interest, Ottawa proceeded unilaterally with the surrender and sale. The federal government's interpretation of the reversionary clause was that it only applied in cases in which the band became extinct. Both Ottawa and Victoria contemplated resorting to the courts for a judgment on the question, and the dispute between the two governments raged until after the federal election of 1911.[11] In the meantime, the McBride administration refused to co-operate in laying out new reserves.

The Indian discontent that had manifested itself in the 1870s was not allayed by the work of the various reserve commissioners over the years. During the 1880s, for instance, the Nishga of the Nass valley and the Coast Tsimshian protested the invasion of their lands by settlers and land speculation companies and the parsimonious reserve allocations of O'Reilly.[12] As federal Indian administration established itself throughout the province, its restrictive features became a further source of irritation and protest. Increasingly, however, the principal focus of disenchantment became the refusal of Victoria and Ottawa (in particular the former) to acknowledge aboriginal title in the province and to provide adequate compensation for its extinguishment. This issue ultimately prompted the creation of native organizations which believed that united action was essential for the effective advancement of the claim. During the new century Indian political action would prove a constant thorn in the side of the federal and provincial governments as they struggled to resolve their differences on the reserve question.

The Nishga Indians, who had long been active in attempting to prevent the encroachment of settlers on their traditional domains in the Nass Valley, had by 1909 created a land committee consisting of sixteen chiefs. In order to protect their interests more effectively, the committee met with coastal groups who shared similar concerns and formed an organization known as the Indian Tribes of British Columbia.[13] They soon received active support from a group of white sympathizers—the Friends of the Indians. The most prominent of these individuals was Arthur E. O'Meara. A native of Ontario and a graduate of the University of Toronto, O'Meara had practised law for twenty years before entering the Anglican ministry in 1906. After working at his new profession in the Yukon for a few years, he became involved in the native land claims agitation in British Columbia.[14] He was to play a major, and controversial, role in that campaign for almost two decades.

The struggle for the recognition of aboriginal rights quickly took the form of petitions and protests to the two governments. Victoria proved particularly intransigent in its response to these overtures. For instance, in March 1911 a delegation of ninety-six Indians presented a petition to the British Columbia government in which they complained of the inadequacy of their reserves and of the non-recognition of their aboriginal title. Premier McBride rejected the very idea of aboriginal claim and dismissed the entire affair as a nuisance which would never have arisen had it not been for "the pernicious advice of some unscrupulous whites."[15] This was a barely disguised reference to O'Meara and his associates, who were to receive much of the blame for the agitation over the years.

The Indians and their supporters soon realized they could make no progress in dealing with the provincial government. Instead they began to look to Ottawa, and even to the imperial government in London, for redress. In fact, an Indian petition to the federal government in 1909 had resulted in some promising developments. Partly in response to this petition and partly to break the impasse over reserve allocation, the dominion authorities introduced Section 37A to the Indian Act in 1910 authorizing Ottawa to initiate proceedings in the Exchequer Court of Canada in cases in which "the possession of any lands reserved or claimed to be reserved for the Indians [was] withheld".[16] And when a deputation of Indians met with Sir Wilfrid Laurier in Ottawa in 26 April 1911, the prime minister acknowledged the seriousness of their grievances and said it was the government's duty to inquire into the case.[17] Consequently, an order-in-council was adopted on 17 May indicating the government's intention of obtaining a decision in the Exchequer Court as soon as an appropriate test case arose. But it never transpired. Laurier's government fell in the autumn of 1911, and the contemplated court action was abandoned by its Conservative successor.[18]

Correspondence between McBride and the new prime minister, Robert Borden, led to arrangements for a negotiated settlement. In May 1912 J.A.J. McKenna was appointed by the federal government as a special commissioner to enter into discussions with Victoria.[19] His mandate extended to all aspects of the Indian question, including aboriginal title. But he discovered that McBride obstinately refused to consider this issue, maintaining that it would cast doubt on all land titles in the province. Nonetheless, by September the premier and the special commissioner had arrived at an understanding which became known as the McKenna-McBride Agreement.

According to its terms, a royal commission with representation from both governments was to be established with power to adjust the acreage of reserves in British Columbia. A reserve found to be inadequate in size could be extended with additions from available crown lands. And reserves that contained more land than was required by their occupants could be reduced. In the latter instance, "cut-offs" were to be sold at public auction and the proceeds divided between Ottawa (for the benefit of the Indians) and Victoria. But no cut-offs were to be made without "the consent of the Indians." In return for these adjustments, the British Columbia government agreed to abandon its reversionary interest in reserve lands, except in cases in which bands became extinct.[20]

In reporting on his mission to Superintendent General R. Rogers in October,

McKenna observed that he had concentrated his efforts on finding a formula for the elimination of the province's reversionary interest. It had long proven a major obstacle to the administration of reserve lands. And the Indian's interests would also be protected by the terms of the agreement. The gross inequalities in reserve acreages would likely be rectified by the commissioners, and there would be "no diminishment of existing reserves" without the Indians' consent.[21]

The Royal Commission on Indian Affairs for the Province of British Columbia was appointed on 31 March 1913. Nathaniel W. White and J.A.J. McKenna were the Dominion's representatives. British Columbia was represented by J.P. Shaw and D.H. MacDowell. E.L. Wetmore, former chief justice of Saskatchewan, was selected as the chairman, but he had to resign the following year for health reasons. S. Carmichael then joined the commission, and White took on the responsibilities of chairman.

The commissioners travelled throughout the province for three years, visiting most reserves and hearing the evidence of hundreds of Indians. They also found time to listen to white farmers, municipal governments, railway companies, and other organizations that coveted Indian land. In several cases, Indians refused to appear before the commission unless it dealt with the question of aboriginal rights. But doing so was outside of the narrow scope of its mandate. Nor would it consider other matters of concern to the Indians, such as fishing, hunting, and water and foreshore rights. The commission's very *raison d'etre* remained suspect in the minds of many Indians throughout. And the frequent assurances that no cut-offs would be made without band consent did little to dispel their suspicions. The commissioners completed their work on 30 June 1916.

The report of the royal commission can be summarized in the following terms:[22]

		approximate value
acreages confirmed	666,640.25	$19,890,000
acreages cut off	47,058.49	$ 1,522,704
additions	87,291.17	$ 444,838

Thus while reserve lands actually increased, the value of the lands cut off exceeded that of the additions by more than three times. These were, of course, only recommendations. Both governments would have to endorse the report before action could be taken on its proposals, and, presumably, the Indians would have to give their consent to the cut-offs.

According to the McKenna-McBride Agreement, the work of the royal commission was to bring about "a final adjustment of all matters relating to Indian Affairs in the Province of British Columbia." This finality was unacceptable to Indian leaders because the commission did not deal with questions of aboriginal title and other issues which they considered important. In fact, during the time that the commissioners were conducting their hearings, Indian agitation took on a new militancy.

Meeting at Kincolith on 22 January 1913, the Nishga chiefs adopted a petition for submission to the Judicial Committee of the Privy Council in London. The petition outlined the territory laid claim to by the Nishgas on the basis of having occupied it from "time immemorial." It acknowledged British sovereignty but argued that by virtue of the Royal Proclamation of 1763, the Indians' title had been recognized by the Crown. In spite of the fact that no surrenders had ever been agreed to, the British Columbia government had expropriated and sold some of the Nishga lands—an action that was explicitly condemned. The petitioners urged the Judicial Committee to "adjudge and determine" their rights to their lands and to assess the constitutionality of the British Columbia Land Act under the authority of which the much criticized sales had taken place.[23]

Arthur E. O'Meara likely played a key role in drawing up the petition. He had evidently come to the conclusion that only a direct appeal to the Judicial Committee of the Privy Council, the highest judicial authority in the empire, would bring redress. Employing the services of a London law firm, Messrs. Fox and Preece, the petition was lodged with the Privy Council in May 1913. Its fate was predictable. On 19 June, it was referred back to the Canadian government.

When D.C. Scott became deputy superintendent general of Indian affairs some months later, the Nishga petition was among the many problems requiring his attention. A few interviews with the Indians' advisers suggested to him that their claims were unwarranted and exaggerated. As he observed upon reflecting on the situation during the following decade:

> I became convinced that the expectation of receiving compensation of a very large value either in money or privileges was influencing to a great extent the strength of the pressure being brought to bear on the government.[24]

Scott gave the matter further consideration, and in a memorandum to the superintendent general dated 11 March 1914 he made a number of observations and recommendations. He pointed out that the Indians held erroneous views regarding the nature of the aboriginal title. For instance, they claimed to retain "such portions of our territory as are required for the future well-being of our people" and proposed that they be compensated for lands already alienated. These were unacceptable demands as far as the deputy superintendent was concerned, and he noted sarcastically, "From these words it will become apparent what fancies occupy the minds of the Indians when they think of the aboriginal title and its purchase." He suggested that the Indian title was merely a "usufructuary right dependent on the good will of the sovereign." Native people were only entitled to what the Crown elected to grant.[25]

Scott, however, was prepared to submit the question to the Exchequer Court of Canada, with right of appeal to the Privy Council, under certain conditions:

1. That the Indians accept beforehand "in a binding way" that in the event that the Exchequer Court or Privy Council agreed that they had a legitimate claim to the lands, that they would surrender them "receiving from the Dominion benefits to be granted for extinguishment of title in accordance with past usage of the Crown." They were also to agree to accept the findings of the royal commission as the full allotment of reserve lands.
2. That by granting reserves the British Columbia government would be deemed to have satisfied all claims against it.
3. That the British Columbia government be represented by counsel and that the Indians be represented by counsel, in the latter case "nominated and paid for by the Dominion."

In establishing these prior conditions, Scott was attempting to overcome the anticipated objections of Victoria and to mitigate the demands that might be made on the public coffers in the event of a favourable judgment. He observed in his memorandum that "it would be a serious matter if the Dominion were to assume the undetermined liability which might arise if the Indians' claim were upheld by the courts."[26]

The memorandum was endorsed by the cabinet, and on 20 June 1914 an order-in-council (P.C. 751) was handed down recommending that the Nishga claim be referred to the Exchequer Court of Canada, with right of appeal to the Privy Council, under the conditions outlined by Scott.

The Nishga chiefs gathered again at Kincolith on 4 December to consider the latest government gambit. At the conclusion of their deliberations, they issued a statement rejecting the conditions set forth. The royal commission was unacceptable because the terms of the McKenna-McBride Agreement made it clear that additional reserve lands could only be allocated from unoccupied crown lands. This meant that the Nishga claims in the Nass Valley could not be upheld. The chiefs demanded a real voice in deciding what lands could be retained for their own use.[27]

During March and April 1915, a delegation consisting of Nishga chief W.J. Lincoln, A.E. O'Meara, and interpreter R.S. Woods spent six weeks in Ottawa occasionally meeting with Scott and Superintendent General William Roche in an effort to resolve their differences. On one of these occasions, in Scott's office on 6 April, O'Meara pointed out that one of the principal difficulties lay in the fact that the provincial government had already sold some of the Nishga lands. The natives were willing to let the colonial secretary adjudicate the issue and in the event that he found in favour of the Indians, the purchasers of the land ought to be compensated by Ottawa. This was unacceptable to the deputy superintendent. The Indians then produced maps on which the lands they claimed were marked. Scott suggested that they take their case to the royal commission, which might give them what they wanted. It was their "only hope." He said that his department would even be willing to give the commissioners "special directions with reference to their report on the Nishgas." And he reiterated the superintendent general's assurance (given at an earlier meeting) that going before the commission would not prejudice their larger claim to aboriginal title.[28]

This was not sufficient to assuage the Indians completely; nevertheless, they appeared before the commission in October only to be told that it had no power to deal with the way in which their lands had been disposed of.[29] In the meantime, however, there was some encouraging news. The work of the royal commission had won little support among the native peoples of the province in general. In fact, it had served only to alienate them further from both levels of government. And it was pointing the way to the necessity of greater co-operation among the native groups if they were to defend their rights. Consequently, at a meeting at Spence's Bridge, 27 February 1915, the chiefs representing the Chilcotin, Kootenay, Lillooet, Okanagan, Shuswap, and Thompson Indians demanded recognition of their rights to their ancestral lands and endorsed the Nishga petition of 1913 as a test case which would establish those rights.[30]

That meeting led to the formation in the following year of the Allied Tribes of British Columbia—an organization of coastal and interior Indians whose primary purpose was the advancement of the land claim.[31] The new organization was led by Andrew Paull and Peter Kelly, two of the most effective native spokesmen of the day.[32] At one of its first meetings in June 1916, the Allied Tribes denounced the work of the royal commission, demanded reserves of 160 acres per capita, recognition of aboriginal title, and compensation for lands already alienated.[33]

A.E. O'Meara also came to play a leading role in the Allied Tribes, acting as its legal counsel. He succeeded in convincing Paull and Kelly that his favourite notion, a direct appeal to the imperial Privy Council, was the tactic most likely to bring results. He continued to insist that the Nishga petition of 1913 still lay with the Privy Council and that it would ultimately be referred to the Judicial Committee. It was simply a matter of persuading the federal government to support this course of action or, at least, to withdraw its opposition. To what extent O'Meara was being honest with his clients in giving this advice is not clear. The minister of justice, C.M. Doherty, had told him in November 1914 that a direct appeal to the Privy Council was unconstitutional. Such matters had first to be adjudicated by Canadian courts.[34]

Scott hoped to blunt the impact of the rising agitation by securing agreement to the report of the royal commission by both governments prior to its release to the public. That would settle the reserve question. The thornier issue of aboriginal title might then proceed to the courts under the conditions he had specified in 1914.[35]

But political developments in British Columbia frustrated his plans. Richard McBride had retired unexpectedly in December 1915, and one of his ministers, W.J. Bowser, had replaced him. The new premier was unable to revive the sagging fortunes of the Conservative Party, and in the election of September 1916, he was swept from power by the Liberals under H.C. Brewster. There had been no opportunity during that fateful summer to consider the recommendations of the royal commission.

Scott continued to seek a secret accord. He urged the Brewster government to consider the commission's report favourably and to maintain confidentiality while doing so. In these negotiations, he came to rely heavily on the services of W.E. Ditchburn, chief inspector of Indian agencies in the province, whose office was conveniently located in Victoria.[36] Both federal officials quickly came to realize that Brewster did not share their sense of urgency. On two visits to Ottawa during 1917, the premier met with Scott but remained noncommittal. Subsequent discussions with Ditchburn revealed the cause of Brewster's reticence. Brewster admitted that he had received complaints about some new reserves and additions recommended by the commission, especially that at St. Mary's Flats in the Kootenay Agency.[37] It was obvious that Victoria was not treating the report with the confidentiality that Scott had desired and that additions to reserves posed an obstacle to agreement.

Brewster died in March 1918 and was succeeded by his minister of agriculture and railways, John Oliver. A Delta farmer with little formal education, "Honest John," as the new premier was called, posed as a champion of the common man.[38] On the question of native rights, however, he would prove as intransigent as his predecessors. Oliver's minister of lands throughout his lengthy premiership was T. Duff Pattullo, a former mayor of Prince Rupert who was equally hostile to Indian claims. Throughout the subsequent decade, much of the negotiations between Ottawa and Victoria would take place between Scott and Pattullo.

On 20 March 1918 Scott wrote to Oliver urging immediate action on the report of the royal commission. As a result of this representation, the premier travelled to Ottawa in May and met with Scott and Superintendent General Arthur Meighen. Oliver proved unco-operative, and nothing came of the meeting.[39] The premier was evidently under the impression that the issue was far more complex than Ottawa supposed and that vital provincial rights were at stake. His government would examine the matter carefully and make no hasty decisions.

In the following months T.D. Pattullo gave the report of the royal commission his attention and discovered what appeared to be a further obstacle to settlement. He wrote to Meighen in December asking if it were indeed true that Indian consent was required before cut-offs could be made to reserves as per subsection 2a of section 1 of the McKenna-McBride Agreement. The superintendent general replied in the affirmative, but assured the provincial minister that once the report was accepted, it would be the responsibility of Indian Affairs to secure that consent.[40]

But Victoria remained hesitant. The government had received numerous complaints from residents of the province regarding the retarding effect that Indian reserves were having on settlement and development. A secret agreement with Ottawa to endorse the report of the commission might result in an outcry from constituents and create further difficulties for a regime with enough troubles on its shoulders.[41] During the early months of 1919, Pattullo distributed maps to members of the legislature showing how reserve lands in their constituencies were affected by the report. And on 4 March the provincial government abandoned any further pretence at confidentiality and released the report to the public.[42] Victoria was giving notice that there would be no secret agreement and that certain aspects of the report would be open to re-negotiation.

But by autumn the province was ready to make some concrete proposals. Pattullo arrived in Ottawa on 10 November having arranged beforehand to meet both Meighen and Scott. A brief meeting was arranged between the three men on the 12th, and they agreed that Pattullo would draw up a memorandum embodying his government's position to present the following day.

The memorandum indicated Victoria's willingness to adopt the report of the commission under the following conditions:

1. The federal government should secure the consent of the Indians to cut-offs.
2. The following additions should not be made: Andimal, Decker Lake, Burns Lake, Anaham Lake, Marysville, Creston.
3. If additions are not occupied by the Indians, they should be sold at public auction.
4. Should any reserve to which additions are made not contain the acreage estimated by the Commission, the province would not be obliged to provide extra land; should any such reserve be larger than the estimated acreage, it should be reduced to the estimation.
5. Indians should have the same water rights as non-Indians.[43]

Pattullo presented his proposals to Scott on the 13th, and the deputy superintendent later characterized them to Meighen as "foreign to the spirit of the original agreement." Scott and Meighen were evidently losing their patience with the provincial government at that stage. Pattullo stayed in Ottawa for two weeks hoping to meet with Meighen once more to discuss his proposals. But the superintendent general made sure that he was never available. Scott pretended that he was trying to arrange such a meeting but was somehow unable to do so. Pattullo finally left for home in frustration. In an angry letter to the superintendent general, he withdrew his proposals of 13 November.[44]

Meighen was unimpressed by this outburst of indignation and responded in an equally irate manner. Having recited the history of his government's dealings with Victoria on the land question, emphasizing the latter's penchant for vacillation and procrastination, he observed that he did not understand the need for urgency in meeting with Pattullo or why his time "should be continually occupied in discussions that were manifestly intended to be fruitless." On the question of Pattullo's proposals, he noted: "I may add that the withdrawal of these proposals is not with me a very serious matter, as the position you took certainly was impossible of consideration by this Department." He said that the position of the federal government had always been perfectly clear while that of the provincial government had always been shrouded in mystery. Now that the memorandum was withdrawn, Victoria's position was even more mysterious.[45]

In spite of the sharp tone of these exchanges, both sides were eager for a mutually acceptable settlement. In fact, early in 1919 the British Columbia government had introduced legislation (The Indian Affairs Settlement Act) empowering it "to give effect" to the report of the royal commission and to negotiate with the federal government or with the Indians to settle outstanding differences.[46] In January 1920 Scott informed Meighen that he was preparing similar legislation, which he hoped would lead to renewed negotiations with British Columbia.[47]

The legislation in question became known as the British Columbia Indian Lands Settlement Act and was introduced into Parliament as Bill 13. It enabled the federal government to adopt the recommendations of the royal commission, but its most important provision was as follows:

> For the purpose of adjusting, readjusting or confirming the reductions or cutoffs from reserves in accordance with the recommendations of the Royal Commission, the Governor in Council may order such reductions or cutoffs to be effected without surrenders of the same by the Indians, notwithstanding any provisions of the Indian Act to the contrary.[48]

An essential aspect of the McKenna-McBride Agreement, that no cut-offs would be made without Indian consent, was thereby overturned. And promises to the same effect made to the Indians by members of the royal commission as they travelled throughout the province were reneged upon. The legislation also overruled a long-established feature of the Indian Act—that reserve lands could only be alienated with band consent.

There was much criticism of the bill in the House of Commons in March and

April. Opposition members cited a petition from the Allied Tribes demanding a withdrawal of the measure. But Meighen denied that that organization really represented Indian opinion. He dismissed the protests as the work of O'Meara and insisted that he would not delay the bill because of such "leaders of Indian trouble." When asked if the Indians had in fact been consulted, he admitted that they had not been. Nor could he see that it was even necessary: "I do not think it makes much difference to them."[49]

Scott was equally insensitive to the criticism levelled at Bill 13. He told Meighen that making the cut-offs without Indian consent was acceptable since the Indians did not really need those lands in any case.[50] The bill passed its third reading on 12 April and was assented to 1 July.

In March, while the legislation was being pushed through Parliament, Scott sent a copy to Pattullo, drawing his attention to the provision regarding cut-offs. The provincial minister of lands was evidently pleased with this concession by Ottawa. After all, the cut-offs had been among the issues raised by him in his memorandum of the previous November. He wrote in a conciliatory manner to Meighen in April proposing that one representative of Indian Affairs and another of his Department of Lands review the entire report. He noted that it contained "innumerable errors" and that while the Indians ought to have enough land for their legitimate requirements, there was no point in granting them lands "for their future speculative value" or in such a way as "to retard white settlement." Meighen responded favourably and said he would act on the suggestion as soon as statutory authority was at hand.[51]

Scott took a brief vacation in the Rocky Mountains that August and travelled on to Victoria where he met Pattullo on 15 September. In what appears to have been an amicable encounter, they arranged for the review of the royal commission's report that Pattullo had suggested in April. W.E. Ditchburn for Indian Affairs and Major J.W. Clark for the province were the individuals selected to conduct it.[52] J.A. Teit was also appointed to represent Indian interests, but he died before the review was completed.[53]

From its very inception the Ditchburn-Clark inquiry was plagued by a seemingly intractable difficulty between the two governments: the status of reserves in the Railway Belt. Ottawa contended that when the belt had been conveyed to the Dominion, the province had lost all claim to reserves already granted and to those that might later be granted within its boundaries. In other words, its reversionary interest did not apply. The royal commission, however, had examined such reserves and had recommended cut-offs in a number of instances. Ottawa suggested that this had been done merely for the sake of consistency and that the cut-offs should not be made. Victoria's viewpoint was quite the opposite. It held that when the Railway Belt had been created under the act of 1884, its reversionary interest in reserves already laid out within the boundaries of the belt had not been cancelled. The adjustments to these reserves recommended by the royal commission should therefore proceed.[54]

This issue remained a source of contention as Ditchburn and Clark conducted their inquiry. But Ditchburn stubbornly refused, with Scott's full support, to consider the case of Railway Belt reserves and he blamed Clark for the lack of progress, saying his grudging and parsimonious attitude was the cause of unnecessary delay. As Ditchburn reported to Scott:

> I would have greatly preferred if the Provincial Government had appointed somebody with broader views on Indian matters than Major Clark has. While he is a very decent fellow, still he is inclined to be very cheese-paring where a few acres of land are concerned.[55]

During the inquiry Ditchburn received requests from a number of Indian bands and organizations for additional lands. The Indians of the Nass Agency, for instance, demanded 160 acres per person, which was immediately rejected as "out of all reason." The Allied Tribes submitted a list of lands required by various bands throughout the province. Ditchburn examined this list, eliminating from it those lands already alienated. He felt that certain demands, those for vacant crown land, coastal fishing stations, and land covered by timber licences were reasonable and should be considered. But Clark objected to most of them on the grounds that they contained the potential for water-power development, resource exploitation, or harbours.[56]

The inquiry was completed by 19 March 1923. Ditchburn and Clark had effected a large number of adjustments to reserves as recommended by the royal commission. In the majority of cases, the adjustments took the form of reductions or the elimination of entire reserves.[57] Scott and Ditchburn continued to press for additional grazing lands for the bands in the Kootenay Agency, and some of these appear to have been granted.[58]

Pattullo was somewhat irritated that Ditchburn had refused to deal with reserves in the Railway Belt, but he felt that it was not of sufficient importance to impede settlement.[59] Provincial order-in-council 911, handed down on 26 July 1923, accepted the report of the royal commission as amended by Ditchburn and Clark for British Columbia. Federal approval, delayed by Indian agitation which shall be examined shortly, came a year later. Order-in-council 1265, handed down 19 July 1924, confirmed the report of the royal commission for Ottawa. And it did more. It reaffirmed the federal position on the Railway Belt reserves:

> As the lands in the Railway Belt are under the sole jurisdiction of the Dominion, the Minister recommends that the findings of the Royal Commission with reference to reserves within the Railway Belt be confirmed, but that no reduction or cut-off be made in the areas of the reserves, as recommended by the said Royal Commission.

Scott sent a copy of P.C. 1265 to Pattullo, who immediately objected to the clause cited above. He pointed out that the provincial order-in-council had made no such distinction between reserves and reasserted Victoria's claim to cut-offs recommended in the Railway Belt. He could not accept Ottawa's confirmation of the royal commission report as a result.[60] Nonetheless, there was substantial agreement between the two sides, at least enough to allow the survey of reserves to proceed. But whenever the question of conveying the surveyed reserves from the province to the Dominion arose, the old irritant of the Railway Belt cut-offs would also appear. Before examining further developments in this federal-provincial contest, it is necessary to give some attention to the increasingly effective Indian agitation which accompanied the appearance of the royal commission report and the subsequent deliberations of Ditchburn and Clark.

The Allied Indian Tribes had not stood idly by as the federal and provincial governments deliberated on the question of their lands and rights. They had no reason to trust either side, and the secrecy surrounding the negotiations was a cause of continuing concern. The time-honoured tactic of protest and petition continued to be employed.

In February 1919 the Allied Tribes submitted a statement to the federal government demanding that no order-in-council be passed adopting the report of the royal commission until the larger issue of aboriginal title be adjudicated by the Privy Council in London. It was rumoured at the time that Ottawa planned to settle thousands of returned soldiers on some of the best lands in British Columbia and that reserves might be expropriated for that purpose. The statement objected to any such settlement until native claims were accounted for.[61]

When the report became available to the public, the Allied Tribes had the opportunity to examine it, and in November they presented their views on the matter to the provincial government. The Indians objected to the fact that the lands to be added to reserves were of inferior quality to those designated as cut-offs. And they pointed out that the inequalities between reserve allotments had not been eliminated. They were aware that in the spring of 1916 the Victoria legislature had adopted a measure enabling it to reclaim about two million acres of land from white farmers because of default in payment. Yet none of this had been made available to Indians. But the principal fault of the commission was that it failed to consider the question of aboriginal title—which had never been surrendered.

In addition to these criticisms, the Indians offered a number of proposals as the basis for a just settlement. They suggested that they be granted 160 acres of agricultural land per capita, taking into account such factors as climate and topography. Where this was not possible, adequate alternatives in the form of grazing or timber lands should be provided. Lands already occupied by non-Indians should be compensated for. Fishing, hunting, and water rights, all ignored by the commission, should be fully recognized. In the negotiations which they hoped to enter into on these issues with the two governments, they asked that the secretary of state for the colonies be the final arbitrator.[62]

But neither federal nor provincial officials felt that negotiations with the Indians were necessary or desirable. The protests and petitions received perfunctory bureaucratic acknowledgment and were promptly ignored. By 1922, however, with a new government in Ottawa, it seemed reasonable to assume that some progress might be made. After all, while in opposition Mackenzie King had been highly critical of Bill 13 and had cited one of the Indians' petitions in the Commons debate on the question.

In January 1922 the Allied Tribes expanded into a larger and more representative organization. Kelly and Paull retained their leadership roles, but there was evidently some opposition to O'Meara. He was nevertheless retained as counsel, but with less influence than previously.[63] On 31 May the Indians presented a memorandum to Mackenzie King which argued for real negotiations and the abandonment of a settlement based on agreement between the two governments.[64] Superintendent General Charles Stewart was receptive, and a meeting with the native leaders was arranged for 24 July in British Columbia. At this meeting the Indians gained the impression that Stewart would attempt a new initiative and that Scott's rigid adherence to the order-in-council of 1914 would no longer be sustained.[65] Further meetings were arranged for the following summer.

In July 1923 Scott and Stewart travelled to Vancouver where they met with representatives of the Allied Tribes. Peter Kelly, who was chairman of the executive committee of the native organization, was unable to be present at the initial meeting on the 25th because of illness, and the Indians were consequently hesitant to make any commitments. He was able to attend two days later and served as the principal Indian spokesman. Kelly was highly critical of the royal commission's failure to allocate adequate reserves, and he condemned Bill 13 as "an instrument of oppression and injustice." On the question of aboriginal title, he said that the Allied Tribes still wished to press forward to the Privy Council for a decision, but that they would prefer a negotiated settlement in Canada. Laurier had seemed sympathetic in 1910, but the Conservative regimes in the interim had been intransigent. Now that the Liberals were back in power, he was optimistic of receiving "British justice."

Stewart was willing to acknowledge the Indians' moral claim to the lands they had not ceded, but he felt that their legal claim was another matter. The Terms of Union and the province's attitude complicated matters. He doubted that Victoria could be persuaded to repurchase occupied lands in order to enlarge reserves. He insisted, nevertheless, that the federal government was on the side of the Indians and would back their demands for "a square deal." He asked for specific proposals with which Ottawa could approach the province.

Kelly, who was still not feeling well, was unwilling to be specific at the time.

Stewart had to leave for Ottawa that afternoon and therefore suggested that the Indians meet later with Scott, who was staying on the west coast for another few weeks.[66]

The meetings between Scott, accompanied by Ditchburn, and the executive committee of the Allied Tribes began in Victoria on 7 August and lasted for five days. An atmosphere of mutual suspicion prevailed, and there was much futile debate and the reiteration of irreconcilable positions. Finally, the Indians did spell out the conditions under which they would be prepared to relinquish their aboriginal claims:

> The right to fish without restriction, and possibly the right to sell the fish to anyone. The right to hunt for food without restriction.
> Access to timber for personal use from public lands.
> Reserves on the basis of 160 acres per capita.
> Full control of reserve foreshores to low-water mark.
> Improved systems of medical care and education.
> Reimbursement of about $100,000 which they had already spent over the years in advancing their claims.
> Annuities of $5 per capita retroactive over the previous twenty years. It would work out at a lump sum of $2,474,400.[67]

These conditions were completely unacceptable to Scott and, as it turned out, to his superiors in Ottawa. Yet they were not substantially different from the terms offered under the numbered treaties. Federal officials, nonetheless, were cognizant of the need for a negotiated settlement and were anxious to prevent a test case in the courts or an appeal to the Privy Council. Scott believed that either course of action would be "a matter of grave moment" even though it probably would not succeed.[68] When Kelly, Paull, and another Indian leader, Alex Leonard, visited Ottawa in March 1924, he introduced them to the deputy minister of justice, E.L. Newcombe. Newcombe explained that he doubted the legal validity of their aboriginal land claims and said that in all probability the courts would not uphold them.[69]

The Indians were not easily dissuaded, however. When Mackenzie King visited Prince Rupert in October, he was met by a delegation of the Nishga tribe, accompanied by O'Meara. The Nishga spokesman, Arthur N. Calder, informed the prime minister of their determination to seek redress from the Privy Council. He spoke of Laurier's promise to allow the case to proceed in 1910. He also recalled visiting Ottawa in 1915 as part of a delegation which had been assured by Dr. Roche that co-operation with the royal commission would not prejudice their case with the Privy Council. And he observed that in the House of Commons on 8 July, Stewart had denied that the government was preventing an appeal to the Privy Council. Yet, in spite of these assurances, obstacles were constantly being placed in their path. Band funds, for instance, could not be employed to finance the case. The prime minister agreed to stand by statements made by Laurier, Roche, and Stewart and promised that the matter would be reconsidered by the Indian Department.[70]

Results were predictably slow. In April 1925 representatives of the Allied Tribes arrived in Ottawa with yet another memorandum, and they succeeded in interviewing the prime minister. They reiterated their willingness to negotiate, noting that the proposals they had made to Scott in Victoria in 1923 had never been answered. But they insisted on retaining the option of an appeal to the Privy Council.[71]

One consequence of these persistent representations was that a subcommittee of the cabinet consisting of Stewart, Justice Minister E. Lapointe, and Public Works Minister J.H. King was appointed to consider the matter.[72] To assist the ministers in their deliberations, Scott prepared an extensive report on the question, dated 14 July 1925, in which he outlined its history and offered his own observations. He argued that the British Columbia Indians had been "fairly compensated" for their aboriginal title by the provision of reserves and the services of his department. If Victoria's policy had been "more considerate," there would likely have been little complaint. But the provincial government had treated native water rights "without sympathy," had attempted to claim cut-offs and a reversionary interest in Railway Belt reserves, and had granted a timber licence on a confirmed reserve.

Scott thought that it was inadvisable to take British Columbia to court on these issues or on the larger one of aboriginal title. Should the Indians win, "there [would] be a cloud on all the land titles issued by the province, and this point [had] always been an obstacle in the way of the reference." Going to the courts became less practicable with the passing of time and was even less so now that the report of the royal commission had been confirmed by both governments. He advised that it was best to avoid judicial proceedings and instead to continue the prevailing policy of increasing expenditure on education and health, thereby "nominally according full compensation for any aboriginal title in the lands." He pointed out that, after all, his department was spending far more on the Indians of British Columbia than they could ever get from a treaty and that the annuities paid under the treaty system were "a questionable benefit."[73]

Nothing came of the deliberations of the cabinet subcommittee, and in June 1926 Kelly and O'Meara were back in Ottawa with yet another petition. It was presented to Parliament on the 10th and was read in the House of Commons the following day. In addition to the already familiar demands for recognition of aboriginal rights and Ottawa's co-operation in securing a hearing before the Privy Council, the petition proposed that a special parliamentary committee consider the matter.[74]

This latest episode in the seemingly interminable agitation came at a rather difficult moment. A few weeks later, on 28 June, Mackenzie King's government resigned. On the day afterwards, Arthur Meighen, though he lacked a majority in the Commons, attempted to form a government and appointed a number of acting ministers. Kelly and O'Meara remained in Ottawa during these months of political turmoil in what Scott later characterized as "a perfectly useless sojourn."[75] On 21 July they met with R.B. Bennett, who was acting superintendent general of Indian affairs. Bennett promised that if the Conservatives won a majority, he would arrange further discussions on aboriginal title claims.[76] But in the general election of 14 September, the Liberals were returned, and Charles Stewart donned the mantle of superintendent general once again.

Kelly raised the issue of a parliamentary inquiry with Stewart in November, adding that the executive committee of the Allied Tribes had unanimously approved this course of action on 29 October. And he noted that the Conservatives had promised immediate attention to the matter if they were returned.[77] Scott advised against such an inquiry, preferring the reinstitution of the cabinet subcommittee.[78] But his counsel was spurned, and by the end of February 1927, the cabinet had decided to create a joint committee of the Senate and House of Commons to investigate the claims put forth by the Indians.[79] The decision was announced by Stewart in the House on 8 March. The special joint committee, consisting of seven senators and seven members of Parliament, convened on 27 March and proceeded to hear the evidence of witnesses such as Scott, Ditchburn, Kelly, Paull, and O'Meara.[80]

Scott was the first to be heard. Quoting extensively from a report he had prepared for the occasion, which was similar to that which he had presented to the cabinet sub-committee two years earlier, he regaled his listeners with a historical treatise on the claim. He attempted to demonstrate that the Indians of British Columbia had been "fairly compensated for the aboriginal title" by the provision of reserves and by the extension to them of "the policy which obtains in the other provinces of the Dominion." This was tacit recognition that aboriginal title did exist, but, throughout, Scott tended to minimize its value. He argued that if the terms offered by Sir James Douglas in the Vancouver Island treaties of the 1850s were taken as a standard, the "Indian title" would be worth less than one dollar per square mile. Since there were 251,097 square miles of unceded territory in the province, the title could only amount to a total value of $251,097.

The deputy superintendent, an experienced treaty-maker in his own right, was unable to see the symbolic importance of treaties to native people and viewed the process purely in monetary terms. He claimed, for instance, that under Treaty No. 6 in Saskatchewan, the federal government was obliged to pay $43,000 per annum but that in 1924-25 it had spent $439,000. This additional expenditure was not mandatory but was "for the most part actuated by humane motives and by a desire to raise the natives of the country to full citizenship."

And he continued to dazzle the committee members with further examples of Ottawa's generosity. The millions spent on the Indians of British Columbia since Confederation were proof that they had been as fairly treated as if they had signed a formal land surrender.[81] Nor would a treaty, even at this late stage, be of much advantage to them. Treaty terms were, after all, settled beforehand by the government and were not subject to meaningful negotiation.

Scott warned the committee of the dangers of a court referral. How would it affect the relations between the Indians and the British Columbia government? What would happen to the agreement between the two governments on the royal commission? And were the Indians to win, what would happen to existing land titles in the province? Would they not all be of dubious legality?[82]

The deputy superintendent was raising practical difficulties that taking the case beyond the committee might entail. Yet these were hardly compelling reasons, on purely ethical grounds, for not proceeding. But questions of principles and fundamental rights were not major factors in the committee's deliberations. Its members were apparently entranced by Scott's rhetoric and by the evidence he marshalled of Ottawa's magnanimity. Most of them had probably made up their minds on the question even before the hearings began, and many seemed to be convinced that the problem would never have arisen but for the meddling of that *bête noir* of Indian politics, A.E. O'Meara.

H.H. Stevens, a Conservative M.P. from Vancouver, was most conspicuous in that respect, and his treatment of the representatives of the Allied Tribes throughout the hearings virtually amounted to harrassment. British by birth and an ardent Methodist, prohibitionist, imperialist, and member of the Orange Order, he shared all the proverbial prejudices associated with such a background.[83] In his determination to keep his province British, he was an unrelenting foe of oriental immigration and native rights. As the self-proclaimed expert on British Columbia, he tended to dominate the proceedings with his hostile cross-examination of the Indians and their lawyers and with his frequent outbursts of indignation. He was an unfortunate choice for the committee, and his presence banished any semblance of objectivity that the inquiry might otherwise have displayed.

As counsel for the Allied Tribes, O'Meara was treated with unprecedented discourtesy. He attempted to present a historical argument for aboriginal title citing legal precedents, but he was constantly interrupted. "Piffle," "rubbish," "rot," "nonsense," and similar remarks punctuated his presentation, in sharp contrast to the reception that Scott had received.[84]

Andrew Paull and Peter Kelly were also interrupted although somewhat less rudely, in the course of their presentation. The Indian leaders raised the issue of hunting and fishing privileges for Indians in the province, and some committee members seemed receptive. They had less success with the question of aboriginal title, which Stevens dismissed as O'Meara's invention.[85] Kelly argued that the country would be getting off lightly by paying $2,500,000 in compensation for the aboriginal title. And he stated that the Indians would agree to a hearing on the matter before the Canadian courts, prior to taking it to the Privy Council.[86]

Although he was a witness and not a member of the committee, Scott remained present throughout most of the hearings and interjected his opinion as he saw fit. He had opposed the establishment of the committee initially, but once the decision to proceed had been made, he had come to the conclusion that it should settle the question for good. There would be no subsequent appeals to the courts or the Privy Council. O'Meara and his Indian clients held the opposite view. They were evidently under the impression that the hearings were a mere prelude to a judicial review and a possible appeal to the Privy Council.[87]

Scott's interpretation ultimately prevailed. The committee's report concluded that the claim to aboriginal title had only been advanced for about fifteen years. The entire difficulty was attributed to the "mischievous" agitation by "designing white men" such as counsel for the Indians. O'Meara had persisted with his activities in spite of the "generous offer" embodied in the order-in-council of June 1914. And he had been informed bluntly by Justice Minister C.J. Doherty that the case could not be taken to the Privy Council without prior consideration by the Canadian courts and that no further progress could be made until the conditions set forth in the order-in-council were accepted. It was the unanimous decision of the committee members that the petitioners had "not established any claim to the lands of British Columbia based on aboriginal or other title." And since the Indians had refused to take advantage of the government's offer of June 1914, they concluded "that the matter should now be regarded as finally closed."[88]

In November 1919 the Allied Tribes had submitted a list of specific claims to the provincial government which they argued could form the basis of a negotiated settlement. In addition to pronouncing on the question of aboriginal title, the committee reviewed these claims and made recommendations on each one. The report rejected the demand for 160 acres of "average agricultural land" or its equivalent on the grounds that the Indians did not normally make a living from agriculture. It was more sympathetic on the question of hunting and fishing rights but stressed that game laws would have to be obeyed. It endorsed the prevailing policy of leniency in the enforcement of regulations. The demand for better health and education services was supported by the committee report, but it noted that the existing system was good. The Indians had asked that the money spent in pursuing the claim ought to be reimbursed. This was rejected. The report recommended that instead of the annuities paid under the treaty system, an additional sum of $100,000 be spent annually in the province on education, health services and agriculture.[89]

Largely on the basis of the evidence presented by Scott, the committee members came to the conclusion that the Indians of British Columbia were receiving as many benefits as those who had signed treaties. Their reserves were "sufficient for their needs," and the obligations the Dominion assumed upon the province's entry into confederation had been "generously fulfilled."[90] And in order to prevent a recurrence of this difficulty, the committee recommended that the Indians be informed of their decision and be advised that "no funds should be contributed by them to continue further presentation of a claim which has now been disallowed."[91]

That was the end of the matter as far as the federal government was concerned. As Scott observed in his annual report for 1927: "The claims referred to are of long standing, and relate to a supposed aboriginal title of the Indian tribes to the lands now forming the province of British Columbia, and various rights alleged on behalf of the Indians in connection therewith." After a "thorough investigation of the whole question," it was concluded that no such aboriginal title ever existed.[92]

The investigation had been decidedly partisan, and it had been conducted with the covert intention of preventing the case being heard before the Canadian courts and, ultimately, the Privy Council. And it was no coincidence that the notorious Section 141 of the Indian Act, which prevented the solicitation or collection of funds from Indians in order to pursue claims on their behalf, was adopted in 1927. One of the many anticipated benefits of this piece of legislation was that individuals such as A.E. O'Meara, who was held responsible for the entire episode, would be silenced for good.

And for a while it seemed that the force of the law would indeed be necessary in order to curb the agitator's activities. In October Scott learned that O'Meara had been in the Nass area once more and was still hoping to take the case to the Privy Council. In January 1928 Ditchburn informed him that O'Meara had been in correspondence with the Nishga Indians asking for money. Scott encouraged him to try to acquire a copy of O'Meara's letter, saying that with "reliable evidence" at hand they could invoke the force of the law. A copy of the incriminating letter fell into the hands of the department in February,[93] but before further evidence could be compiled, O'Meara died.[94]

By this time Kelly and Paull had evidently accepted the report of the special committee,[95] and the Allied Tribes disintegrated shortly afterwards. The Nishga Land Committee remained in existence, but it accomplished little.[96] The death of O'Meara effectively ended the agitation for the recognition of aboriginal land title in British Columbia for several decades.

While the final chapter in the aboriginal title drama was being played out, Ottawa and Victoria continued their discussions of the reserve question. To bring matters to a conclusion, it would be necessary for the province to convey title to the Indian lands to the Dominion. Before this could be done, all reserves

would have to be surveyed and the surveys checked and approved by both
governments. And the dispute over the cut-offs in the Railway Belt would also
have to be resolved. Federal officials soon discovered that the province would
create further difficulties and that the conveyance of title would not be a simple
procedure.

Correspondence between Pattullo and Scott in 1926 and 1927 showed that in
making the proposed conveyance, British Columbia was hoping to retain rights
to Indian lands that did not prevail elsewhere. The draft order-in-council sent
to Ottawa in May 1927 allowed the province to reclaim any part of reserves
needed for roads, canals, bridges, and other such public works without
compensation. Such materials as water, timber, and stone could also be taken
from reserves for public works, and again, without compensation. Scott informed
Pattullo that these were unacceptable conditions which would give the province unprecedented control of Indian lands, contrary to the BNA Act. He
argued that the Indian Act had ample provisions to deal with public works, and
he demanded that the transfer be made "without any restrictions whatever."[97]

Pattullo could not shake off his suspicion that a straight transfer would turn
Indian lands into "a kingdom unto themselves," and his view was supported by
the provincial attorney general, who warned that any conveyance "should
contain proper provisoes to protect administration by the Provincial Crown in
matters such as highways, water, etc."[98]

Ottawa, however, had an important card to play in these negotiations—its
control of the Railway Belt and Peace River Block.[99] The British Columbia
government had wanted to regain possession of these lands for some time. They
had long since served their original purpose, but they might now be used to
finance railway construction into the Peace River area.[100] When Pattullo was in
Ottawa during the summer of 1928, he raised this issue, and in discussions with
Scott many of the differences between the two parties were resolved.[101]

But the advent to power in Victoria of S.F. Tolmie's Conservatives a few
months later made further negotiations necessary. Scott travelled to British
Columbia in March 1929 as the principal representative of the federal government. Together with Ditchburn he worked out an agreement with provincial
officials Henry Cathcart (superintendent of lands) and O.C. Bass (deputy
attorney general) whereby reserves would be conveyed to the Dominion without unusual restrictions. But the Scott-Cathcart Agreement, as it became known,
applied only to reserves outside the Railway Belt and Peace River Block. Ottawa
assumed that it already held title to reserves within those areas and that
therefore no conveyance was necessary.

According to the agreement, the conveyance would be made subject to the
condition that if a band became extinct, its reserve would revert to provincial
control. In addition, the province would be entitled to reclaim up to 5 per cent
of any reserve for public works with the exception of lands on which buildings

or gardens were located. The province would also be entitled to take materials from reserves for public works in return for "reasonable compensation."[102] Federal and provincial orders in council subsequently sanctioned the agreement.[103]

In February 1930 the two governments agreed on terms for the return of the Railway Belt and the Peace River Block to the province, and federal legislation, assented to on 30 May, made the transfer official. Indian reserves within those areas were explicitly excluded from the transfer.

Indian Affairs had every reason to assume that a rapprochement had been achieved. By April 1931 Scott was informed that all surveys had been completed with the exception of three cut-offs. Another encouraging sign was that British Columbia had adopted legislation permitting the registration of Indian land patents in the province's land registry offices. Scott was clearly concerned that the conveyance take place before his retirement, and he sent a number of appeals to Victoria to "expedite" the process. But in March 1932, his final month in office, he discovered that the province's procrastination was intentional. In transferring the railway lands prior to the conveyance of reserves, Ottawa had overplayed its hand, allowing Victoria to bargain once more for "better terms."

The discouraging news came from Ditchburn, who had recently been informed by Cathcart that there would be no conveyance until the question of the cut-offs in the former Railway Belt was settled.[104] Scott's response to the eleventh hour resurrection of this wearisome imbroglio can only be imagined. He believed that this claim had been abandoned for some time and explained the reasoning behind the federal position to Superintendent General T. Murphy. He pointed out that his agreement with Cathcart in 1929 had explicitly excluded Indian reserves from the proposed transfer of the railway lands to provincial control. He also noted that the federal order-in-council of 19 July 1924, which had refused to sanction cut-offs in the Railway Belt reserves, had been an integral part of the agreement. And the attached schedule of reserves had shown no reductions.[105]

There was an unassailable logic to the case that Scott made. It mattered little. Cathcart remained adamant and was supported by the provincial minister of lands, N.S. Lougheed. When the deputy superintendent retired at the end of March, the problem still remained in abeyance.

During the following months the matter continued to be debated between the two governments in volleys of acrimonious correspondence. Upon further investigation Indian Affairs discovered that the cut-offs claimed by the province were of considerable value and size. 5,554 acres valued at $452,791.80 were at issue.[106] Seabird Island, 1,690 acres valued at $121,820, was the prize which had whetted provincial greed most conspicuously. It was mentioned several times in the correspondence and in October Cathcart admitted to Murphy that his government had already promised that cut-off to "certain public bodies."[107] Ottawa refused to be moved, however, and continued to insist that the province had no claim.

The impasse remained until August 1934. In that month T.R.L. MacInnis, acting secretary of the department, and C.C. Perry, assistant commissioner of Indian affairs in British Columbia, entered into discussions with officials of the new Liberal government of the province, including Cathcart, who was deputy minister of lands. As a result of these deliberations, Victoria's claim to the disputed cut-offs was abandoned.[108]

It seemed that the major obstacle to a final settlement had at last been removed. The surveys had been completed by 1931, and the schedules were still being checked by both governments, eliminating discrepancies and errors. Disputes over small parcels of land occasionally appeared, but they were easily resolved. Nevertheless, the elusive official conveyance failed to materialize. Ottawa was evidently perplexed at the province's procrastination, and by 1937 this had turned to irritation.

In February 1938, D.M. MacKay, Indian commissioner for British Columbia, met with Cathcart and Premier Pattullo and discovered the reason behind the delay. The spoilt brat was still seeking "better terms." Cathcart had drawn up a new proposal which would have excluded base and precious metals, timber, and other natural resources from the conveyance. Pattullo was somewhat more flexible. He was prepared to include timber in the transfer, but he wished to retain some control of minerals for the province. MacKay found these new demands unacceptable and recommended their rejection. He observed that Cathcart's attitude was impossible and that progress could only be made in direct negotiations with Pattullo.[109]

As a result, R.A. Hoey, a senior Indian Affairs official, went to Victoria in June where he worked out a compromise with the premier. They agreed that the conveyance would include timber and minerals with the exception of precious metals.[110] The long-awaited transfer took place shortly afterwards on 29 July by provincial order-in-council 1036. 592,296.897 acres of reserve land were involved. After sixty-seven years of irresolution and vacillation, British Columbia had finally fulfilled its obligations under Clause 13 of the Terms of Union. And the province's troublesome reversionary interest in Indian lands, except in cases wherein a band became extinct, was finally put to rest.

Though Scott was not around for the concluding episode of this protracted dispute, he did play a pivotal role during its critical years. The beginnings of agitation for recognition of aboriginal title and the establishment of the royal commission coincided with his elevation to the position of deputy superintendent. He maintained throughout that the agitation was motivated by greed and that it was largely fomented by white troublemakers. And it was he who formulated a procedure for dealing with the problem. An appeal to the courts and ultimately to the imperial Privy Council would be permitted, but only if the Indians accepted self-defeating conditions beforehand.

The Indians wisely rejected this course of action. And they were sufficiently astute to view with scepticism Scott's suggestion that the Royal Commission would deal fairly with their land requirements.

The petty attitude of Victoria and the persistent Indian agitation prolonged the dispute indefinitely. The British Columbia government was undoubtedly the villain of the piece. And it seemed to make little difference whether Liberals or Conservatives held the reins of power in the province. Settlement of the dispute was postponed time and again as Victoria found new excuses to concede the least amount of land possible and even then to retain unprecedented control over the lands grudgingly granted. The economic and business interest was always paramount.

Though it acted in a more reasonable manner, the federal government was hardly the champion of native rights. Its officials were anxious to quell discontent and agitation and thereby stifle embarrassing publicity. But perhaps their primary objective was the elimination of the troublesome issue of the province's reversionary interest and the acquisition of the same title to Indian lands in British Columbia that prevailed elsewhere. In a revealing memorandum to Arthur Meighen in 1920, Scott probably best summed up the reasoning behind federal policy. Referring to the report of the royal commission, which he hoped would soon be confirmed, he observed: "the vexatious reversionary interest of the Province, which is now involved in all our dealing with Indian lands in British Columbia, will disappear, and the Department will be able to sell, lease and otherwise deal with Indian reserves in British Columbia not subject to any other interest."[111] Creating uniformity of administrative practice was the real issue. The rights and needs of native people were scarcely considered.

9

"Senseless Drumming and Dancing"

Transforming the native population into civilized and productive members of the "industrial and mercantile community" was one of the major objectives of federal Indian policy throughout this period. It was deemed particularly critical to effect this change successfully in western Canada, and all the more so as settlement advanced. In British Columbia, it was envisaged that Indians would make the transition from their traditional economic pursuits to wage labour in fishing, fish processing, lumbering, and mining. On the prairies, where reserves were substantially larger, agriculture was touted as the key to self-sufficiency. In both instances, department officials and their missionary allies believed that such characteristics as "steadiness" and "regularity of habits" would have to be internalized by the Indians as a prerequisite to such a transformation.

Chapter Five showed how education, especially that provided in the residential setting, was the favoured mechanism of behavioural and cultural modification. The effects of schooling, nonetheless, were often minimized or even eradicated by the persistence of native customs which tended to undermine the values imparted in the classroom. The potlatch and winter dance ceremonies of the Pacific coast tribes were anathema to officials of both church and state for that reason. On the prairies, the sun dance, thirst dance, and related activities were the major objects of condemnation. Dancing and potlatching allegedly kept children from school, interfered with steady labour, fostered paganism, barbarism, and a disrespect for property, and generally impeded the advancement of civilization and Christianity. Those who had accorded themselves responsibility for the transformation of the native population concluded that these customs ought to be discouraged or suppressed, and they were prepared to invoke the arm of the law to that end.

The suppression of the potlatch has been described by F.E. La Violette in *The*

Struggle for Survival and elsewhere.[1] On the other hand, attempts to stamp out the dances of the prairie Indians have largely been ignored by historians and they will therefore be the principal consideration here. The prohibition of both dancing and potlatching came under the same clause of the Indian Act, and so some preliminary observations regarding developments in British Columbia will help to set the stage.

The decision to employ the powers of the Indian Act to prohibit native customs was first taken in response to protests by missionaries and agents against the perceived evils of the potlatch. In the potlatch ceremony of the Indians of the northwest Pacific coast, a host entertained guests and distributed goods following elaborate rituals and protocols. One of its principal purposes was to establish or confirm rank in what were complex hierarchical societies.[2] Missionaries invariably failed to comprehend its significance. Blinded by a puritanism that equated enjoyment with evil, they denounced it as an orgy of drunkenness, debauchery, idleness, and idolatry. And, of course, the Victorian idea of progress, which encouraged the individual accumulation of material goods, was the direct antithesis of the values implicit in the potlatch.

The campaign against this integral component of west coast native culture brought a ready response from Ottawa. An amendment to the Indian Act in 1884 made the celebration of the potlatch and of the Tamanawas dance a misdemeanor subject to a prison sentence that could range from two to six months.[3] Much to the annoyance of the missionaries, who had been most vociferous in demanding this course of action, the prohibition proved impossible to enforce. Some Indian agents refused to seek prosecutions because they believed that the forbidden customs were harmless. Others feared that repressive measures would precipitate an Indian uprising. The minimal police presence on the coast, the reluctance of the provincial authorities to co-operate, and the absence of jails and guard-houses were additional factors that rendered the legislation meaningless.

Alert Bay, in the Kwawkewlth agency, was the principal centre of potlatching. And the local agent, R.H. Pidcock, was one of the custom's most intransigent opponents. In 1889, acting on his powers as justice of the peace, he arrested an Indian named He-ma-sak for engaging in a potlatch and sentenced him to six months' imprisonment. The case was subsequently appealed to the provincial supreme court. Chief Justice Sir Matthew Baillie Begbie, whom the Indians had come to know and respect over the years, ruled that the prisoner should be released on account of a technicality in the manner of his arrest.[4] The chief justice also observed, however, that the law was vague and did not clearly define the acts that were forbidden. This opinion was brought to the attention of the federal deputy minister of justice who concluded that the clause in the Indian Act would probably have to be rephrased in order to make it effective.[5]

Meanwhile on the prairies, missionaries and government officials were engaged in a similar struggle—the self-imposed burden of weaning the Indians from their "Heathenish customs" and transforming them into model Anglo-Canadian citizens. The sun dance of the Blackfoot and the thirst dance of the Crees were perceived as the major obstacles to progress in that part of the country. The two ceremonies were sufficiently similar in purpose and procedure that a description of one will largely suffice for the other.

The Indians of the Blackfoot confederacy (Blood, Peigan, and Blackfoot proper) held the sun dance during the months of June and July. It was designed "to propitiate the Sun and other lesser spirits."[6] A woman of good character sponsored the event, having made a vow to do so previously, perhaps in a time of need. In preparation, she began to collect buffalo tongues, which were cut into slabs, dried, boiled, and subsequently consumed as a sacred food during the dance. As part of the ritual, she was obliged to remain in her teepee abstaining from food for four days.

The men constructed the circular dance lodge with elaborate ceremonies, especially when they were selecting and raising the centre pole. Each tribe contained a number of different societies, and they took turns officiating at the sun dance. The songs and dances performed were often the exclusive property of the individual societies. Gifts were generously distributed to visitors.[7]

The most controversial feature of the sun dance was the custom known as "the making of a brave." It was not necessarily performed by everyone who wished to become a brave, as has been generally believed, but rather by individuals who wanted to make a special sacrifice to the sun in the hope of receiving a favour. A man might go through the rite several times during his life. Clad in breech cloth and moccasins, his body plastered with white clay, and his head, wrists, and ankles adorned with sage bush, he had his breasts pierced, sticks placed through openings, and the sticks fastened by rawhide thongs to the top of the centre pole. He danced in a backward motion until the flesh broke, and he was freed.[8]

The thirst dance of the Crees was remarkably similar, except that it was sponsored by a man. For example, Fine Day, a leader of the Sweetgrass Cree and a warrior with a formidable reputation, held seven during his lifetime, in spite of official disapproval.[9]

The sun dance and thirst dance were only two of a vast array of dances performed by the plains Indians. The smoking tipi dance, rain dance, prairie chicken dance, beer dance, grass dance—these are the names of a few.[10] Most of them involved some form of gift-giving, which reflected the high regard in which generosity was held among these people. Prestige was acquired by giving goods away rather than by hoarding them. Similar values existed among the west coast tribes where they were associated with the potlatch. Among the plains Indians, however, the gift-giving did not take the form of a single ostentatious display of generosity. Instead, it was done constantly and in a more modest manner.[11]

Government officials began to see dancing in a particularly dangerous light in the aftermath of the Rebellion of 1885. After visiting the sun dance of the Bloods in July 1889, Sam Steele, Superintendent of the North-West Mounted Police, wrote a report to his superiors urging that the festival be discouraged since it tended to revive old associations "too vividly:"

> Old warriors take this occasion of relating their experience of former days, counting their scalps and giving the number of horses they were successful in stealing. This has a pernicious effect on the young men; it makes them unsettled and anxious to emulate the deeds of their forefathers.[12]

The Indian Department shared Steele's concern. In fact, in 1890 headquarters gave credence to rumours that a "messiah craze" was spreading among the western Indians. Followers of the once-dreaded Sitting Bull were reported to be responsible for the movement, which was said to be connected with the ghost dance. Indian agents were warned to be on the lookout for evidence of the craze, but nothing came to their attention.[13] The incident illustrates the nervousness of officialdom in the years following the rebellion. Renewed violence was still a possibility, and the "excitement" generated by dancing might precipitate it.

Even as the danger of rebellion faded, the Indian Department found further reasons to discourage dancing. Commissioner Hayter Reed observed in 1892 that when the Indians congregated for the purposes of these festivals, they lost from four to six weeks of work. And this was during the vital summer months when they ought to be busy repairing fences, breaking new land, and summer fallowing.[14] The proposition that dancing and farming were fundamentally incompatible was a refrain that would be repeated *ad nauseum* in subsequent decades by department officials in the west.

Although Indian agents and the police agreed that dancing should be discouraged if not suppressed, they were initially at a loss on how to proceed. At that time, the department attempted to control its charges by allowing them to leave their reserves only after obtaining a special pass from their agent.[15] The pass system was not sanctioned by law, but the Mounted Police tended to co-operate in enforcing it. Dance gatherings could be restricted somewhat if they were confined to Indians of only one reserve. The requirement for passes, however, was frequently ignored by Indians when they wished to attend a dance. And this method of control became even less effective after 1892 when the police were advised that the pass system would not be sustained by the courts in the event of a challenge.[16]

Agents evidently found this ambiguity disconcerting. Requests for clarification regarding their powers began to reach Ottawa with increasing frequency in the early 1890s. Some wondered if the clause outlawing the potlatch applied to the prairie dances and obviously hoped for an affirmative reply. Headquarters was far from reassuring. Even Hayter Reed, who had been promoted to deputy superintendent general in 1893, could offer little that was concrete beyond advising discretion and caution.[17]

The advocates of repressive measures were undoubtedly relieved to read the revised version of Section 114 of the Indian Act which was adopted in the summer of 1895. The new wording offered a definition of what was forbidden and sought to extend the prohibition on the potlatch to the dances of the plains. Indian ceremonies involving the giving away of "money, goods or articles" or "the wounding or mutilation of the dead or living body of any human being or animal" became indictable offences liable to prison sentences ranging from two to six months.[18] The wounding clause was aimed at "the making of a brave." It also applied to the dog feast and arm-biting rites of some coastal tribes.[19] With the power of the law clearly behind them, officials hoped that Indian agents throughout the west would meet with more success in eradicating these unacceptable aspects of culture.

Senior officials within the department did not view the amended legislation as a *carte blanche* for immediate measures of repression. They did not anticipate that dancing and potlatching would now be stifled by the mass incarceration of participants. In fact, Hayter Reed, who was no stranger to coercion, was quick to emphasize that agents ought to proceed "with great circumspection" and that persuasion was preferable to prosecution: "we have to proceed very cautiously in order to guard against evoking a mutinous spirit among the Indians, who are quick to resent anything that might be regarded as a harsh interference with their customs."[20] Several of the more enthusiastic agents on the prairies had to be advised on a number of occasions to invoke the law only as a last resort and reminded that it only applied to the "give away" and torture features of dances.

The co-operation of the North-West Mounted Police was critical to the success of the policy of persuasion. A police presence at sun and thirst dances always ensured that the forbidden features did not take place. And the police were sometimes successful in convincing the Indians to abandon dances even after they were underway.[21]

There was no question, however, of forsaking dancing permanently. Some bands were prepared to modify the duration of their ceremonies as well as the content in order to appease officialdom. In May/June 1897, Agent G.H. Wheatley, with the approval of Commissioner Forget, agreed to permit the Blackfoot to hold a sun dance under the following conditions: it would last for five days; there would be no torture or giving away; no one would be forced to join in; and children would be encouraged to remain in school. Wheatley later reported to the Regina office that all the conditions had been fulfilled except that regarding the school children. The Indians had "behaved admirably," and no liquor had been present.[22]

But not all agents were as conciliatory. Some were determined to show that the revised Section 114 was no empty gesture. P.J. Williams, agent at Battleford, reported in January 1897 that he had arrested five Indians of Thunderchild's reserve for holding a "give away" dance. Two had been given suspended sentences while three had been given a two-month prison term. J. Cotton, the commanding officer of the Battleford division of the Mounted Police, felt that the minimum sentence of two months' imprisonment was too harsh and would prove injurious to the health of the elderly Indians. He advised Forget that the convictions alone had dealt a death blow to the "nefarious" dances, and he urged that the prisoners be released after two weeks. The commissioner agreed, and Ottawa arranged the release of the Indians with the Ministry of Justice on 10 February 1897.[23]

The incident illustrates a certain difference of opinion between the NWMP and Indian agents on the question of dancing. While the police were willing to co-operate in upholding the law, they tended to take a more tolerant view of the situation and were lacking in that punitive zeal that agents frequently exhibited.[24] When David Laird became Indian commissioner in 1898, he examined the correspondence regarding dancing and noted this element of friction. He approached the assistant commissioner of the Mounted Police and asked that his men work more closely with agents in discouraging aboriginal festivals. Laird reported his observations and actions to headquarters in January 1901.[25] Upon receiving this information, Deputy Superintendent James Smart wrote to Fred White, comptroller of the NWMP, urging him to inform his officers of the need to assist agents in enforcing the law. White was irked by this implied rebuke. In replying, he defended the work of his men, noting that the Indians had always viewed the police as their friends. In the following remark, he suggested that the Mounties were less than enthusiastic about the demands being made upon them by the department:

> If you will, by Departmental instructions, or through the Indian Commissioner, clearly define what dances, if any, the Indians are to be allowed to partici- pate in, either on or off their Reserves, the Police will endeavour to enforce your legislation.[26]

The dilemma facing the police was clear. The law expressly forbade the giving away and torture elements of the Indian festivals, but not dancing itself. The police were quite willing to act when these illegal activities took place. In fact, the "brave making" had largely disappeared by the new century as a result. They were understandably reluctant, however, to co-operate in the suppression of all dancing, as the department evidently wished.

Nevertheless, the law had sufficient teeth to allow for an occasional arrest to take place, and department officials believed that convictions served to discour- age dancing in general. Wanduta, a member of the Oak River Sioux band of

Griswold, Manitoba, was convicted of engaging in an illegal dance in January 1903 and sentenced to four months' imprisonment. Appeals for clemency on his behalf to Ottawa went unheeded. Commissioner Laird and Deputy Superintendent Pedley were adamant that the full sentence be served since Wanduta was said to be the ringleader of the "discontented Indians" and the prison term would undermine his activities.[27]

In March 1903 an "agitator" named Etchease, of Muscowpetung's band, appeared on Piapot's reserve and started "circle dances," at which nothing was given away except a supper. *The Globe* reported that this was a "crafty effort" to evade the law. The local agent, W. M. Graham, became alarmed and took proceedings against Etchease. In spite of an able legal defence, the Indian was found guilty and sentenced to three months' imprisonment.[28] In reporting the trial to headquarters, Assistant Commissioner J.A.J. McKenna observed that the conviction had put an end to dancing in the agency. He also pointed out that if such tough measures were adopted in all western agencies, the problem would soon disappear.[29]

But the enthusiasm of some department officials for the mailed fist could sometimes backfire. This was certainly true in the case of Tapassing, a member of the Fishing Lakes band who was sentenced to two months' imprisonment with hard labour for dancing in January 1904. Upon the intervention of the NWMP at Regina, who had discovered that the prisoner was over ninety years old, feeble, and almost blind, the department consented to his release.[30] The incident nonetheless found its way into the press with the *Winnipeg Telegram* proclaiming it under the following headline: "Injustice to Poor Old Indian—He had deserved better treatment from Canada."[31]

Such embarrassing publicity was the predictable consequence of a misguided policy which was administered in a clumsy and uneven manner. Headquarters in Ottawa and, to a lesser extent, the commissioner's office in Winnipeg were often vague and evasive in the directions given to agents regarding the dancing prohibition. They were frequently advised to use their own discretion, which automatically meant that the degree of permissiveness varied from agency to agency.

Two of the most intransigent opponents of dancing among department officials in the west were W.M. Graham of the Qu'Apelle agency and J.A. Markle of the Blackfoot agency.[32] They both believed that the Indians ought to become self-sufficient farmers and that agriculture and dancing were fundamentally incompatible. Their influence on the course of events was increased during the first decade of the new century when both were promoted to inspector.

Graham's advocacy of repressive measures won the enthusiastic support of Father J. Hugonard, principal of Qu'Appelle industrial school and close collaborator in the forming of the File Hills colony. In November 1903, the Oblate priest wrote a lengthy letter to Laird describing in alarming terms the evil effects of dancing. He was particularly concerned at the ability of the dance to lure school graduates back to paganism—"the change from discipline and a regular life to unbridled licence and debauchery soon transform a promising youth into a shiftless unreliable Indian." If anyone thought otherwise, he ought to attend these events and see for himself the Indians "nearly nude, painted and decked out in feathers and beads, dancing like demented individuals and indulging in all kinds of debauchery." He pointed out that long absences from reserves to attend dances resulted in neglect or loss of crops and farm animals and reiterated the familiar argument that the custom was inimical to progress:

> I am convinced that Christianity and advancement, and paganism and indolence cannot flourish side by side; one or the other has to give way; paganism, dancing and indolence are most natural to the Indian, who has no thought for the morrow.

Hugonard went on to say that since dancing had been prohibited in his agency, great advances in health, education, work, and the accumulation of individual property had taken place. But this was not the case everywhere, and the lack of uniformity in implementing policy was a cause of discontent. The department ought to be as strict on the question of dancing as it was in the case of alcohol.[33]

Shortly after receiving this letter, Laird met with a number of Methodist and Presbyterian missionaries and showed them its contents. They endorsed Hugonard's sentiments completely. This unusual expression of ecclesiastical unanimity impressed the commissioner. He passed the news on to Superintendent General Sifton, noting that the Indian Act ought to be amended once more to facilitate the suppression of dancing. Graham and Hugonard carried the campaign for further coercion to Ottawa in December and succeeded in presenting their views to Sifton in person. The superintendent general agreed with the sentiments they expressed, and it seemed as if the stage were set for another round of harsh measures.[34]

Officials at headquarters were not motivated by the same sense of urgency in the matter as those in the field, however, and little came of Graham's pleadings. In fact, Ottawa sometimes exhibited an element of flexibility that infuriated western agents. An incident illustrating this difference of opinion occurred in 1906. In March of that year thirty-three Indians of the Assiniboine agency signed a petition to Ottawa drawn up with the assistance of Daniel Kennedy, an industrial school graduate. The petition, which was addressed to Superintendant General Frank Oliver, asked that the Indians be allowed to have two special days put aside in which they could hold feasts, sports and "thanksgiving promenades"— "holidays exactly similar to those observed by white people on Dominion Day." Were this granted, they would stay on their reserves and work all through the summer and would abandon the sun dance. Upon examining this request,

Frank Pedley informed Oliver that some western agents had been trying to substitute picnics and sports for the old dances with some success and that what the Assiniboine Indians proposed could not be objected to.[35]

The request of the petitioners was therefore granted, but the decision was not universally welcomed. W. Grant, the Assiniboine agent, informed headquarters that he was suspicious of the proposed picnic because the Indians would likely try to include some of their dances in the program. And he observed that Graham, who was now inspector of agencies for South Saskatchewan, shared his concern.[36] Some church officials also reacted negatively. A group of Presbyterian ministers meeting at Manitoba College on 10 July expressed their opposition to what they believed to be a new permissiveness by the department. They had heard that dances were to be allowed, and they created a committee to approach the department's offices in Winnipeg and Ottawa to make their views known. They feared that in the excitement generated by pow-wows, missionaries might be driven from the reserves.[37]

The Assiniboine sports days were held on 18 and 19 July. Agent Grant was forced to admit that the Indians had kept to their agreement and no dancing had taken place. He hoped, nevertheless, that the event would not be repeated; it had taken up too much time and the participants had spent too much money on beads and ornaments. Commissioner Laird also expressed reservations. He noted that the department's intention had been to allow a sports day in one agency but that invitations to attend had been sent out to Indians in many parts of the west. This had created a potentially troublesome situation. Fortunately, Inspector Graham had taken the matter in hand and had "to a large extent checked the gathering." When Department Secretary J.D. McLean received these comments, he informed Laird that he was satisfied that the Indians had not broken the law. Nor did he believe that they could "be refused permission to indulge, within reasonable limits, in an occasional day of harmless sports."[38]

The attempt to replace dancing with sports days came to nothing. Judging by the attitude of some agents and inspectors, the Indians were not to be allowed any recreation whatsoever. Even had the officials been more flexible, it is doubtful that they would have been successful. There occurred around this time what Frank Pedley described in his annual report as "a certain recrudescence of the sun dance." The deputy superintendent was optimistic, however, that the revival was merely "a spasmodic and expiring effort on the part of the older generation and particularly the surviving medicine men to keep alive superstitions and customs which are doomed to complete disappearance in the near future, but naturally are dying hard."[39]

John McDougall, the veteran Methodist missionary, was also accorded some of the blame for the "recrudescence." In November 1907, he wrote to the *Winnipeg Free Press* complaining about the suppression of dancing. He pointed out that the dances were religious festivals and ought to be tolerated in the spirit of religious liberty![40] This was an astonishing and unique statement from a Christian missionary, most of whom, by the very nature of their calling, viewed indigenous religions with utter contempt.

The Roman Catholic missionaries, for instance, were completely intolerant. In June 1908, Father G. Simonin of the Catholic mission at Hobbema warned the department of a forthcoming sun-dance and urged that it be stopped on moral grounds. He also claimed that McDougall's comments in the previous year had encouraged the Indians to proceed. And in the following month, Father H. Grandin and eighteen other Oblate priests met in Edmonton to discuss ways of suppressing the sun dance—"une practique payenne emminent contraire à tout progrès et à toute civilisation." What emerged from the meeting was a statement outlining the well-known objections of church and state to dancing. It was sent to Bishop Legal of St. Albert who passed it on, with his own stamp of approval, to the superintendent general.[41]

The department needed little encouragement. It had already sent out statements to agents and inspectors in the west confirming its disapproval of dancing and repudiating McDougall's appeal for toleration. But some Indians were now seeking legal advice on the question and knew that dancing itself was not banned. They continued to dance, usually scrupulously avoiding the illegal features. Most agents could do little but rely on their own powers of persuasion. There were some who threatened to withold rations or to depose chiefs and councillors who supported the festivals, but to little avail.

The "recrudescence" of dancing had a further disturbing dimension. Around this time, the organizers of fairs and exhibitions began to invite Indians to perform their dances as a form of entertainment.[42] Country fairs had as their original purpose the promotion of new agricultural methods and the fostering of competition among farmers by the exhibition of crops and livestock. But by the beginning of the twentieth century, this aspect had been overshadowed by the carnival of amusements which had attached itself to the occasion. Horse-racing, vaudeville shows, wheels of fortune, balloon ascensions, dancing girls, and magicians became the major attractions, providing a few days of gaudy diversion to shatter the dull monotony that otherwise prevailed in prairie social life.[43]

Indian dances and parades were to be part of this spectacle. In some ways, this was not surprising. Only a decade or so earlier Buffalo Bill's Wild West Show, the prototype of the exhibition cum circus, had featured Sitting Bull and Gabriel Dumont among its leading stars. It meant that prairie settlers no longer viewed Indians as a menace, but rather as colourful and exotic neighbours who could be relied upon to enliven a festive gathering. Undoubtedly, fair organizers sought to exploit the dancers as inexpensive entertainment. But it is equally certain that the Indians enjoyed participating and being the centre of attention. It was an opportunity to evade, if only temporarily, the oppressive regimen of work imposed by agents and farm instructors. And it must have been reassuring to know that not all elements of the dominant society perceived their dances, songs, and costumes as relics of a barbarism that ought to be ruthlessly stamped out.

The attitude of Indian Department officials to this new obstacle cast across the pathway of progress is not difficult to imagine. In November 1907, Inspector Markle, with characteristic alarm, informed the commissioner's office that a number of Blackfoot Indians had gone on a grand tour of exhibitions during the summer. As a result of their five-week absence, agriculture and stock-raising had suffered. Apart from this neglect, the inspector noted the demoralizing effect that these performances had on the dancers and spectators alike. He was appalled at the very idea of "male Indians in almost nude attire parading streets and other public places, giving so-called war and other dances for the edification of the wives and daughters of people who claim to be civilized and refined." Assistant Commissioner McKenna concurred, and he informed Ottawa that unless the practice was stopped, the Indians might don paint and feathers to appear in the Dominion Exhibition scheduled for Calgary during the summer of 1908. Should this happen, it would be featured in the British and American journals and would give the impression that "aborigines" still wandered "wild over the plains of Alberta." The department might allow "working Indians" to appear "clad as the ordinary people of the Country" and put articles on display which were "the product of their civilized industry."[44]

Indian dances at exhibitions were thus opposed not just because they interfered with farming and had a demoralizing effect on participants and onlookers, but also because they fostered the wrong image of the Dominion abroad. The federal government evidently wished the world to see Canada as a progressive, dynamic society which offered outstanding opportunities for immigrants and investment capital. Indian dances suggested a raw frontier primitiveness that the country's image makers wished to dispel.[45]

Frank Pedley certainly viewed the matter in that way. In June 1908 he heard that Indians had indeed been invited to perform at the Dominion Exhibition. He immediately wrote to G.R. O'Halloran, the federal deputy minister of agriculture, bringing the news to his attention and asking that the government grant to the exhibition be made only on condition that the Indian performance be cancelled. After all, as he explained, "the display of apparently uncivilized savages seems a very questionable form of advertising in the best interests of the country."[46] O'Halloran, it turned out, was unable to oblige since the grant had already been made and the conditions could hardly be changed. Department officials were forced to accept the fact that they could not legally prevent the Indian dances at the exhibition. And their frustration was all the more intense when they learned that the Rev. John McDougall had made the arrangements for the Indian appearance.

The involvement of the well-known missionary tended to undermine department efforts to prevent Indian dancing at public events. In 1909 McDougall was responsible for the presence of about three hundred Stonies at the Dominion Day celebrations at Banff. A few days later, and again with the missionary's involvement, close to six hundred Indians, including Stonies, Crees, Blackfoot, Sarcees, Peigans, and Bloods, attended the Provincial Exhibition in Calgary where they were the main attraction. Department officials viewed these events with dismay and complained bitterly to headquarters both about their inability to control the situation and about McDougall's activities.[47]

David Laird, who had been transferred to Ottawa with the closing of the commissioner's office in Winnipeg, felt that much more could be done even with the powers that were available. Section 208 of the Criminal Code, for instance, which forbade indecent exposure, could be invoked against those wearing aboriginal dress! Or the vagrancy section could be used against those Indians who loitered around town for days. It might be expedient, however, he suggested, to amend the Indian Act in order to "prohibit such exhibitions of Indian savage life in public places." Such displays were "ludicrous and grotesque" and could not "contribute to the refinement of the spectators."[48]

Perhaps Laird's presence contributed to the hardening attitude at headquarters towards Indian dancing and participation at fairs. And the rise to preeminence of D.C. Scott was a further contributing factor. Upon his appointment as superintendent of education in 1909, Scott decided to visit the west to examine conditions in Indian schools and communities for himself. These visits, in fact, became an annual event, and he frequently included a few days vacation in Banff on his itinerary. August 1910 found him in southern Alberta on the first of his western tours. He was already somewhat of a minor celebrity. The *Calgary News* noted his literary accomplishments and his love of the outdoors and acclaimed him as "one of the best Indian authorities in the country." This unaccustomed attention must have been a heady moment for Scott. He issued a statement to the press on the dancing question which, while it reflected his attitude and that of the department, showed a minimal concern with accuracy. His statement reprimanded the organizers of fairs for interfering with the work of the department, and it claimed that during a recent fair in Lethbridge, fifty-five Indians had been arrested for drunkenness.[49]

The latter allegation was immediately repudiated by the *Lethbridge Herald*, which pointed out that the total number of liquor offences during the fair was only five. Scott's statement caused such indignation that at a meeting of the local Agricultural Society on 24 August it was decided to check the records of the Lethbridge courts during fair week for concrete evidence with which to contradict the "slander".[50] The evidence was found and sent to Scott in Ottawa. He was obliged to admit that he had been mistaken and that his statement had been based on the unconfirmed report of an agent.[51]

The incident brought to light a further objection on the part of the department to Indian participation in fairs: the availability of liquor. Even if Indians did not violate the liquor provisions of the act with the alarming regularity that some officials imagined, offences were sufficiently frequent to add fuel to the growing conviction that something would have to be done. In October 1910 western agents and inspectors were asked to report on the effects of Indian attendance at fairs. The majority of respondents had little good to say, and many railed against Indian immorality, intoxication, and the neglect of work which accompanied these events.

The absence of an appropriate clause in the Indian Act meant that coercion could not be employed to solve this problem, at least for the time being. Persuasion, on the other hand, seemed to offer few possibilities. In January 1911, the department wrote to the organizers of agricultural exhibitions in Lethbridge, Calgary, Edmonton, Brandon, Regina, Macleod, and High River asking them to omit Indian performances from their programs. A few positive responses were received, but most ignored the entreaties.[52]

The lack of co-operation of the exhibition organizers was compounded by a growing intervention by politicians, many of whom had vested interests in the success of fairs in their constituencies. The first Calgary Stampede, held in September 1912, illustrates this phenomenon. The Stampede was the brainchild of itinerant cowboy promoter Guy Weadick and was modelled on American wild west shows.[53] Indian participation was therefore deemed essential. The department was initially hostile to the idea and refused to co-operate. But R.B. Bennett, Frank Cochrane, and Senator James Lougheed approached Superintendent General Robert Rogers directly and convinced him otherwise. The fact that the Duke of Connaught planned to attend the event was apparently a major consideration in this change of heart.[54] The *Globe* later reported that six tribes of Indians made up the bulk of the Stampede parade—"a gorgeous display of beads and coloured blankets."[55]

Scott had indicated his antipathy to dancing and parades in aboriginal costume in 1910. Upon his elevation to deputy superintendent in 1913, he quickly showed that nothing had changed in the interim. A memorandum to all agents on 25 October reminded those in the west of the dances forbidden under Section 149 (formerly Section 114) of the Act. And Scott warned them to discourage gatherings which tended "to destroy the civilizing influence of the education imparted to Indian children at the schools" and which worked "against the proper influence of agents and farming instructors."[56]

Scott was all too aware that exhortations of this nature were unlikely to solve the persistent problem. Greater powers of coercion, which had been advocated by some western officials and missionaries for several years, would be required. Consequently, an amendment to Section 149 was drawn up forbidding Indians in the four western provinces and in the territories from participating in "Indian dances" outside of their own reserves and from appearing in shows or exhibitions in "aboriginal costume." Subsection 2, as the amendment was destined to become, provided penalties of $25 or imprisonment for one month "on summary conviction."[57]

Even more astonishing than the absurd repression inherent in this proposed amendment was the fact that it passed through the nation's Parliament with little controversy. One member of Parliament pointed out that Indian dances were superior in his opinion to the tango and the turkey-trot, but this hardly constituted a serious objection. And Prime Minister Borden, who was obliged to explain the measure in the absence of Superintendent General Roche, admitted that he knew little of the evils it was supposed to prevent.[58]

Indian agents were immediately informed of the new powers at their disposal, and they were told to break the news to Indians and to the organizers of fairs and exhibitions.[59] The amendment did not mean a complete ban on dancing; it meant further restrictions. It was envisaged that small gatherings, confined to the Indians of one reserve, could continue, and several dances of this nature took place during the summer of 1914 with department approval.

The discretionary powers allowed under the amendment meant that the law was enforced unevenly. Agents who insisted on a more rigid interpretation were quick to point the finger of accusation at those who favoured a liberal approach. Circulars from headquarters attempted to clarify matters and encourage a degree of uniformity.[60]

During the summer of 1915 a number of convictions were secured by agents in Saskatchewan under subsection 2. Fines and short prison terms were handed down to Indians found guilty of attending dances off their reserves.[61] These manifestations of the strong arm of the law were designed to set an example—to act as a warning to Indians to co-operate with the department. They had little effect. If one is to judge from the persistent complaints of Inspector Graham, dancing was as bad as ever.

The department's attempts to suppress dancing and Indian performances at exhibitions were complicated by the war effort. Scott was eager to persuade Indians to enlist, and he was therefore reluctant to take any action that might antagonize them. Policy implementation therefore remained flexible. Most requests from the organizers of fairs and stampedes for permission to stage an Indian performance continued to be rejected. But when these events had some "patriotic" dimension or when influential political figures were involved, co-operation was usually forthcoming. In July 1916, for instance. R.B. Bennett successfully approached Scott on behalf of the Calgary Returned Veterans' Society which wished to include an Indian race in a stampede they were organizing. In acceding to this request, Scott emphasized that the law was not designed to prevent Indians from entering races, as long as they were not in aboriginal costume:

> The purpose of the amendment to the Act was to prevent the Indians from
> being exploited as a savage or semi-savage race, when the whole administra-
> tive force of the Department is endeavouring to civilize them. . . . I am
> not disposed to administer the law in a puritanical spirit.[62]

While the war effort sometimes required this element of flexibility, it also
gave birth to new powers of prosecution. As the conflict dragged on, the
production of more food and the conservation of existing supplies became a
vital aspect of the patriotic effort. Potlatching and dancing were customs that the
department regarded as inherently wasteful. But they also distracted Indians
from productive activities. The mutilation and "give-away" features had been
declared indictable offences under subsection 1 of Section 149 of the Act, which
meant that agents could only lay charges, not preside at hearings. It was a
complicated and expensive procedure, and convictions had proven difficult to
achieve. Some western officials had been agitating for a number of years for a
change in the act making the outlawed features summary offences. The wartime
exigencies convinced Scott of the wisdom of this course of action, and he
proposed the change to the superintendent general.[63]

Parliament adopted the amendment in the spring of 1918.[64] In informing
western agents of this development, Scott stressed the urgent necessity of
conserving everything, especially food. Those who participated in "give away"
festivals of any kind could now be prosecuted and tried without reference to a
higher court. A renewed vigilance was encouraged in the following manner:

> You should carefully observe the movements of your Indians and check
> any tendency in the direction of preparing for one of these ceremonies;
> and in the event of a performance having actually got underway, vigorous
> steps should be taken to apprehend the offender. . . . I desire to empha-
> size the fact that this policy is now most essential, and it is expected that you
> act accordingly.[65]

Even though the emergency conditions which ostensibly precipitated the
adoption of these latest powers of coercion vanished with the armistice of
November 1918, when attempts to suppress dancing were pursued with renewed
vigour, the summary conviction clause proved eminently useful.

W.M. Graham was largely responsible for the new outbreak of repression.
This adamant foe of dancing was appointed Indian commissioner for the three
prairie provinces in 1920. And his influence was further augmented by the
elevation of Arthur Meighen, with whom he had family connections, to the
office of prime minister. Headquarters would no longer be able to ignore his
calls for harsh measures.

Graham was in Ottawa during the summer of 1920 and conferred with Scott on the matter. The two agreed on the desirability of making a more determined effort to restrict dancing and on using the services of the Mounted Police to that end. Subsequent correspondence between the commissioner and the deputy superintendent revealed that Graham was the more intransigent. He persisted in calling for further amendments to the Indian Act to provide additional extraordinary powers which would enable him to supervise the end of dancing. Scott was not easily convinced that such measures were necessary. The substitution of alternative means of recreation, he believed, was the most positive approach:

> It has always been clear to me that the Indians must have some sort of recreation, and if our agents would endeavour to substitute reasonable amusements for this senseless drumming and dancing, it would be a great assistance.[66]

The difference between Ottawa and Regina was in means; the ends were agreed upon. Nor were the differences of such magnitude to hinder the more vigorous approach which Graham and Scott were determined to pursue. And the Mounted Police were eager to co-operate. Reorganized in 1920 as the Royal Canadian Mounted Police, they were on a new campaign to combat subversion. The dance camps were sometimes the scenes of Indian politicking, and the activities of F.O. Loft in that regard were viewed with deep suspicion. The forces of law and order, then, had their own reasons for taking an interest in the dances.

During 1921, police patrols at dance gatherings increased noticeably. On many occasions, they merely observed the proceedings; on others, they forcibly intervened, sending the participants back to their respective homes. With agents and police working closely together a number of prosecutions for violations of Section 149 took place. With summary procedure, convictions were relatively easy to secure. As a result several Indians found themselves languishing in jail for the heinous crime of holding "give away" dances.[67]

Some Indian leaders reacted with understandable indignation at what they regarded as unwarranted interference with their customs and religion. Among the more eloquent condemnations of the policy of repression was that of Chief Thunderchild, the old Cree warrior who had once supported Big Bear in resisting the treaty process:

> Can things go well in a land where freedom of worship is a lie, a hollow boast? To each nation is given the light by which it knows God, and each finds its own way to express the longing to serve Him. It is astounding to me that a man should be stopped from trying in his own way to express his need or his thankfulness to God. If a nation does not do what is right

according to its own understanding, its power is worthless. . . . why has
the white man no respect for the religion that was given to us, when we
respect the faith of other nations?[68]

1921 and 1922 were the peak years of prosecution for violations of Section
149 on the prairies. On the west coast, the potlatch was being subjected to
similar measures of repression at the same time. The jail terms, fines, and
suspended sentences handed down were supposed to have a salutary effect on
the Indians by convincing them of the folly of resisting the department. But it
quickly became obvious to more astute officials that the mailed fist was too
cumbersome an instrument for the task. In spite of its revisions over the years,
the law remained imprecise, and methods of evasion were not difficult to find.
As police patrols on reserves increased, the Indians sought legal advice and
discovered that dances could be held without breaking the law.[69] It was sometimes even possible to bypass the clause forbidding attendance at dances off
one's own reserve by holding the events on the boundary of adjacent reserves,
where such existed.[70]

On a visit to the west during the summer of 1922, Scott saw for himself the
tenacity with which the Indians clung to their customs. He came to the conclusion that the provisions of the act would not be sufficient in themselves to stifle
dancing. They needed to be supplemented with persuasion and perhaps an
element of compromise. If the dance festivals were restricted in time, for
example, it would be a step in the right direction and would reduce the
accompanying neglect of agriculture. At a meeting with the Blackfoot chiefs at
agent G.H. Gooderhams office, it was agreed that the sun dance of the following
year would last only three days. In May 1923, Scott wrote to the agent proposing
that he remind the Indians of their accord. Gooderham called a meeting, but
his charges bluntly informed him that they needed ten days for the ceremony.
And when the sun dance was organized in July, the Indians took the ten days
that they required.[71]

Scott had more success in seeking limitations on dance festivals with the Cree
of the Hobbema agency. In May 1923, they asked for permission to hold a
two-day dance under police supervision, and the deputy superintendent agreed.
This acquiescence earned the following headline in the *Edmonton Journal*: "By
Special Permission of the Government Red Men Observe Weird Ceremony."
Several photographs accompanied the story which was related in a manner that
speaks for itself:

> A blue curl of smoke drifting upwards from grey ashes at the foot of a giant
> poplar pole that raises up into the sky; tom-toms beating; quick staccato
> jerks of sound from reed whistles; painted dancers in the shadow, swaying,
> jogging; a bright gleam of sunlight striking sharply through the bright open

patch of blue sky above onto moist, yet, copper bodies. The sun-dance of the Crees is on.[72]

Perhaps the journalist was entranced by the occasion. It is even more probable, however, that he merely set out to write a sensational story. Other accounts of the event were decidedly prosaic. The police reported that the dance camp had been orderly and that no contraventions of the act had taken place. The agent, W.G. Askey, was equally satisfied with the way things had gone.

Scott's tactic of granting permission for dances of limited duration met with mixed success. Nor was it universally approved of by those who worked closely with Indians in the west. In July 1923, the deputy superintendent received a letter signed by seventeen Oblate missionaries stationed in Alberta and Saskatchewan, including Father P. Moulin of the Hobbema mission. The priests expressed alarm at the recent revival of the sun dance, which was taking place, they believed, with the approval of the department. They urged Scott to take more vigorous measures to suppress "the old paganism".[73]

The reaction of Commissioner Graham was equally predictable. When he heard that headquarters had permitted the Hobbema dance without consulting him, he wrote an indignant letter to Scott. Not only was he outraged at what he perceived to be an undermining of his authority, but he also predicted that when news got out that the Hobbema Indians had been permitted to dance, there would be an epidemic of dancing everywhere.[74] Graham was undoubtedly aware that the fall of the Meighen government in 1921 had greatly weakened his ability to influence policy matters at headquarters. The fact that he was frequently bypassed on decisions affecting the prairie region was evidence enough that the autocratic powers he wished to assume in his domains were being whittled away. He nonetheless persisted in his campaign for additional authority to suppress dancing. Though he filled his letters with graphic accounts of the triumph of weeds over crops on reserves, Ottawa failed to be moved.[75] Discouraging dancing and fostering the commissioner's beloved "summer fallowing" would have to be done under existing regulations.

In subsequent years, the sun and thirst dance gatherings were as elaborate and well attended as ever. Sometimes permission was forthcoming from the department; frequently, it was not. It did not really seem to matter. The dances went ahead anyway. And the clause forbidding attendance at dances off one's own reserve was openly defied. For instance, in July 1927 there were 951 Indians, including Blackfoot and Peigan, present at the Blood sun dance, which lasted for thirteen days. The police were usually in attendance, and their reports acknowledged the orderly behaviour and the general absence of liquor and fighting. An occasional arrest took place for "giving away," but these acts of illegal generosity were either kept to a minimum or indulged in secretly.

By the latter half of the 1920s, some Indian bands were beginning to hold "modern" dances on their reserves. At school or in everyday contact with the non-Indian world, they had learned jigs, waltzes, and other dances that might be accompanied by fiddle or gramophone Gatherings for this purpose usually took place in specially constructed dance halls during the winter months when the objection that they interfered with agriculture could hardly be raised. Some agents believed that they had a positive side to them because they might prove a viable substitute for aboriginal dances.

E.W. Stephenson, who was in charge of the Moose Mountain agency in Saskatchewan, was of this opinion. In February 1929, Graham heard that dances were taking place in that agency and immediately phoned Stephenson demanding an explanation. The agent pointed out that he had permitted a number of small gatherings involving two-steps and square dances to be held but that he continued to discourage native dances. This was less than satisfactory to the intrepid commissioner, who wrote to Stephenson two days later fulminating against all dancing. The form of the dance was of no consequence, he asserted. All such activities from polkas to pow-wows were injurious to the health of the Indians. He asked for the names of those who were holding dances and demanded to know if any of them were on the ration list. Stephenson felt that Graham was being unrealistic or incorrigibly stubborn. He wrote to Ottawa explaining his actions and enclosing his correspondence with the commissioner. Indians ought to be allowed a simple dance for recreation purposes now and again at the agent's discretion, he said. In this way, they could be induced to get their work done. Headquarters sustained Stephenson's position much to the chagrin of the hapless Graham.[76]

Indian resilience succeeded in negating the department's efforts to suppress their dance festivals throughout the 1920s. And they were equally successful in their defiance of regulations forbidding performances at fairs. The Calgary Stampede was revived in 1919, and it proved to be the principal source of difficulty in this respect. In May of that year, the secretary of the organizing committee wrote to Superintendent General Meighen explaining the plans that were afoot to hold a "grand victory stampede" in August in honour of the veterans. The plans included Indian participation in the parade and an Indian encampment on the fairgrounds. He hoped the department would co-operate. Shortly afterwards, a deputation representing the organizers called upon Scott and made the same request. He turned them down, pointing out that Graham was opposed to the idea and that it would interfere with the harvest. Meighen sustained Scott's objections, and the department refused to sanction Indian participation in the event. This did not deter the organizers. Counting on the department's reputation for irresolution, they defied the law and invited the Indians anyway. For their part, the Indians were only too willing to co-operate, and an elaborate performance in costume was staged at the Stampede. Graham later admitted that nothing would be gained by prosecuting the offenders.[77]

In 1923 the Calgary Exhibition joined with the Stampede organizers to turn the spectacle into an annual event and one of the leading "wild west" shows on the continent.[78] The question of Indian participation was to be a perennial thorn in the side of the department throughout the decade. When approached on the subject by the Stampede promoters in the spring of 1923, Scott displayed his customary obdurancy and refused to co-operate. But a direct appeal to Superintendent Charles Stewart, a former premier of Alberta, was more product- ive, and the deputy superintendent was overruled. Commissioner Graham later reported that the Indians had attended the Stampede in great numbers. Almost the entire Blackfoot tribe had been there, and thirteen days of work had been lost.[79]

Buoyed with the success of the 1923 event, the mayor of Calgary, G.H. Webster, approached Stewart in November regarding Indian performances at the Stampede planned for the following year. He observed that during the previous summer the Indians had been a major attraction and that visitors from the U.S., Britain and all parts of Canada had been very impressed. It was all for the good of Alberta. In commenting on this representation, Scott reminded the minister of the department's objections to exhibitions. But, cognizant of politi- cal reality, he added: "you will probably feel like acceding to the request." That being the case, he suggested that the department ought to keep the situation under control by letting Graham make all the arrangements.[80] This was agreed to, and Scott informed the commissioner of the decision noting, "It would be difficult for us to refuse this request." Graham subsequently met Webster and worked out the conditions of Indian participation. The Stampede would feature an exhibit of school work and handicrafts; about thirty lodges would be located inside the fair grounds; and some Indians would appear in the parade. Officials of the department were to supervise the entire operation.[81]

With the demise of prohibition and the general prosperity of the 1920s, the urge to celebrate became difficult to stifle. The success of the Calgary Stampede inspired many imitations. The organizers of the numerous fairs and exhibitions that enlivened the prairie landscape during the summer months invariably wanted Indian dances in their programs. And they learned from Calgary's example that the department's opposition to these performances could be circumvented by direct appeals to Stewart.

The success of these tactics drove Graham to virtual despair. He complained to Scott in May 1924 that the people of the west had gone "stampede crazy."[82] His persistent appeals for "special powers" and further amendments to the act in order to suppress dancing on reserves were accompanied by calls for similar measures to prevent Indians attending fairs. Scott tended to counsel moderation. He admitted that if Parliament were to pass an amendment making it illegal for Indians to leave their reserves without a permit, it would provide better control. He doubted, however, if such drastic legislation could be passed. Nor did he feel that it was desirable. Persuasion was preferable to coercion, he had decided, since the process of educating Indians "to a realization of the benefits of thrift and industry" was necessarily slow.[83] In his annual report for 1925-26, the deputy superintendent aired similar thoughts:

> The attraction of stampedes, pageants and annual fairs are powerful, and the programs of such celebrations seem opposed to the civilizing influences which are at work on the reserves. It has sometimes occurred to the undersigned that a drastic measure of restriction would be in the interest of the Indian. But reflection has always resulted in a return to the opinion that a policy of suasion and an appeal to reason and experience is best in the long run.[84]

Although Scott's public pronouncements continued to proclaim confidently that the department's policy of gradually weaning the Indians from barbarism through education and moral suasion was meeting with success, he evidently began to harbour some doubts about its efficacy towards the end of his incumbency. Indians continued to attend fairs and stampedes, and the sun and thirst dance festivals were as vibrant as ever. For instance, the police reported that about eighteen hundred Indians were present at the Blood sun dance of 1930, which lasted for eleven days.[85] Commissioner Graham never faltered in his condemnation of these activities or in his appeals for power to stop them.[86]

The doubts sown by the persistence of this evidence led Scott to the belief that Graham may have been right all along and that additional powers were necessary. He confessed his change of heart to Superintendent General T. Murphy in July 1931:

> we are quite powerless to prevent Indians from squandering their time and rendering nugatory our policy of making them self-supporting through farming operations.
>
> It is most necessary the Parliament should give the Superintendent General the power to control aboriginal customs and native restlessness of Indians. We have a feeble clause in the Indian Act which is inoperative, and I hope to be able to discuss with you fully and make recommendations looking forward to obtaining some effective statutory authority in these respects.[87]

It is not clear exactly what Scott had in mind. There were no modifications to the section of the act in question during his remaining months as deputy superintendent. A minor change was made, however, in 1933. In that year the phrase "in aboriginal costume" was deleted from subsection 3 of Section 140 (formerly Section 149).[88] The intent of this amendment was to prevent Indians attending fairs and stampedes without the department's approval. This restriction would apply regardless of whether they dressed themselves in "aboriginal" or in "civilized" costume.

The effect of these new powers was less than earth-shattering. The onset of the Depression had called for less grandiose celebrations and country fairs were experiencing rapid decline.[89] Nor did the restrictions appear to prevent Indians attending those that continued to be held.[90] The sun and thirst dances were hardly affected at all. They continued to play their role in the cultural, social, and religious lives of the prairie Indians.[91] Like all customs, of course, they were subject to change over the years. Photographs of sun dance gatherings on the Blood reserve in the 1940s, for example, show the centre pole being brought to camp in rubber-tired wagons and an automobile forming part of the parade.[92] Mandelbaum reported that during the 1930s the pow-wow was the most common social activity among the Cree. It was a secular dance at which food and tobacco were given away, and it was gradually replacing the older religious ceremonies.[93] The section of the act which forbade Indian dances and festivals was increasingly a dead letter, and it was dropped in the major revision that took place in 1951. Traditional dances and ceremonies are celebrated today without interference.

The attempt to suppress dancing was perfectly consistent with the ultimate goal of government policy — the complete assimilation of the Indians. Dance festivals reflected cultural, social, and religious values that were antipathetic to those of the dominant society, and their persistence tended to counteract the process of transformation that was being pursued.

By the time Scott took charge of the department, the law proscribing certain native customs had become an object of ridicule. As in the case of other aspects of policy, he did not question the fundamental premises of the assault on dancing. He was cognizant, however, of the limited success that had hitherto greeted the experiment, and he resolved to find more effective ways of proceeding. His initial contribution to this struggle was to invoke additional powers for his officials. But during the prosperous 1920s, a decade of dance crazes and general frivolity, the restrictions of Section 149 appeared increasingly incongruous. When the more adamant department officials insisted on pursuing the letter of the law, they merely created incidents which embarrassed the government. Nor did Indian resistance abate. Scott was forced to the realization that coercion was of limited value, and he maintained his support for moderation, at least until shortly before his retirement.[94]

The department consistently underestimated the Indians' determination to prevent the destruction of their traditional culture. The Indians were not amenable to either persuasion or coercion. This is not to suggest that no change was taking place. It was, but prairie Indian culture had never been a static entity. The transformation was as much the product of conscious adaptation as it was the result of the department's designs.

10

The Ambitions of Commissioner Graham

It has been clearly shown that Scott's relations with the Indians were invariably strained and frequently openly antagonistic. This tension was inevitable considering his persistent refusal to take Indian wishes into account when formulating policy or implementing it. He was also obliged to deal with a veritable army of subordinate officials in the department and here, in spite of shared aims, relations were not always harmonious. The spirit of mutual co-operation was often conspicuously absent in Scott's dealings with William Morris Graham, a man who aspired to be his successor. This relationship is interesting for its entertainment value, but it also reveals important features of the internal dynamics of the department and another side of Scott's behaviour as a bureaucrat.

Graham's career in the Indian service paralleled Scott's. Both men were ambitious, and they shared that unquestioning belief in the wisdom of established policy which is the hallmark of the effective official. Graham, who served as Indian commissioner for the prairie provinces throughout the 1920s, was determined to carve out the maximum degree of autonomy for himself in his western domains. Scott, long an advocate of centralized decision-making, resisted this tendency. This difference of opinion was compounded by their personal incompatibility. And each was gripped with the fear that the whims of political fortune would work to the advantage of the other. W.M. Graham was born in the Ottawa Valley on 11 January 1867, one of nine children fathered by James F. Graham. The elder Graham went west with the Wolseley expedition in 1870. He joined the Indian department some years later and ultimately became a senior official in the Manitoba superintendency.[1] Both the challenge and the security of his father's occupation attracted W.M. Graham, and in December 1885 he found employment with the Department of Indian Affairs as a clerk in the Moose Mountain agency. Following a decade of satisfactory service, he was transferred to the commissioner's office in Regina in March 1895. A year later, an unexpected opportunity arose for the ambitious young clerk. An immediate replacement for the agent at File Hills was required, and Graham was chosen. His performance impressed his superiors, and in July 1897 he was appointed agent on a permanent basis.[2]

This was a time of reorganization and retrenchment in the department. Superintendent General Clifford Sifton's campaign to reduce expenditure and increase efficiency was well underway. Incompetent officials were being weeded out of the service while greater responsibility was being thrust on the shoulders of those who displayed initiative. In February 1901, Sifton decided to fire J.A. Mitchell, the agent at Muscowpetung, and to amalgamate that agency with File Hills. The new agency was to be known as Qu'Appelle, and it was placed in the hands of Graham, who had "shown particular ability in leading the Indians to become self-supporting."[3]

While agent at Qu'Appelle, Graham established the File Hills colony. The evident success of this experiment did not go unnoticed in Ottawa, and he was promoted to the position of inspector of Indian agencies for the South Saskatchewan Inspectorate in February 1904.[4] Graham proved to be a tireless and efficient administrator. He devoted himself energetically to the promotion of education and agriculture among the Indians—the twin pathways to civilization and self-sufficiency. And yet he was always ready to sell off "surplus" Indian land—a process that was counterproductive to the achievement of the latter objective. John Tootoosis recalled how Graham used to stack money on a table in an effort to entice Indians to part with their land.[5]

The Indians had little love for the man who attempted to control their every thought and action. He was widely feared and was perceived as "harsh, domineering and inflexible." The Saskatchewan Cree knew him as Kes-Ke-Kat—"the man with the cut-off leg"—since Graham hobbled about on a wooden leg as a result of a childhood accident.[6] Perhaps his intransigent opposition to dancing in all its forms arose from this unfortunate affliction.

Graham's devotion to the department's aims was coupled with intense personal ambition. By 1904 he could be reasonably satisfied with the progress he had made through the bureaucratic echelons. The abolition of the commissioner's office in Winnipeg in 1909, however, eliminated the next logical step on the promotional ladder. This did not stop him looking further afield, to the very pinnacle of the department, the deputy superintendency. Political patronage was one of the keys to advancement in the public service, and Graham was blessed with a connection of impeccable pedigree. His wife, Violette, was a sister of Arthur Meighen's wife's step-father.[7] Although the relationship was somewhat tenuous, Violette Graham was regarded in the family as Meighen's aunt and in her correspondence with him (in which she addressed him as "Dear Arthur") she signed herself "Aunt Vi."[8] Alice Tye, who served as Graham's secretary throughout most of his career, provided a further connection. She was a cousin of Violette Graham and was also related to Meighen, with whom she corresponded regularly. By attaching themselves to the rising star of the Conservative politician, the Grahams had reason to believe that the possibilities were limitless.

The Conservative victory in 1911 and the appointment of Meighen as solicitor general were omens of good fortune. But hopes were dashed when Scott was selected as deputy superintendent in 1913. Relations between Graham and Scott were soon strained. Much of the blame lay with the former, who had acquired a paranoid delusion that officials at headquarters, including Scott, were plotting against him and were determined not only to prevent further promotions, but also to force his resignation.

Graham wrote to Meighen in January 1914, revealing the sordid conspiracy which he believed was afoot. He also implicated Scott in the blatant patronage which he claimed characterized the department's business dealings.[9] Meighen did not keep the letter confidential; he showed it to Superintendent General W.J. Roche asking that Scott and McLean be advised to use "reasonable judgement" in dealing with Graham. Roche, who was already aware of the tension between his officials, asked Scott to comment on the most recent accusations and received the following reply:

> When last session during your absence I promised that correspondence with Mr. Graham should be void of offence so far as possible. I undertook a somewhat difficult task as Mr. Graham cannot be written to as we would write to another inspector, but our directions must be expressed with as much care as if we were diplomatists addressing a foreign power.[10]

Graham's touchiness and penchant for finding insult and reproach where none was intended was part of the problem. It affected not only his relations with headquarters, but also those with his subordinates. In fact, so bad was the state of affairs between himself and the agent at Qu'Appelle that he did not visit the agency for three years.[11]

Graham craved greater autonomy in directing operations in South Saskatchewan. It irritated him that so many decisions, especially those involving expenditure, required the approval of Ottawa. The decentralization that he advocated was contrary to the longstanding trend of administrative practice within the department. But he believed that it would result in greater efficiency and more immediate results. After all, officials such as himself were infinitely more familiar with western conditions than the distant mandarins in Ottawa. There was a certain logic to this argument, but it made little impression at headquarters. Scott and his senior officials were insistent on controlling the purse-strings, and their dilatoriness in dealing with requests from the west tended to infuriate the impatient inspector.

In August 1917, Graham appealed to Ottawa for authority to hire additional clerical help. When he was refused he was so indignant that he threatened to resign. If he expected his superiors to be shocked into a state of contrition, he was soon disappointed. The prime minister's office informed Scott of the pending calamity, but he assured his superiors that the department would survive Graham's departure:

> Mr. Graham is in some respect an excellent officer and has done good work in the Department. He has received very cordial support from me and I have as far as possible advanced his schemes and interests, but I do not always share his extraordinary opinion of his own ability and importance.[12]

Scott went on to say that he had received no official notice of Graham's intention of resigning, but that if it were submitted, it would be carefully considered. A few days later, in a letter to W.J. Roche, he observed:

> I do not think that Inspector Graham's resignation would have a disastrous effect on the Indians, in fact, we might have a rearrangement of the work to the distinct benefit of the Department. Mr. Graham is labouring under the delusion that he is indispensible; if he resigned, a couple of telegrams would be all that would be necessary for me to send in order to make the necessary arrangements for the time being to carry on the work.

There was no official letter of resignation. Graham had written to Meighen threatening to leave if he did not get more support. This message had reached the Prime Minister's office, from whence it was passed on to the department. Superintendent General Roche resented Graham's attempts to circumvent the normal channels of communication and authority and he sent the inspector a stiff rebuke, accusing him of employing the same political influence that he was so quick to condemn in others.[13]

Graham was but temporarily chastized. Shortly afterwards, Meighen replaced Roche as superintendent general, and the temperamental inspector could no longer be ignored. It was under these circumstances that Graham proposed the Greater Production Scheme. His appointment as commissioner for greater production led in 1920 to the re-creation of the position of commissioner of Indian affairs for the three prairie provinces. The post was especially created for Graham, and it seemed to give him that extra authority he had long coveted. He was also pleased to discover that Scott's attitude to him had changed and was now supportive and even friendly. Scott's visit to Regina (where the commissioner's office was located) in September 1920 appears to have been extremely cordial and in the following months the two officials exchanged letters bearing warm greetings and kindest regards.[14]

But the halcyon days of power and influence were short-lived. Before 1921 was out, Mackenzie King's Liberals had come to power in Ottawa, and Meighen, who had briefly served as prime minister, was banished to the opposition benches. It was quickly brought home to Graham that his grandiose schemes had been tolerated by Scott for only as long as Meighen remained in office. In February 1922, the deputy superintendent informed the commissioner that it was the department's policy to close the greater production farms as soon as possible. The practice of leasing reserve lands to white farmers was to be abandoned because such lands had often been neglected, abused, and rendered useless. Seeking the surrender of "surplus Indian lands" and selling them to settlers was to continue as before.[15]

The demise of his agricultural empire was a serious blow to Graham's pride, and it seemed that capricious fortune had once again thwarted his ambitions. There was no doubt in his mind that Scott was entirely to blame for this adverse turn of events, and relations between the two visibly deteriorated. So concerned was the commissioner about the situation—his fear of a conspiracy had been resurrected again—that he took the matter up with Superintendent General Charles Stewart. He explained that the strained relations had existed before the war but that in the interim they had improved. Nevertheless, "from the very day that the present Government came into power, Mr. Scott has again assumed his former attitude and began to make things unpleasant for me." The phasing out of the Greater Production Scheme was clear evidence of this.

The commissioner was never reticent in alluding to his own expertise, as the following passage in his letter illustrates:

> Scarcely a day passes without a letter indicating the antagonistic attitude of Mr. Scott towards me. Mr. Scott was always opposed to such wide powers being given to me, but as the problem here is almost entirely an agricultural one, I think you will agree that in order to put into effect an agressive policy it is necessary that someone with practical experience should have such powers and authority.

Graham cited several instances in which Scott interfered with the plans he had formulated for implementing policy. The real problem, he believed, was the deputy superintendent's refusal to delegate real responsibility to him.[16]

Stewart passed the letter to Scott asking him to respond to the allegations therein. The deputy superintendent admitted that differences of opinion existed between himself and Graham. But they arose, he pointed out, because the latter sought "autocratic control" while the department was only prepared to concede that which was consistent with effective adminstration. And he expressed serious doubts about the Greater Production Scheme: "the success of the grain-growing features of the scheme do not seem to me very remarkable." In fact, he had proposed the closure of the government farms in May 1920, since the ultimate aim was to get the Indians to work their own individual holdings. Indeed, he had evidence that the general work of the department had been neglected because of Graham's devotion to Greater Production:

> Mr. Graham is always prone to refer to a past with which he was not connected as an era of failure and incompetency, but so far as his own responsibility goes, he neglected Manitoba for five years and paid but little attention to it.

Scott felt obliged to inform the minister that Graham was difficult to work with and had always been so:

> Unfortunately, it has been my duty for a long time to keep him smoothed out, and my papers contain evidences of friction and trouble which I have endeavoured to allay. If my strenuous experiences with this gentleman have resulted in a somewhat cooling of my personal feeling towards him, he himself is to blame.[17]

As in most matters, Stewart accepted Scott's judgment. The unfortunate Graham found himself increasingly alienated from headquarters, and his delusions of a conspiracy were constantly reinforced by slights, real or imagined.

His frequent complaints about being overworked and underpaid tended to be ignored. In 1923, for instance, he asked that the department pay the rent on his house as well as the fuel, light, and water bills. Scott estimated that these benefits, when added to his salary of $4,800 and the $60.00 per month he was paid for the use of his car on government business, would give him a total remuneration of $7,200 per annum—an extravagant rate of pay. In fact, the deputy superintendent proposed that the car allowance be withdrawn and that a mileage rate be substituted. Stewart agreed and informed Graham of the decision.[18] The commissioner's reaction can only be imagined.

The friction between Scott and Graham continued in the following years, and the question of the latter's authority was usually at issue. In May 1924, for example, Scott disallowed expenditure that had already been approved by the commissioner. That action brought the following exasperated response from Regina:

> the difficulty is that I can scarcely make a move without obtaining authority. In many cases I know perfectly well that there are lots of funds and it is just a matter of writing to ask "May I do this?" I am not entrusted with the necessary authority. No business concern could function successfully under these conditions.[19]

The animosity persisted until May 1927, when Graham became ill. Scott approved a leave of absence of five weeks' duration. Shortly afterwards, Mrs. Graham, who had been in poor health throughout the winter, was advised to go to the Atlantic coast in order to recuperate, and Scott agreed that Graham should accompany her. This incident improved relations between the two officials. Scott was in Regina in September and his discussions with the commissioner were friendly and mutually supportive.[20] He even listened sympathetically while Graham indulged in his habitual complaints about his financial situation. And he indicated that he would attempt to have the rent on Graham's house readjusted favourably.[21]

Scott was conscious that such a readjustment would cause "a fuss" with the auditor general and he was hesitant to act upon his promise when back in Ottawa. Graham continued to make demands, and his letters to headquarters indicated that he believed Scott was supporting him. By April 1929, the commissioner was asking for a salary increase and that the rent and fuel costs for his house be paid entirely by the department. Scott informed him that the Civil Service Commission would probably not agree to a salary increase unless it could be shown that the rent charged on his house was excessive. Upon making inquiries with a Regina real estate firm, Scott was advised that the estimated annual rental value of Graham's house was $1,200, which was precisely what was being paid for it.

Even when he was told that nothing could be done about his situation, Graham continued to complain. He pointed out in one instance that the police commissioner was far better off financially than he was. This line of argument ultimately tried the patience of officials at headquarters. Scott's irritation was evident in June 1929 when he asked Graham to spell out the precise nature of his demands. The commissioner replied that he would be satisfied were his salary increased from $4,800 to $6,400. Scott found this unacceptable and told Graham that there was little likelihood that the Civil Service Commission would consider such a raise. And he informed Stewart that the commissioner was the highest paid government official in the west and that his salary was "fair and reasonable."[22]

Graham's failure to improve his financial sitution caused his relations with Scott to deteriorate once more, and the delusions of a conspiracy against him appeared again. But there was a glimmer of hope on the not too distant horizon. It was rumoured that Scott was likely to retire in 1932 when he reached seventy, although this was by no means a foregone conclusion. Graham would be sixty-five in that year, and he believed that he was the logical and deserving candidate to take over as department head. Five years as deputy superintendent would at once put him on a firmer financial footing, and it would be a fitting reward for a life devoted to the service.

A further portent of good fortune was the return to power of the Conservatives in 1930. It was regrettable, of course, that Arthur Meighen was no longer at the helm. After the debacle of 1926, he had lost his seat in the Commons and had abandoned politics for a career in business. His relations with the new party leader, R.B. Bennett had always been strained, but Meighen still had many friends in politics. When the Conservatives again formed a government, he could not be ignored. The Depression had dulled the lustre of his business ventures, and when Bennett offered him a Senate appointment with a cabinet post of government leader in that chamber early in 1932, he accepted.[23] Even though he was only fifty-eight at the time, he had acquired the status of elder statesman and could be expected to wield some influence with the prime minister. It seemed that the stage was set for Graham's ultimate promotion. And were it not for the scandal that marred his reputation on the eve of Scott's retirement, the dream might indeed have been realized. The Antapa Shooting Club affair sealed his fate.[24]

In 1924 the Antapa Shooting Club of Regina, of which Graham was a member, attempted to secure a lease for duck-hunting purposes to Antapa Point, part of the Pasqua Indian reserve. A document was drawn up offering the sum of $150 per annum to the band for these rights, and it was submitted to Indian Affairs headquarters for approval. In January 1925, Scott returned the proposed lease to Graham explaining that it had not been properly executed since the Indians had not agreed to the terms.

In the following year a rival claim to the property was made. Local politician D.H. McDonald brought forward an offer of $550 per annum for shooting privileges and won the approval of the Pasqua band. Ottawa refused to sanction the agreement, however, alleging that McDonald represented a group of New York millionaires. Scott, who was now on good terms with Graham, likely rejected the lease because he knew of the commissioner's interest in the property. Some time later he wrote to E.B. Jonah, an official of the Antapa Club, enclosing a copy of the McDonald agreement and suggesting that the club draw up a similar document and obtain the signature of a majority of voting band members. A new Antapa lease, which raised the rental to $550, was subsequently put together.[25]

News of this underhanded manoeuvre apparently got out. McDonald was furious, and the Indians refused to co-operate. When Scott visited Regina in September 1927, he found "quite a demonstration" against the lease. But he was entertained lavishly by Graham and other local dignitaries who were members of the Shooting Club, and he evidently agreed to approve the Antapa lease in spite of the furore. He confided later to Graham:

> Judge McKay[26] whispered to me at the luncheon that they would like to elect me an honorary member of the Club, but I think that it would be

unwise owing to the friction and I having to take the responsibility of approving the lease. You might mention this to the Judge.[27]

And Graham responded:

I think you are quite right, but I do not anticipate any trouble at all. McDonald may try to start something, but this is expected. I will give Judge McKay the message that you sent me. I appreciate your position in this matter.[28]

Scott was conscious of the irregularities involved in this transaction, but he did approve the lease, and it became effective 14 January 1928. It was not an unusual course of action, given well-established departmental highhandedness with Indian land. The Indians continued to protest, but they discovered that they were powerless in the face of an unbudging bureaucracy. Typical of the department's response to their representations is this excerpt from a letter which Scott wrote to Chief Ben Pasqua in February 1931.

It has been decided that this lease is of decided advantage to your band and sufficient reason has not at any time been advanced which, in our estimation, would justify cancellation.[29]

The department's authoritarianism was only part of the problem. Clause 6 of the Antapa Club's lease harboured the embryo of far greater controversy. It read as follows:

It is further agreed that the lessee shall not nor will sell or permit or suffer to be sold on the said premises any spirituous liquors, ale, beer, or any intoxicating liquors whatever, except to members of the said Club.[30]

Even though prohibition had met its unmourned demise early in the decade, public phobia about the availability of alcohol was still stubbornly alive. And the association between Indians and alcohol was as contentious as ever. In fact, the Indian Act expressly forbade the taking of liquor onto reservations. Yet here was a lease, secured for a privileged club through the influence of a leading government official, which appeared to allow intoxicants on Indian land. The Antapa clubhouse was located on private property, but the usual means of access was by a road that crossed the Pasqua reserve. The lease implied that liquor could be taken to the clubhouse, thereby crossing Indian land. And its phrasing was sufficiently ambiguous to permit members to take liquor to the reserve property leased for hunting purposes. It was a situation rife with potential controversy.

It might never have entered the public domain but for the intervention of J.S.

Woodsworth, MP for Winnipeg North Centre. He was apprised of the Antapa affair by P.N.B. Galwey-Foley, an Irishman of allegedly unstable disposition who was critical of the government's Indian policy. On 4 May 1931 Woodsworth asked a series of questions in the House of Commons regarding the Antapa lease and demanded a copy of the document and of all related correspondence. With this information in his hands, he exposed the sordid details of the affair in the House on 13 July 1931. Graham was depicted as the prime villain:

> I would charge this: That there has been a series of misrepresentations by the Department; that Commissioner Graham, a member of the Antapa Club, through misrepresentations, managed to secure the refusal of the lease to one party, and to secure the lease for the Club of which he was a member. I think that is a matter which requires departmental action. I know this cannot be settled today, but I have taken this occasion to lay it before the house, and I think the minister would be well advised to consider the statement that his own commissioner, a public official, who is a member of the Club, has managed to secure these privileges through misrepresentation of the general situation.
>
> I have already pointed out that the clause with regard to liquor violates the terms of the Indian Act, a copy of which I have under my hand and which I can read if necessary. The lease is illegal as being granted without the consent of the band and undoubtedly the whole transaction constitutes a grievance which the Indians feel deeply.[31]

These accusations were as much directed at the previous regime as they were at the government of the day. The events that Woodsworth related had taken place when the Liberals had been in power, and, after all, the Winnipeg socialist had long been a critic of corruption in Mackenzie King's administration. Nonetheless, Prime Minister R.B. Bennett took a particular interest in the case. In his previous role as leader of the Opposition, he had been critical of the Indian Department and its policies in the west. His attitude may have been influenced by letters he had received on the subject, such as the one addressed to him in early May 1930 by Regina building contractor, J. Mayoh. Mayoh disclosed that Graham was known locally as the "Kaiser of the West." The commissioner was allegedly a "job holder" who knew nothing of Indians even after more than forty years in the service. He generally avoided reserves, except for File Hills, his special project, where he was wont to dispense supplies lavishly. His advancement in the department, Mayoh claimed, had been mainly due to the connection with Arthur Meighen.[32] There was an element of hyperbole in this attempt at defamation, but it introduced Bennett to the negative features of Graham's activities and led him to greet with some scepticism the representations he received on behalf of the commissioner when the question of Scott's replacement arose.

Graham's most vigorous and persistent promoter was his long-serving secretary, Alice Tye. She took the initiative in advancing his claim to the deputy superintendency in January 1932 in letters addressed to the prime minister. She argued that the commissioner deserved the position. In her opinion, Scott was "fonder of Arts and Letters than of Indians" while Graham was "fonder of Indians than of Arts and Letters." She urged Bennett to permit Graham to plead his own case since forces "near the centre of the wheels" were conspiring not only to block his appointment, but to force his early retirement.[33] This was the first of many indications from the Regina faction that it believed that Scott was deliberately attempting to sabotage the ultimate promotion that Graham so ardently desired.

The prime minister's reply was far from reassuring. He commended Tye for her loyalty to Graham, but he was obviously less than happy with the commissioner's role in the Antapa affair:

> That you desire to help Mr. Graham is comprehensible; that he deserves to be helped is incomprehensible. During the last session of parliament the allegation that he was a member of a Club, the members of which, with his knowledge, were carrying liquor across the Indian Reserve, caused the government much embarrassment, and I have seen no adequate explanation of the fact.[34]

Graham was evidently shocked at Bennett's response. He contacted his friends in the Antapa Club and appealed for their support. The membership of the club was drawn from the local elite—lawyers, judges, businessmen, politicians—individuals whose opinions carried some weight in Ottawa. As a consequence of Graham's request, several letters from Regina dignitaries were sent to Bennett in February exonerating the commissioner in the affair. Some of the correspondents even attempted to blame Scott because he had signed the lease containing the liquor clause.

The prime minister was intially sceptical at what appeared to be an orchestrated campaign. He was impressed, however, when one of Graham's supporters turned out to be Sir Frederick W.G. Haultain, chief justice of the Saskatchewan Court of Appeal and the former chairman of the North-West Executive Committee in the days of territorial government in the west. Like the others, Haultain argued that the commissioner had not been involved in the lease negotiations, and he expressed surprise at Scott's acquiescence in such an agreement in view of prevailing liquor laws. Bennett replied that "so far as Mr. Graham is concerned, the explanation apparently affords a complete answer to any complaints that may be made against him."[35]

Meanwhile, Graham had protested his own innocence to the prime minister. He insisted that the lease negotiations had taken place between department officials in Ottawa and club members without his personal involvement. He claimed that prior to Woodsworth's questions in the House the previous July, he had never seen the lease and was surprised to learn that it contained the liquor clause. He had received a telegram from Scott on 15 July (two days after Woodsworth's revelations) asking him to consult with club officials to see if they would consent to the cancellation of the controversial clause. Only then had he set eyes on the document. If anyone was to blame for the embarrassment to the government, it was Scott. The deputy superintendent, after all, had signed the lease and must have been aware of its contents. Graham ended his letter by saying that it probably was not the first time that erroneous impressions of his character had been conveyed to Bennett—an oblique reference to the conspiracy by Scott that was supposedly afoot.[36]

Graham was being less than honest. He had been involved in the lease negotiations right from the start. His discussion with Scott during the latter's visits to Regina in September 1927 is ample proof. His ignorance of the liquor clause is therefore improbable. And he must have been aware that alcohol was consumed regularly on the Antapa Club premises, a fact that was frankly admitted by several of the members who wrote to Ottawa on his behalf. Shifting responsibility for the episode to Scott was hardly fair, although the deputy superintendent was certainly implicated. Both men had arrogantly assumed that they could bend the rules to their liking, and if what they did was dishonest or even illegal, there was little likelihood of having to account for it someday. Scott, however, had been shrewd enough to distance himself from the centre of any potential controversy by refusing Judge McKay's offer of honorary membership in the Antapa Club. And, being located in Ottawa, he was in a better strategic position to protect his interests when the scandal erupted.

Scott's political influence, in fact, continued to be the principal source of concern to the Regina faction. As weeks passed and anxiety mounted, Graham's wife and secretary realized that the Meighen card was the one to be played. Violette Graham wrote to Meighen on 30 January, urging him to intercede with Bennett on behalf of her husband. The family had hoped that the commissioner's "wonderful record" would be recognized now that the Conservatives were back in power and that he would get the promotion he deserved. Mrs. Graham was convinced that the entire Antapa affair and the hostility evident in the prime minister's recent letter to Alice Tye was the sinister work of D.C. Scott, who had always had "an uncanny ability to make Bill [Graham] appear in a wrong light." She felt that the deputy superintendent was manoeuvring mischievously behind the scenes to prevent her husband's promotion. It made her sick that "a sneak like Scott" could put that over.[37]

Alice Tye was equally convinced of a Scott conspiracy. She wrote twice to the former Conservative leader at the beginning of February appealing for his intervention. She explained that she had been shocked by Bennett's letter. Upon reflection, nevertheless, she felt that the episode might have a silver lining "if it proves to the powers that be just what sort of man is blocking cousin Bill's progress." She even accused the deputy superintendent of deliberately inserting the liquor clause in the Antapa lease in order to discredit Graham! Now that Meighen was in the Senate, he could surely make certain that justice was done. "We know that Scott would do anything to keep cousin Bill from being Deputy, and it may be too late now to counteract his influence—I hope not."[38]

As these frantic appeals made their way to Ottawa, Graham received an ominous indication that Scott was indeed working against him. On 3 February, the deputy superintendent wired, ordering him to close the Muscowpetung greater production farm and to discharge all staff. This was the surviving remnant of Graham's grandiose scheme of 1918. Was its enforced demise a portent of his own fate? He protested against Scott's orders, explaining the difficulty of selling stock during the Depression, but to no avail. Scott was adamant, and further instructions arrived demanding the immediate sale of the farm regardless of the arrangements that would have to be made.[39] This was depressing news for Graham, and he too felt obliged to take up his case with Meighen, objecting to Scott's attitude and outlining the agricultural progress he had made with the Indians.

Senator Meighen was willing to help his despairing friends and impressed upon the prime minister that Graham had been "for many years the best man in the Indian service" and would not dream of tolerating violations of liquor regulations. In their discussions, Bennett mentioned that the commissioner's office in Regina was likely to be closed. Meighen again objected, but he was reluctant to interfere too much with another man's portfolio.[40]

News of the possible closure of the office was a further blow to the Graham morale. And worse was to come. By mid-March the newspapers were announcing Scott's imminent retirement. Graham was prominent on the list of his possible successors, but it was believed that his age was against him and that he would be superannuated. Tye and Violette Graham were outraged at this suggestion; they both felt that "Bill" could serve the department for at least another five years. Tye appealed once more to Meighen, this time, with a sense of urgency that bordered on desperation. She claimed that retirement would break Graham's heart, and she urged the senator to press for his promotion even if he was accused of nepotism: "Now is the chance to make all come right and you really must not fail us."[41]

Violette Graham was equally frantic. When she read in the newspaper on 17 March that her husband was to be retired, she made a hysterical phone call to Meighen. She was calmer, if not more rational, on the following day and put her thoughts on paper for the benefit of the senator. She complained of the way in which Scott was able to "hypnotize" everyone into doing his bidding. He had been planning to close the Regina office ever since it had opened, and at last he was succeeding. She believed that he would have retired years ago but that he could not stand that thought of "Bill" going to Ottawa in his place. Now that her husband had reached his sixty-fifth birthday and would soon be "safely out of the Department," Scott himself would retire. She begged Meighen to do anything that he could.[42]

Meighen responded to these eleventh hour pleadings by taking up the matter with Superintendent General Thomas Murphy. He even showed the minister Mrs. Graham's letter containing the allegations against Scott. And in a note scribbled on the back of the letter, he added that Scott was "a mere child in business capacity compared to Graham—and [had] the jealousies inevitable in that relationship."[43] Murphy informed the senator that the office of the commissioner of Indian affairs in Regina would be closing on the last day of the month—the same date as Scott's retirement. Graham would be retiring on that date as well, and the work of his office would be divided among three inspectors. The Superintendent General insisted that the decision to close the office had been entirely his. He assured Meighen that Scott had always "spoken well of Mr. Graham's ability as a businessman" although he was aware that relations between the two men "were not of the best."[44]

One of Graham's motivations in seeking the office of deputy superintendent had been to improve his financial situation. At retirement he was granted an annual pension of $4,200—a considerable sum in those days and all the more so given the prevailing economic circumstances. He was, nonetheless, dissatisfied. Bitter and disillusioned, he took the advice of his doctor and spent a few months vacation in England during the summer of 1932. Upon his return in September, he met Meighen in Toronto and complained again of Scott—"a most impractical man" who had never given him any assistance "in carrying on a most difficult work."[45]

Graham spent his retirement living quietly in Regina. His wife died in December 1939, and he followed her to the grave in March of the following year. The *Regina Leader Post* observed his passing with an editorial bearing the headline "W.M. Graham, Friend of Man." There was nothing here of the temperamental, autocratic official who treated Indians as mere pawns in the schemes with which he advanced his career. "Here was a man among men—a kindly, genial, helpful spirit who sent about doing good."[46]

Graham's obsession about a conspiracy at headquarters to impede his work and his career were probably groundless. Whatever Scott's faults, it is difficult to imagine him harbouring the vindictiveness and personal animosity of which he was accused. He did favour a more centralized authority structure in the department. The decision to close the commissioner's office in Winnipeg in 1909 had been made upon his recommendation.[47] He probably opposed its reopening in Regina in 1920. But while he worked throughout the 1920s to restrict the autonomy of the commissioner and thereby ensure uniformity of adminstrative practice, there is no evidence that he was conspiring to abolish the position.

The reorganization of the department that took place at the end of March 1932 was effected in the interests of economy. It was Thomas Murphy who ordered the commissioner's office to be closed. It is likely that he was influenced by Scott, who was always ready to reduce government expenditure. In fact, it was Scott who drew up the plans for the reorganization at Murphy's request. In a memorandum presented to the minister on 1 February 1932, the deputy superintendent proposed replacing the commissioner with an inspector for each of the three prairie provinces and a travelling auditor for the entire region. He recommended that Graham, Tye, and six other employees in Regina and Winnipeg be retired. Scott estimated that these measures would "certainly promote economy" without impairing efficiency and that the savings to the department could amount to $21,000 annually.[48] The reorganization paved the way for the modern adminstrative structure of the department.

Scott, then, had a hand in Graham's retirement, but hardly for reasons of petty jealousy. When both men left the service on 31 March 1932, A.S. Williams, the department's solicitor and assistant deputy superintendent, took charge in a temporary capacity while Scott's permanent successor was being chosen. Williams himself was a candidate for the job, and Scott, it seems, favoured him. But his reputation was tarnished in a letter to the prime minister from H.H. Stevens, minister of trade and commerce. Stevens told Bennett that Scott had secured Williams's elevation to the position of assistant deputy when J.D. McLean had retired in 1930. The deputy superintendent had added "Solicitor of the Department" to the job description, and since Williams was the only senior official around with the legal background, he could not avoid being selected by the Civil Service Commission. The appointment, Stevens added, had been "sneaked through" on 6 August 1930, the very last day of the old government.[49]

A considerable amount of lobbying took place over the vacant position. Some wanted a Catholic, arguing that Catholics were underrepresented in the department. A group based in Caughnawaga proposed the appointment of an Indian — specifically William B. Newell of that reserve who had graduated from Syracuse University. Among the hopeful candidates was the "Indian expert" Diamond Jenness. He applied directly to the prime minister, outlining his experience as an ethnologist with the Department of Mines and his extensive publications. They were all disappointed. Harold W. McGill, a physician based in R.B. Bennett's home town of Calgary, was the ultimate choice. His appointment was approved 13 October 1932.[50]

Scott's retirement was a long and pleasant affair. With his new wife Elise, he indulged in his passion for travel, visiting Europe on a number of occasions. England and Italy were his favourite destinations on the old continent. As the western world struggled with the exigencies of the Depression, he could be seen touring European capitals "doing theatres and music."[51] The Second World War put a halt to such pleasures, and the Scotts turned instead to the United States to satisfy their wanderlust. The "burden of the Indian" and the rancorous disputes with Commissioner Graham were long forgotten.

These years of retirement produced more poetry. Many of the poems in *The Green Cloister*, a collection of verse published in 1935, had European settings and were obviously inspired by the extensive sightseeing. Shortly before Scott's death, three more books appeared. *Walter J. Phillips* was a biographical tribute to the Canadian painter of that name; *The Selected Poems of Archibald Lampman* provided further evidence of Scott's tireless efforts on behalf of the literary reputation of his long-departed friend; and *The Circle of Affection* was an anthology of essays, poems and short stories, some old and some new.[52]

Duncan Campbell Scott died on 19 December 1947. His wife Elise left for Ceylon in the following year. She later moved to India where she came under the influence of Swamiji Yogeshwaranda.[53] The house on Lisgar Street, which had been Scott's home for most of his life, was demolished in 1957, to make way for commercial development.

Conclusion

Canadian Indian policy found its principal inspiration in the assumptions of nineteenth-century evangelical religion, cultural imperialism, and laissez-faire economics. The Indians were to be led, by whatever means possible, to "civilization." In less ambiguous terms, they were expected to abandon their own traditions and beliefs for the trappings of Euro-Canadian culture, including Christianity. Economic self-sufficiency was also part of this agenda. Successful adaptation to agriculture or wage labour would ensure that the native population no longer constituted a burden on the public purse. And this transformation would be accompanied by "amalgamation" with the rest of the populace so that the end result would be the disappearance of the Indians as a separate people. While the reserve system created a degree of isolation from society at large, it was perceived as an integral component of a transitional phase during which Indians still required the paternal guidance of church and state.

Most Indians did not share the policy makers' enthusiasm for the advantages of "civilization." They understood that civilization came in many shapes and sizes and that the edition being forced upon them was by no means preferable to that which they already possessed.

The absence of shared aims meant that Indian administration was constantly beset by difficulties and that Indians were generally regarded as "a problem." The intolerant ethnocentrism of the Anglo-Canadian elite, which was closely linked to prevailing notions of racial superiority, precluded the possibility of the co-existence of culturally diverse peoples within the same political entity. Tolerance, after all, would have implied a residue of self-doubt, and in the heyday of an empire upon which the sun supposedly never set, there was little likelihood of such ambivalence. Instead, the lingering guilt arising from conquest and expropriation was assuaged by the myth of duty and the delusion of paternal responsibility.

Duncan Campbell Scott, who never questioned the aims and assumptions of policy, took control of the Indian Department at a critical phase in its history. It was a period in which the first stirrings of a new Indian militancy was making itself felt. The old generation of war chiefs was passing away. Those who had acquired their status in battle were being replaced by new leaders educated in the white man's schools and increasingly able to manipulate the political and legal system of the dominant society. Men like Deskeheh, F.O. Loft, and Andrew Paull were of a new and troublesome breed who not only rejected the methods and objectives of the department, but who also knew how to oppose them effectively.

The catalogue of Indian grievances was lengthy. Although they varied from region to region, they included in one form or another the following: land claims, hunting and fishing rights, treaty rights, the erosion of reserves, religious freedom, cultural integrity, and the all-pervasive bureaucratic control of their lives. Agitation for redress created the first glimmerings of a pan-Indian consciousness. The vision of F.O. Loft, that all Indians shared common experiences and that only by creating an organization that transcended tribal boundaries could they overcome their disabilities, was potentially the most serious difficulty encountered by the department in Scott's day. It suggested that Indians were attempting to cast off the shackles of subjugation and reassert their autonomy and the importance of their own traditions. In these circumstances, the reserve was no longer a mere "pied à terre" as Scott called it,[1] but an embryonic national homeland. Nowhere was this more evident than in the case of the Six Nations, who went so far as to assert their own sovereignty.

Scott invariably underestimated the resilience of native culture. He continued to insist, in spite of evidence to the contrary, that the Indians were a "weird and waning race," destined ultimately to disappear. At the end of his career, he was as stubbornly convinced of this eventuality as he had been at its inception.

Organized opposition to the department generally prompted Scott to seek additional powers under the Indian Act. Clauses of a draconian nature were introduced to give the department's officials greater control of their charges. Existing clauses that had proven ineffective were amended so that they could no longer be circumvented or ignored. Even so, Scott was by no means the most inflexible or authoritarian official of his day. Had the incorrigible Commissioner Graham had his way, the western reserves would have been transformed into virtual penitentiaries. Scott was at least cognizant that there was a political price to be paid for powers of repression, and he was only prepared to support those measures which would bear the scrutiny of Parliament without undue controversy. He also believed that persuasion was a useful and necessary corollary of coercion.

In administering his department, Scott remained an almost obsessive penny-pinching book-keeper. Disbursing the public's money was a sacred trust. All expenditure had to be accounted for and justified. In his dealings with some issues, such as native health, this parsimonious approach was a disaster. In spite of this general restraint, however, the parliamentary vote for Indian Affairs increased steadily during Scott's incumbency. It doubled, in fact, between 1921 and 1931. But these gains were not a product of a new concern for native well-being or of a sudden conversion to generosity on Scott's part. The 1920s was a decade of prosperity and of increasing government expenditure in many areas, and it marked the beginnings of the welfare state in Canada. If more money was spent on Indians, it was not because they were receiving special attention.

The centralization of decision-making was a tendency which Scott encouraged. As communications with the west improved, it became possible to insist upon the approval of headquarters for decisions of even minor significance, especially those involving expenditure. Centralization was part of an ongoing effort to impose a degree of uniformity on Indian administration throughout the country. And yet complete uniformity was never really achieved. Nor was it actually sought. Certain clauses in the Indian Act, for instance, applied only to the western provinces and to the territories. Moreover, the terms of the various treaties were not identical, and many Indians had never been party to the treaty system.

Apart from these legal distinctions, Scott was convinced that not all Indians were at the same level of progress on the road to civilization. He believed that those in eastern Canada were the most advanced. Those in British Columbia came next in rank; those on the prairies were further down the scale; and those in the northern forests were at the most primitive stage. Uniformity in adminstrative practice was therefore out of the question. Scott was of the opinion, in fact, that most Indians in southern Ontario and Quebec no longer needed the protection of the state or of the reserve system and could be enfranchised immediately. It had been with this in mind that he had introduced compulsory enfranchisement in 1920. Abandoning wardship and their reserves would come later for the others, depending on how rapidly they progressed. The end result, of course, would be the same for all.

If Scott did not impose uniformity, he certainly provided continuity. He succeeded in winning the confidence of the various regimes that held power in Ottawa during his lengthy incumbency. The superintendent general invariably bowed to his superior knowledge and experience of Indian matters and accepted the prevailing policies and methods of the department. Amendments to the Indian Act were almost always instigated at the behest of the deputy superintendent; rarely did they come from the minister. As a result, Indian policy in 1932 was easily recognizable as the curious anachronism it had been nineteen years previously.

Duncan Campbell Scott was certainly a capable and efficient administrator. To his credit, he was not prone to the corrupt practices that had abruptly terminated the careers of some of his predecessors. Nonetheless, he lacked the vision to transcend the account books and the narrow strictures of the Indian policy that he inherited. The explanation, if there is one, may be in the fact that his position in the government was to Scott a mere source of income rather than an abiding passion. It provided him with the means to indulge in his real interests, the arts. As his friend, E.K. Brown, said of him:

> His work in the civil service interested him; but the centre of his life was not in his office, where he seldom came early, and never stayed late. After he retired his conversation did not run on the Indian department.[2]

Notes

NOTES TO CHAPTER ONE

1. David T. McNab, "Herman Merivale and Colonial Office Indian Policy in the Mid-Nineteenth Century," in Ian A.L. Getty and Antoine S. Lussier, eds., *As Long as the Sun Shines and Water Flows* (Vancouver: University of British Columbia Press, 1983).
2. *The Historical Development of the Indian Act*, Treaties and Historical Research Centre, P.R.E. Group, Indian and Northern Affairs (Ottawa, 1978), p. 3.
3. John L. Tobias, "Protection, Civilization, Assimilation: An Outline History of Canada's Indian Policy," *Western Canadian Journal of Anthropology* 6, no. 2 (1976): 13.
4. Alan G. Harper, "Canada's Indian Administration: The Treaty System," *America Indigena* 7, no. 2 (April 1947): 134.
5. G.F.G. Stanley, "As Long as the Sun Shines and Water Flows: An Historical Comment," in Getty and Lussier, *As Long as the Sun Shines and Water Flows*, p. 8.
6. *Historical Development of the Indian Act*, p. 12. In 1830 the Indian department was divided into two offices, one for Upper Canada under the lieutenant-governor and one for Lower Canada under the military secretary.
7. J.E. Hodgetts, *Pioneer Public Service: An Administrative History of the United Canadas* (Toronto: University of Toronto Press, 1955), pp. 213-18.
8. L.F.S. Upton, "The Origins of Canadian Indian Policy," *Journal of Canadian Studies* 8, no. 4 (November 1973): 51-60. See also J.W. Grant, *Moon of Wintertime: Missionaries and the Indians of Canada in Encounters since 1534* (Toronto: University of Toronto Press, 1984), pp. 71-86.
9. Alan G. Harper, "Canada's Indian Administration: The Treaty System," p. 135.
10. *Historical Development of the Indian Act*, pp. 23-24.
11. Ibid., pp. 27-29.
12. John S. Milloy, "The Early Indian Acts: Developmental Strategy and Constitutional Change," in Getty and Lussier, *As Long as the Sun Shines and Water Flows*, pp. 60-61.
13. Hodgetts, *Pioneer Public Service*, pp. 211-13.
14. L.F.S. Upton, *Micmacs and Colonists: Indian-White Relations in the Maritimes 1713-1867* (Vancouver: University of British Columbia Press, 1979), pp. 25-26.
15. Ibid., pp. 47-53.
16. Ibid., pp. 90-97. See also Joseph Howe, "Report on Indian Affairs" in H.F. McGee, ed., *The Native Peoples of Atlantic Canada* (Toronto: McClelland and Stewart, 1974), pp. 90-101.
17. Ibid., pp. 104-6.
18. Ibid., pp. 113-23.
19. Ibid., p. 149.
20. Robin Fisher, *Contact and Conflict: Indian-European Relations in British Columbia, 1774-1890* (Vancouver: University of British Columbia Press, 1977), pp. 44-45.
21. Ibid., pp. 66-67.
22. Ibid., pp. 95-96.
23. Ibid., pp. 160-65.
24. Ibid., p. 168.
25. Tobias, "Protection, Civilization, Assimilation," pp. 16-17.
26. T.L. MacInnes, "History of Indian Administration in Canada," *Canadian Journal of Economics and Political Science* 12 (February-November 1946): 388.
27. *Historical Development of the Indian Act*, p. 53.
28. Milloy, "The Early Indian Acts," p. 62.

29. Upton, *Micmacs and Colonists*, pp. 172-74.
30. Fisher, *Contact and Conflict*, p. 180.
31. Wilson Duff, *The Indian History of British Columbia* (Victoria: Provincial Museum of Natural History and Anthropology, 1964), p. 63.
32. G. Brown and R. Maguire, *Indian Treaties in Historical Perspective* (Ottawa: Research Branch, Department of Indian and Northern Affairs, 1979). There was a significant Metis or half-breed population in the west that also had to be considered. Some were admitted to the treaties and thereby acquired the legal status of Indians with all of its attendant benefits and disabilities. Others, however, were granted "scrip"—an entitlement to land or money designed to satisfy their historic claims. Those in the latter category no longer came under the jurisdiction of the federal Indian department and therefore are not of immediate concern in this study.
33. G.F.G. Stanley, *The Birth of Western Canada* (Toronto: University of Toronto Press, 1960), pp. 227-28.
34. Initially, the commissioner's office was located in Winnipeg but it was moved to Battleford when Dewdney became lieutenant governor of the North-West Territories. When Regina was selected as the new capital in 1883, the office was transferred to that city.
35. Jean Larmour, "Edgar Dewdney: Indian Commissioner in the Transition Period of Indian Settlement, 1879-1884," *Saskatchewan History* 33 (1980): 20. A provocative reinterpretation of developments at this time has suggested that Dewdney ruthlessly used his control over the distribution of rations to convince recalcitrant Indians to adhere to the treaties. It also implied that he deliberately thwarted the plans of some chiefs to establish an autonomous Indian territory. See John L. Tobias, "Canada's Subjugation of the Plains Cree, 1879-1885," *Canadian Historical Review* 64 (December 1983).
36. *The Indian Act, 1876*, S.C. 1876, c. 18 (39 Vict.).
37. It is worth observing that Indians were subject to civil and criminal laws in addition to the Indian Act.
38. *Historical Development of the Indian Act*, pp. 72-73.
39. Vankoughnet was born in Cornwall, Upper Canada, on 7 October 1836, of an old Loyalist family with important ties to the establishment. He became a junior clerk in the Indian department in February 1861 and rose in the ranks to succeed William Spragge as deputy superintendent general in 1874. See Douglas Leighton, "A Victorian Civil Servant at Work: Lawrence Vankoughnet and the Canadian Indian Department, 1874-1893," in Getty and Lussier, *As Long as the Sun Shines and Water Flows*, p. 105.
40. Ibid., pp. 108-9.
41. *Historical Development of the Indian Act*, p. 79.
42. Stanley, *The Birth of Western Canada*, p. 269.
43. Leighton, "A Victorian Civil Servant at Work," pp. 114-16.
44. For an analysis of Reed's career, see Brian Titley, "Hayter Reed and Indian Administration in the West," paper presented at the Western Canada Studies Conference, University of Alberta, November 1985.
45. *Historical Development of the Indian Act*, p. 97.
46. *An Act further to amend the Indian Act 1880*, S.C. 1884, c. 27 (47 Vict.).
47. *An Act further to amend the Indian Act*, S.C. 1895, c. 35 (58-59 Vict.).
48. *Historical Development of the Indian Act*, pp. 96-97.
49. Hall, "Clifford Sifton and Canadian Indian Administration, 1896-1905," *Prairie Forum* 2 (1977): 127.
50. Canada, House of Commons, *Debates*, 44, cols. 1984-85 (10 May 1897).
51. Hall, "Clifford Sifton and Canadian Indian Administration, 1896-1905," p. 129.
52. John W. Chalmers, *Laird of the West* (Calgary: Detselig, 1981), p. 65.
53. Hall, "Clifford Sifton and Canadian Indian Administration, 1896-1905," p. 130.
54. Chalmers, *Laird of the West*, p. 209.
55. Canada, House of Commons, *Debates*, 47, cols. 6854-55 (2 June 1898).
56. Hall, "Clifford Sifton and Canadian Indian Administration, 1896-1905," p. 132.
57. Ibid., p. 132
58. Ibid., p. 140.
59. Canada, House of Commons, *Debates*, 54, col. 2759 (10 April 1901).
60. Ibid., 67, col. 6960 (18 July 1904).
61. Canada, *Sessional Papers, Report of the Department of Indian Affairs for the Year ended 31 March 1908*, pp. xxv.
62. Canada, House of Commons, *Debates*, 60, col. 6422 (10 July 1903).
63. E. Brian Titley, "W.M. Graham: Indian Agent Extraordinaire," *Prairie Forum* 8 (1983): 26-28.
64. Canada, House of Commons, *Debates*, 67, col. 3054 (18 April 1902).
65. Ibid., 67, col. 6943 (18 July 1904).
66. Morris Zaslow, *The Opening of the Canadian*

North, 1870-1914 (Toronto: McClelland and Stewart, 1971), pp. 94-100.

67. Ibid., p. 146.
68. Canada, House of Commons, *Debates,* 60, cols. 7266-67 (23 July 1903).
69. Ibid., 74, cols. 948-49 (30 March 1906).
70. Ibid., 76, cols. 5422-23 (15 June 1906).
71. *Historical Development of the Indian Act,* p. 108.
72. With regard to the Oliver Act, see Public Archives of Canada (hereafter PAC), RG 10 (Records of the Department of Indian Affairs), vol. 6809, file 470-2-3, pt. 5.
73. *Report of the Department of Indian Affairs for the Year ended 31 March 1908,* p. 196.
74. *Report of the Department of Indian Affairs for the Year ended 31 March 1909,* pp. xx.
75. Canada, House of Commons, *Debates,* 93, col. 784 (1 December 1909).
76. Ibid., 100, cols. 5837-64 (22 March 1911).
77. Richard C. Daniel, *A History of Native Claims Processes in Canada, 1867-1979* (Ottawa: Research Branch, Department of Indian and Northern Affairs, 1980), pp. 116-17.
78. Laird was seventy-six years old in 1909, but there was no compulsory retirement age for public servants and pensions were negligible (Chalmers, *Laird of the West,* pp. 252-55).
79. "The Alienation of Indian Reserve Lands during the Administration of Sir Wilfrid Laurier, 1896-1911," a report prepared for the Federation of Saskatchewan Indians by Tyler and Wright Research Consultants Ltd., Ottawa, March 1978, pp. 223-25. The story of Pedley's demise is also told (with predictable inaccuracy) by Pierre Berton in *The Promised Land* (Toronto: McClelland and Stewart, 1984), pp. 245-49. The *Globe and Mail* (6 September 1984) reprinted Berton's version.

NOTES TO CHAPTER TWO

1. The Rev. William Scott had served as a missionary to the Indians in his early years in Canada. In 1882 he was called in as an arbitrator in a land dispute between the Indians of Oka and the Seminary of St. Sulpice. See Richard C. Daniel, A *History of Native Claims Processes in Canada, 1867-1979* (Ottawa, Research Branch, Department of Indian and Northern Affairs, 1980), pp. 79-80.
2. E.K. Brown, "Duncan Campbell Scott: A Memoir," in E.K. Brown, *Responses and Evaluations: Essays on Canada,* edited with an introduction by David Staines, (Toronto: McClelland and Stewart, 1977), p. 112.
3. Ibid., p. 113.
4. Ibid., p. 114.
5. *Ottawa Citizen,* 4 August 1945.
6. These details are found in the annual reports of the department. They are recounted here for the sake of accuracy and to dispel a number of misconceptions. For example, in the biographical note at the beginning of Glenn Clever, *Duncan Campbell Scott: Selected Poetry* (Ottawa: Tecumseh Press, 1974), it is claimed that Scott was made secretary to the department in 1896. This is untrue. The mistake is repeated by Gerald Lynch citing Clever as the authority. Gerald Lynch, "An Endless Flow: D.C. Scott's Indian Poems," *Studies in Canadian Literature* 7 (1982): 39.
7. In D.J. Hall's opinion, Scott had "the outlook of an economizing bookkeeper, expressing concern for cutting costs, living within budgets and demonstrating absolutely no sympathy for the realities of administration at the reserve level," Hall, "Clifford Sifton and Canadian Indian Administration, 1896-1905," pp. 129-30.
8. Brown, "Duncan Campbell Scott: A Memoir," p. 127.
9. Barrie Davies, ed., *At the Mermaid Inn: Wilfred Campbell, Archibald Lampman, and Duncan Campbell Scott in The Globe, 1892-93* (Toronto: University of Toronto Press, 1979), pp. 145-46.
10. James Doyle, "Duncan Campbell Scott and American Literature," in K.P. Stich, ed., *The Duncan Campbell Scott Symposium* (Ottawa: University of Ottawa Press, 1979), p. 102.
11. Davies, *At the Mermaid Inn,* p. 249.
12. Carl Berger, *The Sense of Power: Studies in the Idea of Canadian Imperialism, 1867-1914* (Toronto: University of Toronto Press, 1970).
13. Pelham Edgar, "Duncan Campbell Scott," *Dalhousie Review* 7 (April 1927): 40.
14. Davies, *At The Mermaid Inn,* xvii-xix.
15. Doyle, "Duncan Campbell Scott and American Literature," p. 105.
16. Brown, "Duncan Campbell Scott: A Memoir," p. 120.
17. Sandra Campbell, "A Fortunate Friendship: Duncan Campbell Scott and Pelham Edgar," in Stich, *The Duncan Campbell Scott Symposium,* pp. 113-15.
18. Scott to P. Edgar, 6 May 1901, in Arthur S. Bourinot, ed., *More Letters of Duncan Campbell Scott* (Ottawa: A.S. Bourinot, 1960).
19. Scott to P. Edgar, 2 January 1905, ibid.
20. A.B. McKillop, "Introduction" to W.D. Le Sueur, *William Lyon Mackenzie: A Reinterpretation* (Toronto: Macmillan, 1979), pp. ix-xvii.
21. Duncan Campbell Scott, *John Graves Simcoe*

(Toronto: Morang, 1909), pp. 227-28.

22. Ibid., p. 128.

23. G. Sylvestre, B. Conron and C. Klinck, eds., *Canadian Writers/Ecrivains Canadiens*, (Toronto: Ryerson, 1964), pp. 139-40.

24. Stan Dragland, "Duncan Campbell Scott as Literary Executor for Archibald Lampman: 'A Labour of Love,'" *Studies in Canadian Literature* 1, no. 2 (Summer 1976): 144.

25. P. Edgar, "Duncan Campbell Scott," p. 40.

26. S. Dragland, "Duncan Campbell Scott as Literary Executor for Archibald Lampman," p. 156.

27. Duncan Campbell Scott, *Walter J. Phillips* (Toronto: Ryerson, 1947).

28. Madge Macbeth, *Over My Shoulder* (Toronto: Ryerson, 1953), pp. 140-42.

29. Brown, "Duncan Campbell Scott: A Memoir," p. 119.

30. Bourinot, ed., *More Letters of Duncan Campbell Scott*, p. 4. This volume contains a letter from Scott to P. Edgar, 17 July 1907, in which he expressed his anguish at his daughter's death: "We have both suffered too much. I think every fibre of our souls was ingrown and tangled with hers. In no merely rhetorical way I say it seems impossible for us to go on." See also Harry Adaskin, *A Fiddler's World* (Vancouver: November House, 1977), p. 168.

31. Robert L. McDougall, "Duncan Campbell Scott. A Trace of Documents and a Touch of Life," in Stich, *The Duncan Campbell Scott Symposium*, p. 128.

32. Macbeth, *Over My Shoulder*, pp. 135-37, 146-47. See also, PAC, D.C. Scott Papers, John M. Elson, "Onward: Pen Sketches of Canadian Poets - D.C. Scott" (unidentified newsclipping, 16 January 1932).

33. Desmond Pacey, ed., *Ten Canadian Poets* (Toronto: Ryerson, 1958), p. 143.

34. Wilfrid Eggleston, *Literary Friends* (Ottawa: Burealis Press, 1980), p. 108.

35. Scott to E.K. Brown, 24 November 1946, in Bourinot, *More Letters of Duncan Campbell Scott*, p. 77-78.

36. Scott to A. Lampman, 16 September 1898, in A.S. Bourinot, ed., *Some Letters of Duncan Campbell Scott, Archibald Lampman and Others* (Ottawa: A.S. Bourinet, 1959).

37. Scott to E.K. Brown, during 1943, in Bourinot, *Some Letters of Duncan Campbell Scott, Archibald Lampman and Others*, p. 32.

38. E.K. Brown, "Duncan Campbell Scott," in Stan Dragland ed., *Duncan Campbell Scott: A Book of Criticism* (Ottawa: Tecumseh, 1974), p. 83.

39. Susan Beckman, "A Note on Duncan Campbell Scott's 'The Forsaken,'" *Humanities Association Review* 25 (Winter 1974): 32.

40. Roy Daniels, "Crawford, Carman, and D.C. Scott," in Carl Klinck, ed., *Literary History of Canada*, vol. 1, (Toronto: University of Toronto Press, 1976, 2d edition), p. 435.

41. Melvin H. Dagg, "Scott and the Indians " in Dragland, *Duncan Campbell Scott: A Book of Criticism*, pp. 183-90.

42. Keiichi Hirano, "The Aborigine in Canadian Literature," *Canadian Literature* 14 (Autumn 1962): 44-47.

43. Gerald Lynch, "An Endless Flow: D.C. Scott's Indian Poems," *Studies in Canadian Literature* 7, no. 1 (1982): 54.

44. John Flood, "The Duplicity of Duncan Campbell Scott and the James Bay Treaty," *Black Moss*, second series, 2 (Fall 1976).

45. John Flood, "Native People in Scott's Short Fiction," in Stich, *The Duncan Campbell Scott Symposium*, pp. 73-83.

46. E. Palmer Patterson II, "The Poet and the Indian: Indian Themes in the Poetry of Duncan Campbell Scott and John Collier," *Ontario History* 59 (1967): 69-78. A recent article by another historian is of limited value: S.D. Grant, "Indian Affairs Under Duncan Campbell Scott: The Plains Cree of Saskatchewan, 1913-1931," *Journal of Canadian Studies* 18, no. 3 (Autumn 1983). Although Grant makes a number of plausible observations regarding Scott's attitude, her article is replete with factual errors and must therefore be approached with great caution. She gives the years 1913-31 as the years of Scott's incumbency as Deputy Superintendent, rather than 1913-32. She claims that reserve lands were "expropriated" under the Soldier Settlement scheme (p. 30) and that the Greater Production scheme was designed to increase food production "after the war" (p. 32). Both of these assertions are incorrect. And she refers to the power granted to chiefs and councils under the Indian Act to control "obnoxious weeds" (p. 33). The offending plants in question were in fact "noxious weeds"!

47. Duncan Campbell Scott, "Poetry and Progress," Presidential address to the Royal Society of Canada, 17 May 1922, reprinted in Dragland, *Duncan Campbell Scott: A Book of Criticism*, pp. 9-10.

48. D.C. Scott, "Indian Affairs, 1763-1841," in Adam Shortt and Arthur G. Doughty, eds., *Canada and its Provinces*, 4, sec. 2, pt. 2, *British Dominion* (Toronto: Glasgow, Brook and

Company, 1914), p. 706.

49. D.C. Scott, "The Last of the Indian Treaties," in *The Circle of Affection* (Toronto: McClelland and Stewart, 1947), p. 110.

50. Scott, *John Graves Simcoe*, pp. 74-75.

51. D.C. Scott, "Indian Affairs, 1867-1912," in Shortt and Doughty, *Canada and its Provinces*, 7, sec. 4, *The Dominion*, p. 599.

52. Ibid., p. 601.

53. D.C. Scott, "Report of the Superintendent of Indian Education," in *Report of the Department of Indian Affairs for the year ended 31 March 1910*, p. 273.

54. D.C. Scott, "Indian Affairs, 1840-1867," in Shortt and Doughty, *Canada and its Provinces*, 5, sec. 3, *United Canada*, p. 333.

55. D.C. Scott, "Indian Affairs, 1763-1841," p. 695.

56. Ibid., p. 713.

57. D.C. Scott, "Report of the Superintendent of Indian Education," 1910, p. 273.

58. Scott, "Indian Affairs, 1867-1912," pp. 622-23.

59. Ibid., p. 602.

60. Ibid., p. 605.

61. Ibid., pp. 609-10.

62. D.C. Scott, *The Administration of Indian Affairs in Canada* (Toronto: Canadian Institute of International Affairs, 1931), p. 11.

63. Scott, "Indian Affairs, 1867-1912," p. 610.

64. Fisher, *Contact and Conflict*, pp. 124-36.

65. Scott, "Report of the Superintendent of Indian Education," 1910, p. 273.

66. Scott, "Indian Affairs, 1763-1841," p. 696.

67. *Report of the Department of Indian Affairs for the year ended 31 March 1927*, pp. 9-10.

68. Scott, *The Administration of Indian Affairs in Canada*, p. 26.

Notes to Chapter Three

1. *Report of the Department of Indian Affairs for the year ended 31 March 1914.*

2. Ibid.

3. R. Craig Brown and Ramsay Cook, *Canada 1896-1921: A Nation Transformed* (Toronto: McClelland and Stewart, 1974), pp. 198-99.

4. *Report of the Department of Indian Affairs*, appropriate years.

5. PAC, RG10, vol. 3086, file 279,222-1A.

6. Ibid., vol. 1129 (Deputy Superintendent's letterbooks, p. 623), Scott to the Superintendent General, 9 January 1914.

7. One such circular, of 13 January 1925, warned agents against their personal use of alcohol. So serious did the department regard the conduct of agents in that regard that any "well-founded reports of inebriety" would result in "immediate suspension and probable dismissal." Ibid., vol. 3086, file 279,222-1C.

8. James Dempsey, "The Indians and World War One," *Alberta History* 31, no. 3 (Summer 1983): 2.

9. PAC, RG10, vol. 3086, file 279,222-1A, Scott to agency inspectors in Manitoba, Saskatchewan, and Alberta, 29 September 1914.

10. Ibid., file 279,222-1C, Scott to all agents, 12 February 1918.

11. Ibid., Scott to principals of boarding and industrial schools, 19 February 1918.

12. PAC, Arthur Meighen Papers, series 1, vol. 4, 2223, W.M. Graham to A. Meighen, 7 January 1918.

13. *Report of the Department of Indian Affairs for the year ended 31 March 1919*, p. 10.

14. PAC, RG10, vol. 4069, file 427,063, Scott to A. Meighen, 28 February 1919.

15. Ibid., vol. 4070, file 427, 063-A, Scott to W.M. Graham, 21 February 1918. See also House of Commons, *Debates*, 132, p. 27-28 (19 March 1918).

16. *Report of the Department of Indian Affairs for the year ended 31 March 1918*, p. 20.

17. Canada, House of Commons, *Debates*, 132, p. 1049 (19 April 1918).

18. PAC, Meighen Papers, series 2, vol. 31, 17702 and 17692.

19. Ibid., 17709.

20. Canada, House of Commons, *Debates*, 138, pp. 4061, 4063 (25 June 1919).

21. PAC, RG10, vol. 4070, file 427,063-A, Scott to W.M. Graham, 23 February 1922.

22. Canada, House of Commons, *Debates*, 151, pp. 681-82 (4 April 1922).

23. PAC, RG10, vol. 4070, file 427,063-A, the superintendent general to the governor-in-council, 27 April 1920.

24. PAC, R.B. Bennett Papers, Indian Affairs file D-200, Scott to T. Murphy, 15 March 1932. Plans to create the commissioner's position were underway in January 1920: see RG10, vol. 4070, file 427-063-A, Scott to P.H. Myers, organization branch, Civil Service Commission, 12 January 1920.

25. Brown and Cook, *Canada 1896-1921: A Nation Transformed*, p. 321.

26. Desmond Morton and Glenn Wright, "The Bonus Campaign, 1919-21: Veterans and the Campaign for Re-establishment," *Canadian Historical Review* 64, no. 2 (June 1983): 148-51.

27. *An Act to assist Returned Soldiers in settling upon the Land and to increase Agricultural production*, Chapter 21, 7-8 George V (assented

to 29 August 1917).

28. Canada, House of Commons, *Debates*, 137, pp. 3849-50 (23 June 1919).

29. *An Act to assist Returned Soldiers in settling upon the Land*, Chapter 25, 9-10 George V (assented to 7 July 1919).

30. PAC, RG10, vol. 7484, file 25001, pt. 1, Scott to A. Meighen, 15 October 1918.

31. Ibid., A. Meighen to Scott, 8 November 1918.

32. *An Act to amend the Indian Act*, Chapter 25, 9-10 George V (assented to 7 July 1919).

33. PAC, RG10, vol. 3086, file 279,222-1C, Scott to Indian agents, 6 May 1919; and Ibid., vol. 7484, file 25001, pt. 1, Scott to W.M. Graham, 10 June 1919.

34. *Report of the Department of Indian Affairs for the year ended 31 March 1922*, pp. 15-16.

35. *An Act to amend the Indian Act*, Chapter 26, 12-13 George V, Section 197.

36. PAC, RG10, vol. 7484, file 25001, pt. 1, department memos and correspondence.

37. Ibid., vol. 7484, file 25001-1A, department memos and correspondence.

38. Ibid., vol. 7484, file 25001, pt. 1, Scott to A. Meighen, 10 March 1919.

39. Canada, House of Commons, *Debates*, 137, pp. 3877-78 (23 June 1919).

40. PAC, RG10, vol. 7535, file 26,131-1, W.M. Graham to Scott, 21 June 1919.

41. Ibid., Scott to A. Meighen, 13 June 1919.

42. PAC, RG10, vol. 7535, file 26,150-1.

43. The annual reports of the Department of Indian Affairs give the following figures for Indian lands sold:
Between 1 April 1918 and 31 March 1919: 19,010.45 acres
Between 1 April 1919 and 31 March 1920: 114,819.07 acres
Between 1 April 1920 and 31 March 1921: 32,491.71 acres
Between 1 April 1921 and 31 March 1922: 5,804.43 acres
Between 1 April 1922 and 31 March 1923: 6,898.38 acres
Between 1 April 1923 and 31 March 1924: 16,480.43 acres
Between 1 April 1924 and 31 March 1925: 21,622.99 acres

44. *Report of the Department of Indian Affairs for the year ended 31 March 1914*, p. xxvii.

45. *Report of the Department of Indian Affairs for the year ended 31 March 1917*, p. 20.

46. *An Act to amend the Indian Act*, Chapter 26, 8-9 George V (assented to 24 May 1918).

47. *Report of the Department of Indian Affairs for the year ended 31 March 1920*, p. 13.

48. *Report of the Department of Indian Affairs for the year ended 31 March 1919*, p. 32.

49. PAC, RG10, vol. 6809, file 470-2-3, pt. 5, Scott to A. Meighen, 28 January 1920.

50. *The Globe*, 20 March 1920.

51. *Ottawa Journal*, 23 March 1920.

52. PAC, RG10, vol. 6810, file 470-2-3, pt. 7, Scott to W.A. Boys, 3 April 1920.

53. Canada, House of Commons, *Debates*, 144, p. 4029, (15 June 1920).

54. PAC, RG10, vol. 6810, file 470-2-3, pt. 7, Memorandum of the Six Nations and other Iroquois, 30 March 1920.

55. Ibid., evidence of Scott before the Committee of the House.

56. Canada, House of Commons, *Debates*, 144, p. 4029 (15 June 1920).

57. Ibid., pp. 4033-35.

58. *An Act to amend the Indian Act*, Chapter 26, 12-13 George V (assented to 28 June 1922). See also House of Commons, *Debates*, 153, p. 2991 (15 June 1922).

59. Canada, House of Commons, *Debates*, 154, pp. 3192-3 (19 June 1922).

60. Ibid., 152, p. 1221 (27 April 1922).

61. PAC, RG10, vol. 2405, file 84041. J.D. McLean to Mississauga Indians of Mud Lake, Rice Lake and Scugog, 17 January 1901; and to Moses Smoke, 23 November 1901. In protesting the sale of game by Indians, Ontario Commissioner of Crown Lands J.M. Gibson pointed out to the department that the laws were designed to protect animals and that the Indians would have to recognize this. Nor should they complain so incessantly; in the limited hunting season they could earn "good wages" as guides for white hunters. Ibid., J.M. Gibson to J.A. Smart, 27 April 1899.

62. PAC, RG10, vol. 2406, file 84,041, pt. 2, Scott to C. McCrea, Ontario Legislature, 5 October 1916.

63. Ibid. Scott to A. Sheriff, Ontario Deputy Minister of Game and Fisheries, 9 January 1917, and subsequent correspondence.

64. Ibid., Scott to E.L. Newcombe, 29 August 1917.

65. Ibid., Scott to A. Meighen, 6 March 1918.

66. Dan Gottesman, "Native Hunting and the Migratory Birds Convention Act: Historical, Political and Ideological Perspectives," *Journal of Canadian Studies* 8, no. 3 (Fall 1983): 70-72.

67. The treaty was actually signed on Canada's behalf by Sir Cecil Spring-Rice, British ambassador to Washington. Canada's foreign relations were conducted by the imperial government at the time.

68. *The Migratory Birds Convention Act*, Chapter 18, 7-8 George V (assented to 29 August 1917).

69. PAC, RG10, vol. 4084, file 496,658.

70. Ibid., vol. 3234, file 600,245, pts. 1 and 2, correspondence between Scott and J.B. Harkin, Dominion Parks Branch, January 1921. See also Scott, *The Administration of Indian Affairs in Canada*, p. 12 and *Report of the Department of Indian Affairs for the year ended 31 March 1929*, pp. 7-8. In his evidence before the National Conference on Conservation in 1919, Scott said: "Of course, we sometimes get exaggerated reports that the Indians are killing all the moose in certain districts, but, when we investigate them, we usually find that there is little foundation for the reports. On the whole, it may be said that the Indian obeys the hunting and fishing regulations equally as well as the white man." Canada, Commission of Conservation, *National Conference on Conservation of Game, Fur-Bearing Animals and other Wild Life* (Ottawa: J. de Labroquerie Tache, 1919), p. 21.

71. PAC, RG10, vol. 3234, file 600,245, pts. 1 and 2, W.E. Collison, agent at Skeena River, to headquarters, 18 July 1923; J.D. McLean to W.E. Collison, 2 August 1923.

72. Ibid., W. Whitehead and E. Martin to Scott, 5 July 1927.

73. Ibid., A.S. Williams to W.M. Cory, assistant solicitor, Department of the Interior, 21 August 1930. Scott to H.H. Rowatt, deputy minister of the Interior, 5 February 1932.

74. *The Northwest Game Act*, Chapter 36, 7-8 George V (assented to 20 September 1917).

75. Rene Fumoleau, *As Long As This Land Shall Last* (Toronto: McClelland and Stewart, n. d.), p. 246.

76. Ibid., p. 287. See Fumoleau also for the special concessions granted to Indians when Wood Buffalo Park was established in 1922 (pp. 255-56) and when the natural resources of Manitoba, Saskatchewan and Alberta were transferred to provincial jurisdiction in 1929-30 (pp. 288-89).

77. *Report of the Department of Indian Affairs for the year ended 31 March 1929*, p. 8.

78. Canada, House of Commons, *Debates*, 190, p. 4542 (3 August 1931), Charles Stewart said that the establishment of hunting preserves would be "of immense benefit to the Indians and helpful to the exchequer of the federal government."

79. For the full story of this epidemic, see Eileen Pettigrew, *The Silent Enemy* (Saskatoon: Western Producer Prairie Books, 1983).

80. G. Graham-Cumming, "Health of Original Canadians, 1867-1967", *Medical Services Journal Canada* 23 (February 1967): 149. See also, Canada, House of Commons, *Debates*, 138, p. 4062 (25 June 1919).

81. Brown and Cook, *Canada 1896-1921: A Nation Transformed*, p. 325.

82. *Report of the Department of Indian Affairs for the year ended 31 March 1928*, p. 7.

83. Graham-Cumming, "Health of Original Canadians, 1867-1967," p. 125.

84. *Report of the Department of Indian Affairs for the year ended 31 March 1929*, pp. 11-14.

85. Fumoleau, *As Long As This Land Shall Last*, pp. 265-66.

86. *Report of the Department of Indian Affairs*, appropriate years. After 1917, the population was recorded at quinquennial intervals.

87. Graham-Cumming, "Health of Original Canadians, 1867-1967," pp. 138-41.

88. *Report of the Department of Indian Affairs for the year ended 31 March 1931*, pp. 9-10. With the onset of the depression, funds were even more limited than in previous years. Scott wrote to all agents on 1 May 1931 informing them of economies that would have to be made regarding health services. He said that until further notice it would be necessary "to avoid admission of Indian patients to hospital or sanitarium for treatment of tuberculosis or trachoma." PAC, RG10, vol. 3086, file 279,222-1C. Ironically, in a paper prepared for an international audience in the same year, Scott said, "The Department of Indian Affairs has no reason to feel ashamed of its medical service from a remedial standpoint. No appeal for medical treatment from a Canadian Indian goes unheeded, and no expense is spared to give the sick Indian the benefit of the best medical and hospital care available." Scott, *The Administration of Indian Affairs in Canada*, p. 19.

89. Fumoleau, *As Long as This Land Shall Last*, pp. 150-224. The terms of Treaty 11 were similar to those of the other numbered treaties.

90. PAC, RG10, vol. 6810, file 470-2-3, pt. 8, Scott to E.L. Newcombe, 11 April 1924. Scott's initial idea was that the consent of the minister of justice, rather than that of the superintendent general, be required before Indians could hire lawyers for the pursuit of claims. As he explained: "I would not like it

to appear as though the Department itself was preventing the Indians from asserting claims that they may be led to believe they may have."

91. Canada, House of Commons, *Debates*, 175, pp. 324-25 (15 February 1927).

NOTES TO CHAPTER FOUR

1. John Long, *Treaty No. 9: The Half-Breed Question, 1902-1910* (Cobalt, Ont: Highway Book Shop, 1978), pp. 3-5.
2. W.T. Easterbrook and Hugh G.J. Aitken, *Canadian Economic History* (Toronto: Macmillan, 1956), p. 524.
3. A coal strike in the United States in 1902 resulted in a rapid increase in the price of fuel and brought home to Ontario its dependency on foreign sources of energy. Under the circumstances, domestically controlled alternative sources such as hydroelectricity appeared all the more attractive. Brown and Cook, *Canada 1896-1921: A Nation Transformed*, p. 104.
4. Easterbrook and Aitken, *Canadian Economic History*, p. 538.
5. In fact, in 1901 the owners of the Canadian Northern Railway had announced plans to span the continent in competition with the Canadian Pacific and had found ready government support. The Grand Trunk would therefore constitute a third transcontinental system. In the blinkered optimism of the Laurier years, the folly of three such railways was not always appreciated.
6. Easterbrook and Aitken, *Canadian Economic History*, pp. 438-44.
7. Kapuskasing and Hearst were originally known as MacPherson and Grant respectively.
8. A.S. Pain, *The Way North* (Toronto: Ryerson, 1964), pp. 101-13.
9. D.C. Scott, "The Last of the Indian Treaties," in his *The Circle of Affection* (Toronto: McClelland and Stewart, 1947), p. 111. The essay was originally published in *Scribners' Magazine*, December 1906.
10. PAC, RG10, vol. 3033, file 235,225, pt. 1, J. Macrae to the superintendent general, 3 June 1901.
11. Ibid., petition of Isaiah Poo-yah-way and other Indians of Lake St. Joseph to the superintendent general, 12 December 1901.
12. Ibid., T.C. Irving to Sir Wilfrid Laurier, 10 April 1904. Irving said that he represented an exploration company that believed the

area contained great quantities of lignite, gypsum, iron and "boundless" spruce forests waiting to be exploited.

13. McKenna was a native of Prince Edward Island who had been promoted from second-class clerk in the department to Clifford Sifton's private secretary in 1897. As of 1 July 1901, he served as assistant Indian commissioner and chief inspector for Manitoba and the Northwest Territories. Hall, "Clifford Sifton and Canadian Indian Administration, 1896-1905," p. 130 and note, p. 146.
14. PAC, RG10, vol. 3033, file 235,225, pt. 1, J.A.J. McKenna to C. Sifton, 22 February 1902.
15. Ibid., J. Hodder, agent at Port Arthur to headquarters, 6 December 1902.
16. Ibid., F. Pedley to C. Sifton, 17 August 1903.
17. Ibid., F. Pedley to S.C. Chipman, 4 May 1904, and Chipman to Pedley, 11 May 1904.
18. Ibid., F. Pedley to E.J. Davis, 30 April 1904.
19. Ibid., A. White to F. Pedley, 30 May 1904. The province's reluctance to co-operate was largely a result of the action pending in the Court of Exchequer wherein Ontario's liability under Treaty No. 3 was at issue.
20. Ibid., F. Pedley to A. White, 26 June 1904.
21. Ibid., Scott to F. Pedley, 18 March 1905.
22. Ibid., F. Pedley to Sir Wilfrid Laurier, 27 April 1905.
23. Ibid., F. Pedley to Sir Wilfrid Laurier, 2 June 1905.
24. "Agreement Between the Dominion of Canada and the Province of Ontario," 3 July 1905, in Canada, *The James Bay Treaty* (Ottawa: Queen's Printer, 1964, reprinted from the 1931 edition).
25. PAC, RG10, vol. 3033, file 235,225, pt. 1, F. Pedley to F. Oliver, 26 June 1905.
26. Canada, *The James Bay Treaty*, p. 20.
27. Ibid.
28. Scott, "The Last of the Indian Treaties," pp. 111-12.
29. Canada, *The James Bay Treaty*, p. 4.
30. Scott, "The Last of the Indian Treaties," pp. 112-13.
31. PAC, uncatalogued diary kept by an unidentified member of the expedition, pp. 25-27.
32. Scott, "The Last of the Indian Treaties," p. 115.
33. Canada, *The James Bay Treaty*, p. 5.
34. Ibid., p. 6.
35. About thirty half-breeds resident at Moose Factory were excluded from the treaty by Scott and his companions. In spite of subsequent protests to Ottawa, it seems that their

right to "scrip" or similar compensation was never recognized. See Long, *Treaty No. 9: The Half-Breed Question, 1902-1910.*

36. Scott, "The Last of the Indian Treaties," p. 121.
37. Canada, *The James Bay Treaty*, p. 10.
38. Ibid.
39. Ibid., pp. 10-11.
40. Ibid., p. 11.
41. PAC, RG10, vol. 1028, D.C. Scott, "Journal of trip to James Bay, 30 June - 6 September 1905; 22 May - 16 August 1906." Part of Scott's journal has been reproduced in *Copperfield* 5 (1974): 37-45.
42. Scott to P. Edgar, 9 October 1905, in Bourinot, *More Letters of Duncan Campbell Scott*, pp. 29-30.
43. Ibid., Scott to P. Edgar, 17 March 1906, p. 31.
44. Pelham Edgar, "Travelling with a Poet," in Northrop Frye, ed., *Across My Path* (Toronto: Ryerson, 1952), p. 59.
45. Canada, *The James Bay Treaty*, p. 17.
46. In March of the following year Scott wrote to Edgar as follows: "I don't like to hear you talk of working this summer. O for another canoe trip." Scott to P. Edgar, 20 March 1907, in Bourinot, *More Letters to Duncan Campbell Scott*, p. 33.
47. Scott to E.K. Brown, 12 November 1943, in Bourinot, *Some Letters to Duncan Campbell Scott, Archibald Lampman and Others*, p. 18.
48. Edgar, "Travelling with a Poet," p. 60.
49. Ibid., pp. 65-66.
50. Ibid., p. 66.
51. *Ottawa Citizen*, 26 November 1923.
52. PAC, RG10, vol. 3033, file 235, 225, pt. 1, Scott to G.H. Ferguson, 1 May 1926, and Ferguson to Scott 8, May 1926.
53. "Report of the Commissioners re Adhesion to Treaty No. 9 for the year 1929," in *Report of the Department of Indian Affairs for the year ended 31 March 1929*, p. 24.
54. Fumoleau, *As Long as this Land Shall Last*, p. 18.
55. Pain, *The Way North*, p. 125.
56. Ibid., p. 231.
57. Scott, "The Last of the Indian Treaties," p. 115.

NOTES TO CHAPTER FIVE

1. *Report of the Department of Indian Affairs for the year ended 30 June 1903*, p. xxvii.
2. Nicholas Flood Davin (1843-1901) was a native of Ireland who arrived in Canada in July 1872. A poet, journalist and lawyer, he served as Conservative M.P. for Assiniboia West between 1887 and 1900. For a full biographical study see C.B. Koester, *Mr. Davin, M.P.* (Saskatoon: Western Producer Prairie Books, 1980). D.C. Scott evidently did not hold Davin in very high regard, probably because of the pamphlet he had once written attacking Sir John Bourinot. Many years later, in a letter to Sir John's son, Arthur, Scott had the following observations to make about the Irishman:

> He was said to be a brilliant talker but the symphonies always ended when the whiskey bottle was empty. I have heard him make some violent speeches in the House of Commons. He was in some respects a typical Irishman and he was a disappointed one and they are apt to be venomous. . . . By the way, I think some enthusiastic Irish put up a cenotaph to Davin in Beechwood—when I come back early in May, we might go there and hang a wreath of onions around his neck!

Scott to Arthur S. Bourinot, 5 March 1941, in Bourinot, ed., *Some Letters of Duncan Campbell Scott, Archibald Lampman and Others*, p. 48.
3. PAC, RG10, vol. 3674, file 11,422, Nicholas Flood Davin, "Report on Industrial Schools," 1879.
4. The delay was caused by the government's negotiations with the various churches and by the fact that Indian starvation in the west was a matter of more immediate concern. See Jacqueline Gresko, "White 'Rites' and Indian 'Rites': Indian Education and Native Responses in the West, 1870-1910," in A.W. Rasporich, ed. *Western Canada: Past and Present* (Calgary: McClelland and Stewart West, 1975), p. 169.
5. PAC, RG10, vol. 3674, file 11,422, L. Vankoughnet to Sir John A. Macdonald, 17 May 1883.
6. The rules regarding the age of students were extremely flexible; in many cases students much older or younger than the guidelines specified were in attendance at both types of school. The per capita grant system encouraged this.
7. Ibid., vol. 3964, file 149,874, memo of J.D. McLean, 20 July 1897.
8. Ibid., vol. 3922, file 116,820-1.
9. Ibid., vol. 3674, file 11,422, Commissioner E. Dewdney to Rev. T. Clark (principal, Battleford Industrial School), 31 July 1883.

10. Ibid., vol. 3597, file 1350, J.P. Wright (agent, File Hills) to Commissioner H. Reed, 23 December 1890.
11. Ibid., vol. 3818, file 57,799, Hayter Reed to the superintendent general, 14 May 1889.
12. Ibid., vol. 3982, file 161,962, "Statement of Expenditure for Industrial Schools in 1896."
13. Ibid., vol. 3926, file 116,836-1, A.J. McLeod (principal, Regina Industrial School) to Commissioner D. Laird, 10 June 1899.
14. Ibid., vol. 3767, file 33170.
15. Ibid., vol. 3558, file 64, pt. 39.
16. Ibid., vol. 3927, file 116,836-1A, J.A. Sinclair (principal, Regina Industrial School) to J.A. Smart, 27 April 1903.
17. See Gresko, "White 'Rites' and Indian 'Rites': Indian Education and Native Responses in the West, 1870-1910," for an interesting discussion of Indian resistance to cultural change.
18. Ibid., vol. 3926, file 116,836-1, L. Vankoughnet to E. Dewdney, 10 June 1890.
19. Ibid., vol. 3927, file 116,836-1A, M. Benson to F. Pedley, 2 October 1903.
20. PAC, RG10, vol. 3961, file 145,051, memo prepared by D.C. Scott in response to request by J.A. Smart, 1 March 1901.
21. Hall, "Clifford Sifton and Canadian Indian Administration, 1896-1905," pp. 133-34.
22. PAC, RG10, vol. 3926, file 116,836-1, C. Sifton to J.A.J. McKenna, 14 July 1897 and subsequent correspondence.
23. Ibid., vol. 3964, file 149,874, M. Benson to J.D. McLean, 24 March 1902.
24. Ibid., vol. 3927, file 116, 836-1A.
25. Ibid., M. Benson to F. Pedley, 17 March 1904.
26. Ibid., F. Pedley to Scott, 19 March 1904.
27. Ibid., Scott to F. Pedley, 29 April 1904.
28. Ibid., F. Pedley to C. Sifton, 2 May 1904.
29. Ibid., M. Benson to F. Pedley, 24 November 1904.
30. Ibid., F. Pedley to R.P. MacKay, 23 June 1904.
31. Ibid., M. Benson to F. Pedley, 30 December 1904.
32. Ibid., 22 March 1905.
33. PAC, RG10, vol. 3927, file 116,836-1C.
34. For a detailed discussion of this topic, see E. Brian Titley, "Indian Industrial Schools in Western Canada" in N. Sheehan, D.C. Jones and J.D. Wilson, eds., *Schools in the West: Essays on Canadian Educational History* (Calgary: Detselig, 1986).
35. PAC, RG10, vol. 3067, file 254,017-1.
36. Ibid., vol. 4037, file 317,021, F. Pedley to J.D.

McLean, 14 February 1907 and J.D. McLean to P.H. Bryce, 15 February 1907.
37. Ibid., P.H. Bryce, *Report on the Indian Schools of Manitoba and the Northwest Territories* (19 June 1907).
38. *Ottawa Citizen*, 16 November 1907, and *Montreal Star*, 15 November 1907.
39. PAC, RG10, vol. 4037, file 317,021, D. Laird to J.D. McLean, 7 December 1907.
40. Ibid., vol. 3957, file 140,754-1, report of Dr. P.H. Bryce, 5 November 1909.
41. Ibid., D.C. Scott, "Notes on Dr. Bryce's Report— With Suggestions for Future Action."
42. Ibid., Scott to F. Pedley, 29 March 1911.
43. P.H. Bryce, *The Story of a National Crime* (Ottawa: James Hope, 1922).
44. PAC, RG10, vol. 3086, file 279,222-1.
45. Ibid., vol. 4076, file 451,868, Scott to Arthur Meighen, 8 November 1918.
46. Ibid., vol. 4077, file 454,016, O.I. Grain to Scott, 18 January 1914.
47. Ibid., vol. 4076, file 451, 868, Scott to A. Meighen, 8 November 1918.
48. Ibid., vol. 4092, file 546,898, F.A. Corbett to W.M. Graham, 7 December 1920.
49. Ibid., Scott to Sir James Lougheed, 11 December 1920.
50. Ibid., W.M. Graham to Scott, 24 June 1922.
51. Scott, acting on behalf of the deputy superintendent general, to the assistant commissioner at Regina, 16 July 1894, noted that the department's policy was to encourage attendance at industrial schools while closing day schools if necessary. PAC, RG10, vol. 1289 (School Branch Letterbook, 1894).
52. *Report of the Department of Indian Affairs for the year ended 31 March 1909*, pp. xxxiii-xxxiv.
53. PAC, RG10, vol. 4024, file 289,032-2, S.H. Blake to F. Pedley, 7 January 1909.
54. *The Indian Act*, chapter 28, section 74, as amended 1880.
55. PAC, RG10, vol. 3965, file 150-000-8, D. Laird to J.D. McLean, 13 March 1903.
56. Ibid., J.A. Newnham to F. Pedley, 1 October 1907.
57. Ibid., Scott to F. Pedley, 15 October 1907.
58. PAC, RG10, vol. 4043, file 343,016, memo from Scott, 11 June 1909.
59. *Report of the Department of Indian Affairs for the year ended 31 March 1910*, p. 274.
60. *The Indian Act*, chapter 32, sections 137 and 138, as amended 1894.
61. PAC, RG10, vol. 6810, file 470-2-3, pt. 7. See also *The Indian Act*, chapter 50, section 10, as amended 1920.
62. *Report of the Department of Indian Affairs for*

the year ended 31 March 1929, p. 17.

63. Annual reports of the Department of Indian Affairs, appropriate years. The disparity between the two sets of figures is explained by a small number of Indians who attended public schools and who are included in the "total" figures.

64. *Report of the Department of Indian Affairs for the year ended 31 March 1931,* p. 11.

65. *Report of the Department of Indian Affairs for the year ended 31 March 1931,* p. 12. See also *The Indian Act,* chapter 25, section 10, subsection 1, as amended 1930.

66. The best example of the social control interpretation is Michael Katz and Paul H. Mattingly, eds., *Education and Social Change: Themes From Ontario's Past* (New York: New York University Press, 1975).

67. Indian motives for sending their children to school were obviously far more complex than Scott suggested. Undoubtedly the compulsory attendance legislation with its attendant penalties had much to do with it. James Redford has advanced an additional explanation. Noting that large numbers of students attending residential schools in British Columbia during this era were either orphans or came from families in which one parent had died, he concluded that economic necessity was often a factor in allowing the children to be enrolled. See James Redford, "Attendance at Indian Residential Schools in British Columbia, 1890-1920," *B.C. Studies* 44 (Winter 1979-80).

NOTES TO CHAPTER SIX

1. PAC, RG10, vol. 2639, file 129,690-1, Scott to J.A. Macrae, 11 June 1896.

2. Ibid., file 129,690-2, Minutes of 18th Grand General Indian Council of Ontario, Saugeen, 9-13 June 1904.

3. Ibid., Minutes of 19th Grand General Indian Council of Ontario, Saugeen, 12-15 June 1906.

4. *Toronto Daily Star,* 7 May 1919.

5. PAC, RG10, vol. 2639, file 129,690-3, J.D. McLean to J. Carlyle Moore, 9 January 1926.

6. Ibid., file 129,690-3C, A.F. McKenzie to D.W. Osahgee, 3 September 1930.

7. Rick Lueger, "An Introduction to Canadian Indian Political Organizations: a preliminary report," unpublished manuscript, Ottawa, National Indian Brotherhood, August 1972, pp. 40-41.

8. Susan K. Postal, "Hoax Nativism at Caughnawaga: A Control Case for the Theory of Revitalization," *Ethnology* 4, no. 3 (July 1965): 268.

9. Ibid., p. 266.

10. Ibid., p. 269.

11. *Utica Observer,* 21 November 1914.

12. PAC, RG10, vol. 3184, file 458,168, F.E. Taillon to headquarters, 12 November 1914.

13. Ibid., A.C. Parker to Scott, 23 April 1915.

14. Postal, "Hoax Nativism at Caughnawaga," pp. 277-78.

15. *Ottawa Citizen,* 26 October 1917.

16. PAC, RG10, vol. 3184, file 458,168, Scott to A. Meighen, 23 April 1918.

17. Ibid., E.G. Porter to G.I. Gogo, barrister, Cornwall, Ontario, 29 October 1918.

18. Ibid., D.C. Scott to W.D. Scott, 14 February 1919.

19. Postal, "Hoax Nativism at Caughnawaga," p. 271.

20. Ibid., p. 267.

21. PAC, RG10, vol. 3184, file 458,168, *Louisville Times* to Scott, 11 March 1927.

22. *Louisville Times,* 15 March 1927.

23. *The Evening,* circa 1929.

24. PAC, RG10, vol. 3211, file 527,781, undated clipping, *Edmonton Journal* (December 1918 or January 1919).

25. *London Free Press,* 4 September 1919.

26. PAC, RG10, vol. 3211, file 527,781, A.D. McNabb to J.D. McLean, 20 August 1919.

27. Ibid., circular from F.O. Loft, 25 November 1919.

28. Ibid., J.D. McLean to C.P. Schmidt, 16 December 1919.

29. Ibid., Scott to J.P. Wright, 31 December 1919.

30. Ibid., C.F. Hamilton, assistant comptroller, RNWMP, Ottawa, to Scott, 2 January 1920.

31. Ibid., Scott to W.M. Graham, 10 June 1920.

32. Ibid., Scott to G.J. Smith, 8 October 1920.

33. Ibid., G.J. Smith to Scott, 20 October 1920.

34. Ibid., F.O. Loft to Sir James Lougheed with memo by Scott attached, 9 February 1921.

35. Ibid., Scott to Sir James Lougheed, 21 February 1921.

36. Ibid., Scott to Charles Stewart, 3 February 1922.

37. Ibid., J.D. McLean to F.O. Loft, 25 November 1921.

38. Ibid., Scott to C.W. Kirby, 5 June 1922. The Royal North West Mounted Police became the Royal Canadian Mounted Police in 1920.

39. *Regina Leader,* 30 June 1922.

40. PAC, RG10, vol. 3211, file 527,781, RCMP report on Samson reserve rally, 3 July 1922.

41. Ibid., W.M. Graham to Scott, 3 July 1922.
42. *Toronto Sunday World*, 6 June 1920.
43. *Toronto Star Weekly*, 28 August 1920.
44. *Regina Leader*, 4 July 1922.
45. See, for instance, PAC, RG10, vol. 3211, file 527,781, "Report re Convention of Indians," by Cpl. J.S. Wood, "F" Division RCMP, Prince Albert, Saskatchewan, 9 July 1928.
46. Ibid., circular from F.O. Loft, 31 March 1931.
47. Ibid., Scott to T.G. Murphy, 29 April 1931.

NOTES TO CHAPTER SEVEN

1. Ella Cork, *The Worst of the Bargain* (San Jacinto, CA: Foundation for Social Research, 1962), pp. 90-91.
2. Elisabeth Tooker, "On the New Religion of Handsome Lake," *Anthropological Quarterly* 41, no. 4 (October 1968): 188.
3. Ibid., p. 196.
4. Elisabeth Tooker, "The Iroquois White Dog Sacrifice in the Latter Part of the Eighteenth Century," *Ethnohistory* 12, no. 2 (Spring 1965).
5. PAC, RG10, vol. 2286, file 57,169-1, pt. 5.
6. Malcolm Montgomery, "The Legal Status of the Six Nations Indians in Canada," *Ontario History* 55, no. 2 (1963): 96.
7. Department officials of this sort were usually known as "Indian agents."
8. Montgomery, "The Legal Status of the Six Nations Indians in Canada," p. 96.
9. Sally Weaver and Virginia Cooper, "An Early History of the Movement for an Elective Form of Government among the Six Nations of Grand River 1861-1903," 1970 (an unpublished working paper in the authors' possession), p. 19.
10. Ibid., pp. 20-21.
11. Malcolm Montgomery, "The Six Nations Indians and the Macdonald Franchise," *Ontario History* 57, no. 1 (1965): 25.
12. Weaver and Cooper, "An Early History of the Movement for an Elective Form of Local Government among the Six Nations of Grand River 1861-1903," pp. 22-23.
13. Sally Weaver and Virginia Cooper, "An Early History of the Dehorners, 1904-1910," 1970 (an unpublished working paper in the authors' possession), p. 4.
14. Ibid., p. 19.
15. Ibid., p. 11.
16. Sally Weaver, "Iroquois Politics: Grand River, 1847-1975," 1975 (an unpublished manuscript in the author's possession), pp. 417-19.
17. Ibid., pp. 419-24.

18. Ibid., pp. 427-28.
19. Ibid., pp. 430-31.
20. *Brantford Expositor*, 23 March 1920.
21. PAC, RG10, vol. 2285, file 57, 169-1A2, Scott to A. Meighen, 3 May 1920.
22. Ibid., Scott to A.R. Hill, 29 June 1920.
23. Ibid., Scott to Sir James Lougheed, 15 July 1920.
24. Ibid., E.L. Newcombe to Scott, 1 September 1920.
25. Ibid., petition of the Six Nations to the Duke of Devonshire, governor general of Canada, 10 May 1921.
26. Ibid., Scott to David S. Hill, 11 June 1921.
27. Ibid.
28. *Brantford Expositor*, 29 March 1921.
29. PAC, RG10, vol. 2285, file 57,169-1A2, Scott to J. Harold, 6 May 1921.
30. PAC, RG10, vol. 2287, file 57,169-1H6, Scott to Gordon J. Smith, 14 April 1921.
31. PAC, RG10, vol. 2285, file 57,169-1A2, Winston Churchill to Lord Byng of Vimy, governor general of Canada, 23 September 1921.
32. *Canada*, 27 August 1921.
33. PAC, RG10, vol. 2285, file 57,169-1A2, Scott to Walter Lafroy, 26 August 1921.
34. *Montreal Gazette*, 30 September 1921.
35. PAC, RG10, vol. 2285, file 57,169-1A2, Scott to Sir James Lougheed, 30 September 1921.
36. Ibid., vol. 3229, file 571,571, Charles Stewart to the chiefs and warriors of the Six Nations, 13 June 1922.
37. Ibid., Scott to Charles Stewart, 13 September 1922.
38. Ibid.
39. Ibid., C. Stewart to Deskeheh, 4 December 1922.
40. Ibid., Scott to C. Stewart, 21 December 1922.
41. Richard Veatch, *Canada and the League of Nations* (Toronto: University of Toronto Press, 1975), p. 4.
42. Ibid., pp. 6-8.
43. Ibid., p. 17.
44. Ibid., p. 51.
45. PAC, RG10, vol. 2285, file 57,169-1B, pt. 3, petition of Deskeheh to the government of the Netherlands, 7 December 1922.
46. Ibid., Sir Eric Drummond to W.L. Mackenzie King, 3 May 1923.
47. Ibid., Scott to P.C. Larkin, 10 July 1923.
48. PAC, RG10, vol. 2287, file 57,169-1, pt. 6, Duke of Devonshire to Lord Byng of Vimy, 7 April 1923.
49. Ibid., vol. 2285, file 57,169-1B, pt. 3, Sir Joseph Pope to Sir Eric Drummond, 25 May 1923.

50. Ibid., Drummond to van Panhuys, 28 June 1923.
51. Veatch, *Canada and the League of Nations*, pp. 93-94.
52. *Morning Post*, 25 August 1923.
53. PAC, RG10, vol. 2285, file 57,169-1B, pt 3, Inazo Nitobe to Sir Joseph Pope, 6 November 1923.
54. Ibid., G.P. Graham to C. Stewart, 6 October 1923.
55. Ibid., "Statement Respecting the Six Nations' Appeal to the League of Nations."
56. Ibid., Scott to Sir Joseph Pope, 31 January 1924.
57. Ibid., Sir Herbert Ames to Mackenzie King, 28 December 1923.
58. Ibid. See, for instance, British Foreign Office dispatch to British ambassador in Estonia, 7 March 1924.
59. See, for instance, PAC, RG10, vol. 2286, file 57, 169-1, pt. 5, B. Wallis to Ramsay MacDonald, 17 March 1924. For a more detailed account of these events, see Veatch, *Canada and the League of Nations*, pp. 96-98.
60. Ibid., file 57, 169-1, pt. 5, Deskeheh to King George V, 22 October 1924.
61. Ibid., Scott to C.E. Morgan, 19 November 1924.
62. PAC, RG10, vol. 3229, file 571,571, Scott to C. Stewart, 1 March 1923.
63. Weaver, "Iroquois Politics: Grand River, 1847-1975," p. 407.
64. PAC, RG10, vol. 3231, file 582,103.
65. Ibid., *Report of Col. A.T. Thompson re Six Nations Indians*, Ottawa, 22 November 1923.
66. Weaver, "Iroquois Politics: Grand River, 1847-1975," p. 472.
67. Ibid., pp. 457-58.
68. Ibid., p. 474.
69. Ibid., pp. 475-76.
70. Ibid., pp. 477-79.
71. Ibid., p. 481.
72. Ibid., pp. 487-92.
73. Ibid., p. 493.
74. *Toronto Star Weekly*, 14 February 1925.
75. PAC, RG10, vol. 2286, file 57,169-1, pt. 5, C.E. Morgan to Scott, 9 February 1925.
76. Ibid., O.D. Skelton to Scott, 5 June 1925, and Scott to O.D. Skelton, 9 June 1925.
77. *La Tribune de Genève*, 13 July 1925.
78. PAC, RG10, vol. 2286, file 57,169-1, pt. 5, report of Supt. H.M. Newson, "C" Division, RCMP, Western Ontario District, Ohsweken Detachment, re: Mohawk Workers, 7 July 1925.
79. Ibid., Scott to L.F. Heyd, 11 May 1927.
80. Ibid., W.D. Lighthall to Scott, 3 February 1928.
81. Monkman, *A Native Heritage: Images of the Indian in English Canadian Literature*, pp. 136-37.
82. PAC, RG10, vol. 2286, file 57, 169-1, pt. 5, Scott to W.D. Lighthall, 11 February 1928.
83. Ibid., C.E. Morgan to Scott, 11 February 1928; C.E. Morgan to Scott, 30 June 1928; Scott to C.E. Morgan, 3 July 1928.
84. *Detroit Free Press*, 1 July 1928.
85. *Family Herald and Weekly Star* (Montreal), 11 July 1928.
86. *Toronto Globe*, 2 July 1928.
87. PAC, RG10, vol. 2286, file 57, 169-1, pt. 5, Scott to Col. A.W. Duffus, 6 July 1928; Scott to W.J. Egan, 6 July 1928.
88. Ibid., Cpl. E.S. Covell to Supt. G.L. Jennings, Commanding Officer, "O" Division, RCMP, 7 August 1928.
89. Ibid., RCMP Commissioner Cortlandt Starnes to Scott, 30 October 1928.
90. Ibid., E.S. Covell to G.L. Jennings, 7 August 1928.
91. Ibid., report of Cpl. W.W. Jacomb, RCMP detachment, Ohsweken, 7 May 1929.
92. Ibid., Scott to O.D. Skelton, 18 May 1929.
93. Ibid., W.A. Riddell to O.D. Skelton, 15 July 1929.
94. Ibid., C.E. Morgan to Scott, 7 August 1929.
95. Ibid., O.D. Skelton to W.A. Riddell, 28 August 1929.
96. Ibid., C.E. Morgan to Scott, 30 May 1930.
97. Ibid., Scott to O.D. Skelton, 21 August 1930.
98. Ibid., W.A. Riddell to O.D. Skelton, 29 August 1929.
99. Ibid., Scott to O.D. Skelton, 5 September 1929.
100. Ibid., O.D. Skelton to Scott, 6 September 1929.
101. Ibid., W.A. Riddell to O.D. Skelton, 21 September 1929.
102. Veatch, *Canada and the League of Nations*, p. 19.
103. PAC, RG10, vol. 2286, file 57, 169-1, pt. 5, Henri Junod to Senator Raoul Dandurand, 16 May 1930.
104. Ibid., R. Dandurand to Scott, 6 and 29 June 1930.
105. PAC, RG10, vol. 2287, file 57, 169-1, pt. 6, Scott to R. Dandurand, 8 July 1930.

NOTES TO CHAPTER EIGHT

1. Robert E. Cail, *Land, Man, and the Law:*

*The Disposal of Crown Lands in British Colum-
bia 1871-1913* (Vancouver: University of
British Columbia Press, 1974); Phillip
Drucker, *The Native Brotherhoods: Modern
Intertribal Organizations on the Northwest Coast*
(Washington, Smithsonian Institute, 1958);
Wilson Duff, *The Indian History of British
Columbia* (Victoria: Provincial Museum of
British Columbia, 1964); Forrest E. La-
Violette, *The Struggle for Survival: Indian
Cultures and the Protestant Ethic in B.C.*
(Toronto: University of Toronto Press, 1961);
George E. Shankel, "The Development of
Indian Policy in British Columbia," (Ph.D.
diss., University of Washington, 1945).

2. Fisher, *Contact and Conflict*, pp. 176-7.

3. Ibid., pp. 181-91.

4. Ibid., p. 201.

5. Cail, *Land, Man, and the Law*, pp. 226-27.

6. Margaret A. Ormsby, *British Columbia: A
History* (Toronto: Macmillan, 1958), pp.
247-48.

7. Cail, *Land Man, and the Law*, pp. 136-42. It
is sometimes overlooked that Treaty No. 8
(1899), which covered what is now northern Alberta and part of the North-West
Territories, also extended into the north-
eastern corner of British Columbia. The
Fort St. John Beavers, who were signatories to this agreement, were granted reserves
from the Peace River Block, then under
federal control. The Slaves of Fort Nelson,
who were also signatories, did not claim
their reserves until 1956. It required a special conveyance by Victoria to Ottawa in
1961, as the Block had reverted to provincial control in 1930. Duff, *The Indian History of British Columbia*, pp. 70-71.

8. Ormsby, *British Columbia: A History*, p. 283.
See also F.W. Howay, "The Settlement and
Progress of British Columbia, 1871-1914,"
in J. Friesen and H.K. Ralston, eds., *Historical
Essays on British Columbia* (Toronto: Mc-
Clelland and Stewart, 1976), pp. 35-36.

9. Ormsby, *British Columbia: A History*, pp.
330-59.

10. Canada, House of Commons, *Debates*, 82,
cols. 628-29 (13 December 1907).

11. Shankel, "The Development of Indian Policy in British Columbia," pp. 214-19.

12. E. Palmer Patterson II, "A Decade of Change:
Origins of the Nishga and Tsimshian Land
Protests in the 1880s," *Journal of Canadian
Studies* 18, no. 3 (Autumn 1983): 44-46.

13. Paul Tennant, "Native Indian Political Organization in British Columbia, 1900-1969:

A Response to Internal Colonialism," *B.C.
Studies* 55 (Autumn 1982): 27-28. Tennant
points out that residential schools played
the unintended role of fostering pan-Indian
consciousness by bringing different tribes
together (p. 22).

14. E. Palmer Patterson II, "Arthur E. O'Meara:
Friend of the Indians," *Pacific Northwest
Quarterly* 58, no. 2 (April 1967): 91-92.

15. Shankel, "The Development of Indian Policy in British Columbia," p. 194.

16. *An Act to amend the Indian Act*, S.C. 1910, c.
28 (9-10 Edward VII), assented to 4 May
1910.

17. In fact, Laurier had met delegations of
Indians in Prince Rupert and Kamloops
in the previous year and had responded
sympathetically to their overtures.

18. PAC, RG10, vol. 3820, file 59,335, pt. 3A,
D.C. Scott, "Report on the British Colum-
bia Indian Question," presented to C.
Stewart, 14 July 1925.

19. McKenna had been assistant Indian commissioner when the Winnipeg office was
closed in 1909. He had served as inspector
of Roman Catholic schools in the west
since then.

20. Reuben Ware, *The Lands We Lost: A History
of Cut-Off Lands and Land Losses from Indian
Reserves in British Columbia* (Vancouver:
Union of B.C. Indian Chiefs, 1974), pp.
15-16.

21. PAC, RG10, vol. 3822, file 59,335-3A, J.A.J.
McKenna to R. Rogers, 26 October 1912.
McKenna observed that in one agency the
per capita allotment was under two acres
while in another it exceeded 184.

22. *Report of the Royal Commission on Indian
Affairs for the Province of British Columbia*
(Victoria: Acme Press, 1916), p. 26.

23. PAC, RG10, vol. 3822, file 59,335-2, "In the
Matter of the Territory of the Nishga Nation
or Tribe of Indians—to the King's Most
Excellent Majesty in Council—the Hum-
ble Petition of the Nishga Nation or Tribe
of Indians."

24. Ibid., vol. 3820, file 59,335, pt. 3A, D.C.
Scott, "Report on the British Columbia
Indian Question," presented to C. Stewart,
14 July 1925.

25. In giving this interpretation, Scott was rely-
ing on the judgment of the Judicial Committee of the Privy Council in the St. Cath-
erines Milling case in 1888. James S. Friders,
*Native People in Canada: Contemporary Con-
flicts*, 2d Edition (Scarborough, Ont: Prentice-
Hall, 1983), pp. 99-100.

26. British Columbia, Ministry of Lands, Parks and Housing, file 026076, section 1, Scott to the superintendent general, 11 March 1914.

27. PAC, MG 26H, Robert Borden Papers, 16330, "Statement of the Nishga Nation," adopted at Kinolith, 4 December 1914.

28. Ibid., 16532.

29. Ibid., 16405.

30. E. Palmer Patterson II, "Andrew Paull (1892-1959): Finding a Voice for the New Indian," *Western Canadian Journal of Anthropology* 6, no. 2 (1976): 67.

31. Tennant, "Native Indian Political Organization in British Columbia, 1900-1969: A Response to Internal Colonialism," pp. 27-28.

32. Paull was a native of the Squamish reserve in North Vancouver. He had been educated by Catholic missionaries and had acquired a knowledge of law while working in a lawyer's office. Kelly was a Haida from the Queen Charlotte Islands. He became a Methodist minister in 1916.

33. Shankel, "The Development of Indian Policy in British Columbia," pp. 201-2.

34. Patterson, "Arthur E. O'Meara: Friend of the Indians," p. 94.

35. PAC, RG10, vol. 3822, file 59,335, pt. 1, Scott to Hewitt Bostock, 7 February 1917.

36. Ibid., Scott to W.E. Ditchburn, 14 February 1917. Ditchburn was urged to maintain confidentiality: "if those who are agitating the Indian land question get access to the report, they will oppose it vigorously if they can and render it more difficult for the governments to act."

37. Ibid., W.E. Ditchburn to Scott, 29 January 1918.

38. Ormsby, *British Columbia: A History*, p. 398.

39. PAC, RG10, vol. 3820, file 59,335, pt. 3, Scott to A. Meighen, 28 November 1919.

40. B.C., Ministry of Lands, Parks and Housing, file 026076, section 2, T.D. Pattullo to A. Meighen, 17 December 1918 and A. Meighen to T.D. Pattullo, 7 January 1919.

41. The government faced recession in the fishing, mining and manufacturing sectors, and labour agitation, much of it in sympathy with the Winnipeg strikers.

42. PAC, RG10, vol. 3820, file 59,335, pt. 3, Scott to A. Meighen, 28 November 1919.

43. B.C., Ministry of Lands, Parks and Housing, file 026076, section 2, T.D. Pattullo to A. Meighen, 13 November 1919.

44. PAC, Robert Borden Papers, 16480-16483,

T.D. Pattullo to A. Meighen, 26 November 1919.

45. Ibid., 16487, A. Meighen to T.D. Pattullo, 1 December 1919.

46. The act, assented to 29 March 1919, is reproduced in full in R. Ware, *The Lands We Lost*, pp. 202-3.

47. PAC, RG10, vol. 3820, file 59,335, pt. 3, Scott to A. Meighen, 2 January 1920.

48. The act, assented to 1 July 1920, is reproduced in full in R. Ware, *The Lands We Lost*, pp. 204-5.

49. Canada, House of Commons, *Debates*, 141, pp. 787-94 (26 March 1920) and p. 953 (6 April 1920).

50. PAC, RG10, vol. 6810, file 470-2-3, pt. 7, Scott to A. Meighen, 31 May 1920.

51. B.C., Ministry of Lands, Parks and Housing, file 026076, section 2, Scott to T.D. Pattullo, 25 March 1920; T.D. Pattullo to A. Meighen, 21 April 1920; A. Meighen to T.D. Pattullo, 27 May 1920.

52. Clark was the province's superintendent of soldier settlement.

53. PAC, RG10, vol. 3820, file 59, 335 pt. 3, Scott to Sir James Lougheed, 1 October 1920. Teit was a Scottish born trader and ethnologist with a strong interest in Indians.

54. B.C., Ministry of Lands, Parks and Housing, file 026076, section 3, W.E. Ditchburn to J.W. Clark, 21 May 1921; J.W. Clark to W.E. Ditchburn, 6 June 1921.

55. PAC, RG10, vol. 3820, file 59, 335, pt. 3, W.E. Ditchburn to Scott, 23 February 1923.

56. B.C., Ministry of Lands, Parks and Housing, file 026076, section 3, W.E. Ditchburn to T.D. Pattullo, 10 February 1923; J.W. Clark to T.D. Pattullo, 15 March 1923.

57. Most of the reductions are listed in Ware, *The Lands We Lost*, pp. 42-47.

58. B.C., Ministry of Lands, Parks and Housing, file 026076, section 3, W.E. Ditchburn to G.R. Naden, provincial deputy minister of lands, 26 March 1923; Scott to T.D. Pattullo, 9 April 1923.

59. Ibid., T.D. Pattullo to Scott, 6 April 1923.

60. Ibid., 30 August 1924.

61. PAC, Robert Borden Papers, 16477, "Statement of the Allied Indian Tribes of British Columbia to the Government of Canada," 5 February 1919.

62. Ibid., 16501, "Statement of the Allied Indian Tribes of British Columbia for the Government of British Columbia," adopted at Vancouver, 12 November 1919.

63. PAC, RG10, vol. 3820, file 59,335, pt. 3, A.

Paull to W.E. Ditchburn, 25 October 1922. O'Meara's tactic of appealing directly to the Privy Council was somewhat tarnished by then. On 27 May 1918, a London law firm engaged by the Allied Tribes had addressed a memo to the president of the Privy Council urging consideration of the Nishga petition and rejecting the report of the royal commission as a final settlement of the land question. The president had replied that such questions should first go through the Canadian courts. And then it could only go to the Privy Council on the advice of the dominion government and the secretary of state for the colonies. It seems that O'Meara had refused to accept this rebuff and continued to advise the Allied Tribes that a direct appeal to London offered the best prospect for success. Patterson, "Arthur E. O'Meara: Friend of the Indians," pp. 94-95.

64. PAC, MG 26J, W.L. Mackenzie King Papers, vol. 123, 93393ff.

65. PAC, RG10, vol. 3820, file 59,335, pt. 1, "Report of a meeting between Charles Stewart and the Allied Tribes of British Columbia at the Board of Trade Rooms, Vancouver, 25 July 1923".

66. Ibid.

67. Provincial Archives of British Columbia, Add. ms. 997, "Conference of Dr. D.C. Scott, DSGIA of the Dominion Government of Canada, W.E. Ditchburn, Chief Inspector of Indian Agencies of British Columbia, with the Executive Committee of the Allied Indian Tribes of British Columbia." Victoria, beginning on 7 August 1923.

68. PAC, RG10, vol. 3820, file 59,335, pt. 3, memo of D.C. Scott on the British Columbia case, 31 July 1924.

69. Ibid., Scott to W.E. Ditchburn, 1 April 1924.

70. PAC, W.L. Mackenzie King Papers, vol. 123, 93393, "Report of an interview between the Nishga Tribe accompanied by A.E. O'Meara and Richard S. Woods, interpreter, and Prime Minister W.L. Mackenzie King," Prince Rupert, 13 October 1924.

71. PAC, RG10, vol. 3820, file 59,335, pt. 3, "Supplementary Memorandum of the Allied Tribes," 23 April 1925.

72. Ibid., Scott to H.H. Stevens, 30 June 1926.

73. PAC, RG10, vol. 3820, file 59,335, pt. 3A, D.C. Scott, "Report on the British Columbia Indian Question," presented to C. Stewart, 14 July 1925.

74. Canada, House of Commons, *Debates*, 174, pp. 4417-19 (11 June 1926).

75. PAC, RG10, vol. 3820, file 59,335, pt. 3A, Scott to C. Stewart, 23 November 1926.

76. Ibid., R.B. Bennett to P. Kelly, 21 July 1926.

77. Ibid., P. Kelly to C. Stewart, 13 November 1926.

78. Ibid., Scott to C. Stewart, 23 November 1926 and 11 February 1927.

79. Ibid., Scott to C. Stewart, 25 February 1927. There was some support among the opposition for the proposed inquiry and this may have influenced the cabinet decision. See remarks of H.H. Stevens, Canada, House of Commons, *Debates*, 175, p. 174 (10 February 1927).

80. The British Columbia government refused to be represented at the hearings.

81. Scott may have been less than honest in making this assertion. Figures from the annual report of the department for 1925 suggest that the per capita expenditure by Ottawa on the treaty Indians of Manitoba, Saskatchewan, Alberta and the North-West Territories far exceeded the expenditure on the Indians of British Columbia.

	Man. Sask. Alta. NWT	B.C.
appropriation account expenditure	$776,818.02	$290,685.17
Indian population	39,511	23,782
per capita expenditure	$19.66	$12.20

When treaty Indian annuities of $214,360 are also taken into account, the per capita expenditure in Manitoba, Saskatchewan, Alberta and the North-West Territories rises to $25.08—double that in British Columbia." Appropriation account funds were spent on relief, medical services, agricultural supplies, surveys, and so forth and amounted to about half the annual department budget. The other half was spent mainly on education. Unfortunately, educational expenditures were not broken down on a provincial basis in the report; it is therefore difficult to make a conclusive comparison between British Columbia and western treaty Indians.

82. Canada, Parliament, *Appendix to the Journals of the Senate of Canada, First Session of the Sixteenth Parliament, 1926-27; Special Joint Committee of the Senate and House of Commons, Appointed to Inquire into the Claims of the Allied Indian Tribes of British Columbia, as set forth in their Petition Submitted to Parliament in June 1926: Report and Evidence*, Ottawa

1927 (hereafter *Special Joint Committee re: Claims of Allied Tribes*), pp. 3-25.

83. Richard Wilbur, *H.H. Stevens, 1878-1973* (Toronto: University of Toronto Press, 1977). This is a sympathetic biography and Stevens's role in the Joint Committee is ignored.

84. Canada, Parliament, *Special Joint Committee re Claims of Allied Tribes*, pp. 78-93.

85. Ibid., p. 133.

86. Ibid., pp. 161-162.

87. PAC, RG10, vol. 3920, file 59,335, pt. 3A, Scott to H.H. Stevens, 9 March 1927.

88. Canada, Parliament, *Special Joint Committee re Claims of Allied Tribes*, viii-xi.

89. Ibid., xii-xviii.

90. Ibid., xi.

91. Ibid., xviii.

92. *Annual Report of the Department of Indian Affairs for the year ended 31 March 1927*, p. 10.

93. PAC, RG10, vol. 3823, file 59,335-5 correspondence between Scott and W.E. Ditchburn and between Scott and W.E. Collison, agent at Prince Rupert, January and February 1928.

94. *Victoria Times*, 3 April 1928.

95. PAC, RG10, vol. 3820, file 59,335, pt. 3A, C. Perry, agent at Vancouver, to Scott, 18 February 1928.

96. Drucker, *The Native Brotherhoods: Modern Intertribal Organizations on the Northwest Coast*, pp. 101-2.

97. B.C., Ministry of Lands, Parks and Housing, file 026076, section 4, Scott to T.D. Pattullo, 6 December 1927.

98. Ibid., T.D. Pattullo to A.M. Manson, 13 January 1928; A.M. Manson to T.D. Pattullo, 20 January 1928.

99. PAC, RG10, vol. 3820, file 59,335, pt. 3A, W.E. Ditchburn to Scott, 27 January 1928. Ditchburn proposed using the railway lands in the bargaining process.

100. *Victoria Times*, 10 November 1926.

101. B.C., Ministry of Lands, Parks and Housing, file 026076, section 4, correspondence between Scott and G.R. Naden, deputy minister of lands, British Columbia, August and November 1928.

102. Ibid., "Memorandum of Agreement arrived at between Dr. Duncan C. Scott and Mr. W.E. Ditchburn on behalf of the Dominion Government, and Mr. Henry Cathcart and Mr. O.C. Bass on behalf of the Provincial Government," Victoria, British Columbia, 22 March 1929.

103. Dominion order-in-council 208, 3 February 1930, provincial order-in-council 1151, 24 September 1930.

104. PAC, RG10, vol. 7785, file 27150-0-18, pt. 1, W.E. Ditchburn to Scott, 4 March 1932.

105. Ibid., Scott to T. Murphy, 10 March 1932.

106. Ibid., A.S. Williams to T. Murphy, 19 October 1932.

107. Ibid., H. Cathcart to T. Murphy, 19 October 1932.

108. Ibid., Memorandum of interview between H. Cathcart, T.R.L. MacInnis and C.C. Perry, 23 August 1934.

109. Ibid., D.M. MacKay to H. McGill, director of the Indian Affairs Branch, 19 April 1938.

110. Ibid., D.M. MacKay to H. McGill, 13 June 1938.

111. PAC, RG10, vol. 6810, file 470-2-3, pt. 7, Scott to A. Meighen, 31 May 1920.

NOTES TO CHAPTER NINE

1. La Violette, *The Struggle for Survival*, pp. 31-97.

2. There is no shortage of literature on the potlatch. In fact, it has been a favourite subject of investigation for cultural anthropologists since the days of Franz Boas. See part three of Tom McFeat, ed., *Indians of the North Pacific Coast* (Toronto: McClelland and Stewart, 1966).

3. *An Act Further to Amend The Indian Act, 1880*, S.C. 1884, c. 27 (47 Vict.), assented to 19 April 1884.

4. David R. Williams, *The Man for a New Country* (Sidney, BC: Grey's Publishing, 1977) is a biography of Begbie. The judge's attitude towards the Indians is found on pages 100-118.

5. PAC, RG10, vol. 3628, file 6244-1 contains the correspondence on this question.

6. Mike Mountain Horse, *My People the Bloods* (Calgary: Glenbow-Alberta Institute and Standoff, AB: Blood Tribal Council, 1979), p. 567.

7. Ibid., pp. 64-65.

8. Adolf Hungry Wolf, *The Blood People* (New York: Harper and Row, 1977), pp. 20-48 contain detailed accounts of sun dance gatherings including self-torture and sweat lodge elements.

9. Fine Day, *My Cree People* (n.p., n.d., University of Alberta Library), p. 25.

10. David Mandelbaum, *The Plains Cree: An Ethnographic, Historical and Comparative Study* (Regina: Canadian Plains Research Centre, University of Regina, 1979), pp. 199-212.

11. Lucien M. Hanks and Jane R. Hanks, *Tribe Under Trust: A Study of the Blackfoot Reserve in Alberta* (Toronto: University of Toronto Press, 1950), p. 86.

12. Hungry Wolf, *The Blood People*, p. 301. Steele expressed similar views in 1891. See R.C. Macleod, *The North-West Mounted Police and Law Enforcement, 1873-1905* (Toronto: University of Toronto Press, 1976), pp. 145-46.

13. PAC, RG10, vol. 3597, file 1350, L. Vankoughnet to Hayter Reed, 27 November 1890, and subsequent correspondence.

14. Ibid., 3876, file 91, 749, Hayter Reed to L. Vankoughnet, 21 June 1892.

15. John Snow, *These Mountains are our Sacred Places: The Story of the Stoney Indians* (Toronto: Samuel Stevens, 1977), pp. 52-53. Snow claims that the control of rations was used to enforce the pass system.

16. Macleod, *The North-West Mounted Police and Law Enforcement 1873-1905*, p. 146.

17. PAC, RG10, vol. 3825, file 60, 511-1, Hayter Reed to A.E. Forget, 20 June 1895.

18. *An Act further to amend the Indian Act*, S.C. 1895, c. 35 (58-59 Vict.), assented to 22 July 1895.

19. PAC, RG10, vol. 3628, file 6244-1. The brief accompanying the amendment noted the similarities between coastal and plains ceremonies and indicated that the prohibition was to extend to both. All give away festivals were "conductive of extravagance and cause much loss of time and the assemblage of large numbers of Indians with all the usual attendant evils." The Tamanawas were described as "orgies of the most disgusting character, viz. biting the arms of spectators."

20. Ibid., Hayter Reed to C. E. Carbould, M.P., 31 March 1896.

21. PAC, RG10, vol. 3825, file 60, 511-1, A. McNeill to A.E. Forget, 12 June 1896, re: the abandonment of a dance at File Hills. See also Sergeant A.F.M. Brooke, Gleichen detachment, NWMP, to officer in command, Calgary, 14 August 1898, re breaking up the Blackfoot sun dance and preventing the brave-making ceremony.

22. Ibid., G.H. Wheatley to A.E. Forget, 31 May 1897 and subsequent correspondence.

23. Ibid., P.J. Williams to A.E. Forget, 15 January 1897 and subsequent correspondence.

24. The strained relations between James Wilson, the agent in charge of the Bloods, and Superintendent R.B. Deane of the NWMP over the sun dance illustrates this difference of opinion clearly. See Hugh A. Dempsey, *Red Crow, Warrior Chief* (Saskatoon: Western Producer Prairie Books, 1980), pp. 203-14.

25. PAC, RG10, vol. 3825, file 60, 511-1, D. Laird to J.D. McLean, 17 January 1901.

26. Ibid., F. White to J. Smart, 23 February 1902.

27. Ibid., G. Coldwell and G. Coleman (lawyers, Brandon, Manitoba) to C. Sifton, 20 February 1903 and subsequent correspondence.

28. *The Globe*, 27 May 1903.

29. PAC, RG10, vol. 3825, file 60, 511-1, J.A.J. McKenna to J.D. McLean, 15 June 1903.

30. Ibid., file 60,511-1, C. Pearson Bell, assistant surgeon, NWMP, Regina, to officer in command, Regina, 18 January 1904 and subsequent correspondence.

31. *Winnipeg Telegram*, 18 February 1904.

32. PAC, RG10, vol. 3825, file 60, 511-1. Markle had written to Laird, 4 December 1901, advocating withholding rations from Indians who danced. The commissioner had opposed the idea.

33. Ibid., J. Hugonard to D. Laird, 23 November 1903.

34. Ibid., C. Sifton to Archbishop Adelard of St. Boniface, 31 December 1903.

35. PAC, RG10, vol. 3825, file 60, 511-2, F. Pedley to F. Oliver, 30 March 1906.

36. Ibid., W. Grant to headquarters, 2 July 1906.

37. *Winnipeg Telegram*, 11 July 1906.

38. PAC, RG10, vol. 3825, file 60, 511-2, J.D. McLean to D. Laird, 5 September 1906.

39. *Report of the Department of Indian Affairs for the year ended 31 March 1908*, pp. xxi-xxii.

40. *Winnipeg Free Press*, 22 November 1907.

41. PAC, RG10, vol. 3825, file 60, 511-2, Bishop Emile Legal to the superintendent general, 20 July 1908.

42. Hungry Wolf, *The Blood People*, p. 311 features a photograph of Blood dancers in Fort Macleod in 1907.

43. David C. Jones, *Midways, Judges, and Smooth-Tongued Fakirs: The Illustrated Story of Country Fairs in the Prairie West* (Saskatoon: Western Producer Prairie Books, 1983),pp. 3-4.

44. PAC, RG10, vol. 3825, file 60, 511-2, J.A. Markle to D. Laird, 9 September 1907; J.A.J. McKenna to J.D. McLean, 21 February 1908.

45. In fact there were several instances during the first two decades of the twentieth century in which showmen of one sort or another wished to take Indians abroad for exhibition purposes. The department invariably refused to sanction these tours. See ibid., vol. 4010, file 253, 430.

46. Ibid., vol. 3825, file 60, 511-2, F. Pedley to G.F. O'Halloran, 13 June 1908.

47. Ibid., for example, J.A. Markle to J.D. McLean, 3 August 1909.
48. PAC, RG10, vol. 3826, file 60, 511-3, D. Laird to F. Pedley, 30 November 1909.
49. *Calgary News*, 22 August 1910.
50. *Lethbridge Herald*, 25 August 1910.
51. PAC, RG10, vol. 3825, file 60, 511-2, Scott to J.W. McNicol, secretary, Lethbridge Agricultural Society, n.d.
52. Ibid., F. Pedley to J.W. Hyde, Blood agency.
53. James G. McGregor, *A History of Alberta* (Edmonton: Hurtig, 1972), p. 225.
54. PAC, RG10, vol. 3826, file 60, 511-3, G. Campbell, chief inspector of agencies, Winnipeg, to T. Crothers, 12 May 1913.
55. *The Globe*, 4 September 1912.
56. PAC, RG10, vol. 3806, file 279, 222-1A, Scott to all agents, 25 October 1913.
57. Ibid., vol 6809, file 470-2-3, pt. 5. See also *An Act to amend the Indian Act*, S.C. 1914, c. 35 (4-5 George V), assented to 12 June 1914.
58. Canada, House of Commons, *Debates*, 116, pp. 3483-84 (8 May 1914).
59. PAC, RG10, vol. 3086, file 279, 222-1A, J.D. McLean to all western agents, 17 June 1914.
60. Ibid., vol. 3826, file 60, 511-3, circulars to western agents, 26 December 1914 and 23 February 1915.
61. Ibid., 511-4, pt. 1, crime report by J.R. Hooper, RNWMP, Leask, Saskatchewan, 2 June 1915.
62. PAC, RG10, vol. 3827, file 60, 511-5, Scott to R.B. Bennett, 17 July 1916. Scott also allowed Indians to participate in races and dancing contests on Victoria Day, 1916 in Vancouver in order to raise money for the British Columbia Aero Club which was involved in training military pilots. See ibid., vol. 3629, file 6244-2.
63. Ibid., vol. 3629, file 6244-2, Scott to W.J. Roche, 18 December 1916.
64. *An Act to amend the Indian Act*, S.C. 1918, c. 26 (8-9 George V), assented to 24 May 1918.
65. PAC, RG10, vol. 3629, file 6244-2, Scott to western agents, 21 October 1918.
66. Ibid., vol 3826, file 60, 511-4A, Scott to Graham, 4 October 1921.
67. Ibid. An RCMP crime report dated 26 June 1921 at Fort Francis, Ontario noted that Jim Kubinase was sent to Winnipeg jail for two months for organizing a sun dance at Buffalo Point, Manitoba. Another report in November 1921 announced that four Blood Indians were sent to Lethbridge jail for participating in a "give away" dance.
68. Edward Ahenakew, *Voices of the Plains Cree* (Toronto: McClelland and Stewart, 1973), p. 69.
69. PAC, RG10, vol. 3826, file 60, 511-4A. One RCMP officer, reporting on the Blackfoot sun dance of June 1921, blamed Joseph O'Keefe, a lawyer based in Gleichen, for advising the Indians on the matter. The officer suspected that O'Keefe had done so as he was allegedly an "out an out Sinn Feiner."
70. Mandelbaum, *The Plains Cree*, p. 194.
71. PAC, RG10, vol. 3826, file 60, 511-4A, Scott to G.H. Gooderham, 5 May 1923 and subsequent correspondence.
72. *Edmonton Journal*, 21 July 1923.
73. PAC, RG10, vol. 3826, file 60, 511-4A, letter signed by seventeen Oblate fathers to Scott, 23 July 1923.
74. Ibid., W.M. Graham to Scott, 9 July 1923.
75. Ibid., W.M. Graham to J.D. McLean, 24 August 1923; W.M. Graham to headquarters, 11 December 1923.
76. Ibid., W.M. Graham to E.W. Stephenson, 4 February 1929; E.W. Stephenson to headquarters, 26 February 1929; headquarters to E.W. Stephenson, 7 March 1929.
77. PAC, RG10, vol. 3827, file 60, 511-5, Scott to A. Meighen, 5 May 1919; W.M. Graham to Scott, 23 October 1919 and subsequent correspondence.
78. W.B. Fraser, *Calgary* (Toronto: Holt, Rinehart and Winston, 1967), p. 76.
79. PAC, RG10, vol. 3827, file 60, 511-5, Scott to Stoney, Blackfoot and Sarcee agents, 26 June 1923; W.M. Graham to headquarters, 4 August 1923 and 11 December 1923.
80. Ibid., Scott to C. Stewart, 29 November 1923.
81. Ibid., W.M. Graham to Scott, 5 April 1924.
82. Ibid., W.M. Graham to Scott, 29 May 1924.
83. Ibid., Scott to W.M. Graham, 11 November 1925.
84. *Report of the Department of Indian Affairs for the year ended 31 March 1926*, p. 7.
85. PAC, RG10, vol. 3826, file 60, 511-4A, report of Serg. A. Howard, Cardston detachment RCMP, 1 August 1930, re: Blood sun dance.
86. Ibid., W.M. Graham to Scott, 22 June 1931.
87. Ibid., Scott to T. Murphy, 28 July 1931.
88. *An Act to amend the Indian Act*, S.C. 1932-33, c. 4 (23-24 George V), assented to 23 May 1933.
89. Jones, *Midways, Judges, and Smooth-Tongued Fakirs*, pp. 124-26.
90. For example, the *Montreal Gazette*, 14 August 1934, reported that seven hundred Stonies were expected to attend the "Indian Days" celebrations in Banff.
91. In Hanks and Hanks, *Tribes Under Trust*, p.

78, it was observed that the sun dance, tobacco dance and deer dance were very much
alive on the Blackfoot reserve in 1941.

92. Hungry Wolf, *The Blood People*, pp. 323-31.

93. Mandelbaum, *The Plains Cree*, pp. 214-15.

94. It should be remembered that, in spite of
setbacks over the years, Scott's attitude to
dancing did not undergo any fundamental
changes. In a paper prepared for the Bian-
nual Conference of the Institute of Pacific
Relations, October-November 1931, he said:

It may seem arbitrary on our part to interfere with the native culture. The position
of the department, however, can readily
be understood, and it is pointed out that
Indians will spend a fortnight engaging in
it, another fortnight to get over it. Obviously this plays havoc with summer
ploughing.

Scott, *The Administration of Indian Affairs in
Canada*, p. 25.

NOTES TO CHAPTER TEN

1. *Winnipeg Tribune*, 29 March 1940.

2. PAC, MG 26 K, R.B. Bennett Papers, Indian
Affairs file D-200, Scott to T. Murphy, 15
March 1932.

3. PAC, RG 10, vol. 3878, file 91, 839-7.

4. PAC, R.B. Bennett Papers, Indian Affairs
file D-200, Scott to T. Murphy, 15 March
1932.

5. Norma Sluman and Jean Goodwill, *John
Tootoosis: Biography of a Cree Leader* (Ottawa:
Golden Dog Press, 1982), p. 120.

6. Ibid., p. 119. See also Donald B. Smith, *Long
Lance: The True Story of an Imposter* (Toronto:
Macmillan, 1982), p. 91.

7. PAC, MG 26, I, 31, Arthur Meighen Papers,
97594, A. Meighen to T. Murphy, undated
note scribbled on the back of a letter to
Meighen from Violette Graham, 20 March
1932.

8. Annie Helena Violette Graham was born in
Sarnia, Ontario in 1868, the daughter of
J.H. Wood. The family moved to Birtle,
Manitoba when she was a child. She married Graham on 10 December 1890. She
was active in the Red Cross and in women's
organizations. *Regina Leader Post*, 18 December 1939.

9. PAC, RG 10, vol. 4070, file 427, 063-A, W.M.
Graham to A. Meighen, 22 January 1914.

10. Ibid., Scott to W.J. Roche, 7 February 1914.

11. Ibid., Scott to A. Meighen, 4 June 1915.

12. Ibid., Scott to A.E. Blount, private secretary
to the prime minister, 31 August 1917.

13. Ibid., W.J. Roche to W.M. Graham, 25 September 1917.

14. Ibid., Scott to W.M. Graham, 2 October 1920;
W.M. Graham to Scott, 1 October 1920; Scott
to W.M. Graham, 27 June 1921.

15. Ibid., Scott to W.M. Graham, 23 February
1922.

16. PAC, RG 10, vol. 4070, file 427, 063-A1,
W.M. Graham to C. Stewart, 13 June 1923.

17. Ibid., Scott to C. Stewart, 29 June 1923.

18. Ibid. memorandum by Scott, undated; C.
Stewart to W.M. Graham, 5 October 1923.

19. Ibid. W.M. Graham to Scott, 15 May 1924.

20. Ibid., W.M. Graham to Scott, 28 September
1927.

21. Ibid., Scott to C. Stewart, 2 October 1928.

22. Ibid., Scott to W.M. Graham, 4 June 1929
and subsequent correspondence.

23. John English, *Arthur Meighen* (Don Mills,
ONT: Fitzhenry and Whiteside, 1977), pp.
46-48.

24. The author wishes to acknowledge the assistance of Bennett McCardle in bringing this
incident to his attention.

25. Canada, House of Commons, *Debates*, 190,
pp. 3674-77 (13 July 1931). These details
were divulged in the speech by J.S. Woodsworth.

26. Mr. Justice James McKay, president of the
club.

27. PAC, RG10, vol. 4070, file 427, 063-A, Scott
to W.M. Graham, 30 September 1927.

28. Ibid., W.M. Graham to Scott, 5 October 1982.

29. Canada, House of Commons, *Debates*, 190,
p. 3677 (13 July 1931).

30. Ibid., p. 3674.

31. Ibid., p. 3678.

32. PAC, R.B. Bennett Papers, Indian Affairs
file D-200, J. Mayoh to R.B. Bennett, 31 May
1930.

33. Ibid., W.M. Graham file D-207-G, A. Tye to
R.B. Bennett, 13 January 1932.

34. PAC, Arthur Meighen Papers, series 5, vol.
159, 97542, R.B. Bennett to A. Tye, 25 January 1932.

35. PAC, R.B. Bennett Papers, W.M. Graham
file D-207-G, F.W.G. Haultain to R.B. Bennett,
11 February 1932; R.B. Bennett to F.W.G.
Haultain, 15 February 1932.

36. PAC, Arthur Meighen Papers, series 5, vol.
159, 97533, W.M. Graham to R.B. Bennett, 2
February 1932.

37. Ibid., 97526, V. Graham to A. Meighen, 30
January 1932.

38. Ibid., 97545, A. Tye to A. Meighen, 5 February 1932.
39. Ibid., 97544-70, Scott to W.M. Graham, 3 February 1932 and subsequent correspondence.
40. Ibid., 97553, A. Meighen to R.B. Bennett, 18 February 1932.
41. Ibid., 97581, A. Tye to A. Meighen, 17 March 1932.
42. Ibid., 97585, V. Graham to A. Meighen, 18 March 1932.
43. Ibid., 97594, A. Meighen to T. Murphy, undated noted scribbled on the back of a letter to Meighen from Violette Graham, 20 March 1932.
44. Ibid., 97591, 97592, T. Murphy to A. Mieghen, 22 March 1932 and 29 March 1932.
45. Ibid., 97598, W.M. Graham to A. Meighen, 3 October 1932.
46. *Regina Leader Post*, 30 March 1940.
47. PAC, RG10, vol. 3877, file 91, 839-1, Scott to F. Pedley, 3 March 1904. He noted that the department had no guarantee that the commissioner's office supplied all information or carried out all instructions. "It might be independent in spirit as well as in action."
48. PAC, RG10, vol. 4070, file 427, 063-A, Scott to T. Murphy, 1 February 1932.
49. PAC, R.B. Bennett Papers, Indian Affairs file D-200, H.H. Stevens to R.B. Bennett, 29 January 1932.
50. Ibid., correspondence re: position of deputy superintendent general of Indian affairs.
51. Scott to Madge McBeth, 19 November, 1934, in Bourinot, *Some Letters of Duncan Campbell Scott, Archibald Lampman and Others*.
52. Pacey, "Duncan Campbell Scott," in *Ten Canadian Poets*, pp. 160-61.
53. PAC, MG30 D276, Elise Aylen Scott Papers, biographical note. A gossipy account of Scott's relations with his two wives is found in Sandra Gwyn, *The Private Capital: Ambition and Love in the Age of Macdonald and Laurier* (Toronto: McClelland and Stewart, 1984), p. 436-70.

NOTES TO CONCLUSION

1. Scott, *The Adminstration of Indian Affairs in Canada*, p. 26.
2. Brown, "Duncan Campbell Scott: A Memoir," p. 134. In Scott's voluminous correspondence with Brown, which commenced in 1940 and ended only with the former's death, Indians make but one brief appearance. The reference is, however, an interesting one. Writing to Brown on 2 July 1941, Scott noted:

   I had for about twenty years oversight of their [Indians] development and I was never unsympathetic to aboriginal ideals, but there was a law which I did not originate and which I never tried to amend in the direction of severity. One can hardly be sympathetic with the contemporary Sun-dance or Potlatch when one knows that the original spirit has departed and that they are largely the opportunities for debauchery by low white men.

   Readers can judge for themselves if the assertion in the first sentence bears the scrutiny of the historical record. Scott's comment on the sun dance and potlatch should not surprise anyone. Robert L. McDougall, *The Poet and the Critic* (Ottawa: Carleton University Press, 1983), p. 26.

Selected Bibliography

ARCHIVAL MATERIALS

British Columbia, Ministry of Lands, Parks and Housing, Records (file 026076).
Public Archives of Canada:
    Elise Aylen Scott Papers
    R.B. Bennett Papers
    Robert Borden Papers
    W.L. Mackenzie King Papers
    Arthur Meighen Papers
    Records of the Department of Indian Affairs (RG10)
    Duncan Campbell Scott Papers
    Clifford Sifton Papers
Victoria College, University of Toronto (Pratt Library): Pelham Edgar Papers.

GOVERNMENT PUBLICATIONS

Canada. Commission on Conservation. *National Conference on Conservation of Game, Fur-Bearing Animals and Other Wild Life.* Ottawa: J. de Labroquerie Tache, 1919.
Canada. House of Commons. *Debates.*
Canada. Sessional Papers. Department of Indian Affairs. *Annual Reports.*
Canada. Parliament. *Appendix to the Journals of the Senate of Canada, First Session of the Sixteenth Parliament 1926-27; Special Joint Committee of the Senate and House Commons, appointed to Inquire into the Claims of the Allied Indian Tribes of British Columbia, as set forth in their Petition Submitted to Parliament in June, 1926: Report and Evidence.* Ottawa, 1927.
Canada. *The James Bay Treaty.* Ottawa: Queen's Printer, 1964, (reprinted from the edition of 1931).

NEWSPAPERS

Brantford Expositer
Calgary News
Detroit Free Press
Edmonton Journal
Family Herald and Weekly Star (Montreal)
La Tribune de Genève
Lethbridge Herald
London Free Press
Louisville Times
Montreal Gazette
Montreal Star
Ottawa Citizen
Ottawa Journal
Regina Leader
Regina Leader Post
Toronto Daily Star
Toronto Globe
Toronto Star Weekly
Toronto Sunday World
Utica Observer
Winnipeg Free Press
Winnipeg Telegram
Winnipeg Tribune

UNPUBLISHED MATERIALS

Kennedy, Jacqueline. "Qu'Appelle Industrial School: White 'Rites' for the Indians of the Old North-West." M.A. thesis, Carleton University, 1970.

Leighton, J. Douglas. "The Development of Federal Indian Policy in Canada, 1840-1890." Ph.D. diss., University of Western Ontario, 1975.

Looy, A.J. "The Indian Agent and His Role in the Administration of the North-West Superintendency, 1876-1893." Ph.D. diss., Queen's University, 1977.

Lueger, Rick. "An Introduction to Canadian Indian Political Organizations: a preliminary report." Ottawa: National Indian Brotherhood, 1972.

Shankel, George, E. "The Development of Indian Policy in British Columbia." Ph.D. diss., University of Washington, 1945.

Titley, E. Brian. "Hayter Reed and Indian Administration in the West." Paper presented at the Western Canada Studies Conference, University of Alberta, November 1985.

Tyler and Wright Research Consultants, Ltd., Ottawa. "The Alienation of Indian Reserve Lands during the Administration of Sir Wilfrid Laurier, 1896-1911." A Report prepared for the Federation of Saskatchewan Indians, March 1978.

Weaver, Sally M. "Iroquois Politics: Grand River, 1847-1975." Unpublished manuscript in author's possession.

————. and Virginia Cooper. "An Early History of the Dehorners, 1904-1910". Unpublished working paper in authors' possession, 1970.

————. "An Early History of the Movement for an Elective Form of Local Government among the Six Nations of Grand River, 1861-1903." Unpublished working paper in authors' possession, 1970.

Weis, Lyle P. "D.C. Scott and the Desire for a Sense of Order". Ph.D. diss., University of Alberta, 1983.

ARTICLES AND BOOKS

Adaskin, Harry. *A Fiddler's World.* Vancouver: November House, 1977.

Ahenakew, Edward. *Voices of the Plains Crees.* Toronto: McClelland and Stewart, 1973.

Beckman, Susan. "A Note on Duncan Campbell Scott's 'The Forsaken.' " *Humanities Association Review* 25, no. 1 (Winter 1974).

Berger, Carl. *The Sense of Power: Studies in the Idea of Canadian Imperialism, 1867-1914.* Toronto: University of Toronto Press, 1970.

Berton, Pierre. *The Promised Land: Settling the West, 1896-1914.* Toronto: McClelland and Stewart, 1984.

Blake, T.M. "Indian Reserve Allocation in British Columbia." *B.C. Perspectives* 3 (March 1973).

Bourinot, A.S., *Some Letters of Duncan Campbell Scott, Archibald Lampman and Others.* Ottawa: A.S. Bourinot, 1959.

————. *More Letters of Duncan Campbell Scott.* Ottawa: A.S. Bourinot, 1960.

Brown, Dugald. "Indian Hunting Rights and Provincial Law: Some Recent Developments." *University of Toronto Faculty of Law Review* 39, no. 2 (Fall 1981).

Brown, E.K. *Responses and Evaluations: Essays on Canada.* Toronto: McClelland and Stewart, 1977.

Brown, G. and R. Maguire. *Indian Treaties in Historical Perspective.* Ottawa: Research Branch, Department of Indian and Northern Affairs, 1979.

Brown, R. Craig and Ramsay Cook. *Canada 1896-1921: A Nation Transformed.* Toronto: McClelland and Stewart, 1974.

Bryce, P.H. *The Story of a National Crime.* Ottawa: James Hope, 1922.

Cail, Robert E. *Land, Man, and the Law: The Disposal of Crown Lands in British Columbia, 1871-1913.* Vancouver: University of British Columbia Press, 1974.

Chalmers, John W. *Laird of the West.* Calgary: Detselig, 1981.

Chamberlain, J.E. *The Harrowing of Eden: White Attitudes Toward Native Americans.* New York: Seabury Press, 1975.

Clever, Glen, ed. *Duncan Campbell Scott: Selected Poetry.* Ottawa: Tecumseh Press, 1974.

Cork, Ella. *The Worst of the Bargain.* San Jacinto, CA: Foundation for Social Research, 1962.

Daniel, Richard C. *A History of Native Claims Processes in Canada, 1867-1979.* Ottawa: Research Branch, Department of Indian and Northern Affairs, 1980.

Davies, Barrie, ed. *At the Mermaid Inn: Wilfred Campbell, Archibald Lampman, Duncan Campbell Scott in the Globe, 1892-93.* Toronto: University of Toronto Press, 1979.

Dempsey, Hugh A. *Red Crow, Warrior Chief.* Saskatoon: Western Producer Prairie Books, 1980.

Dempsey, James. "The Indians and World War One." *Alberta History* 31, no. 3 (Summer 1983).

Doyle, James. "Duncan Campbell Scott and American Literature," in K.P. Stich, ed., *The Duncan Campbell Scott Symposium*. Ottawa: University of Ottawa Press, 1980.

Duncan Campbell Scott: A Book of Criticism. Ottawa: Tecumseh Press, 1974.

Drucker, Phillip. *The Native Brotherhoods: Modern Intertribal Organizations on the Northwest Coast*. Washington: Smithsonian Institute, 1958.

Duff, Wilson. *The Indian History of British Columbia, Vol. I, The Impact of the White Man*. Victoria: Provincial Museum of Natural History and Anthropology, 1964.

Easterbrook, W.T., and G.J. Aitken. *Canadian Economic History*. Toronto: Macmillan, 1954.

Edgar, Pelham. *Across My Path*. Toronto: Ryerson Press, 1952.

_____. "Duncan Campbell Scott." *Dalhousie Review* 7 (April 1927).

Eggleston, Wilfrid. *Literary Friends*. Ottawa: Borealis Press, 1980.

English, John. *Arthur Meighen*. Don Mills, ONT: Fitzhenry and Whiteside, 1977.

Fine Day. *My Cree People*. n.p., n.d., University of Alberta Library.

Fisher, Robin. *Contact and Conflict: Indian-European Relations in British Columbia, 1774-1890*. Vancouver: University of British Columbia Press, 1977.

_____. "Joseph Trutch and Indian Land Policy." *B.C. Studies* 12 (Winter 1971-72).

Flood, John. "The Duplicity of D.C. Scott and the James Bay Treaty." *Black Moss* 2, no. 2 (Fall 1976).

_____. "Native People in Scott's Short Fiction," in K.P. Stich, ed. *The Duncan Campbell Scott Symposium* Ottawa: University of Ottawa Press, 1980.

Fraser, W.B. *Calgary*. Toronto: Holt, Rinehart and Winston, 1967.

Frideres, James S. *Native People in Canada: Contemporary Conflicts*. 3d ed. Scarborough, ONT: Prentice Hall, of Canada, 1983.

Friesen, J. and H.K. Ralston, eds. *Historical Essays on British Columbia*. Toronto: McClelland and Stewart, 1976.

Fumoleau, Rene. *As Long as This Land Shall Last*. Toronto: McClelland and Stewart, n.d.

Getty, Ian A.L., and Antoine S. Lussier., eds. *As Long as the Sun Shines and Water Flows*. Vancouver: University of British Columbia Press, 1983.

Gottesman, Dan. "Native Hunting and the Migratory Birds Convention Act: Historical, Political and Ideological Perspectives." *Journal of Canadian Studies* 8, no. 3 (Fall 1983).

Graham-Cumming, G. "The Health of the Original Canadians, 1867-1967." *Medical Services Journal* 13 (February 1967).

Grant, John W. *Moon of Wintertime: Missionaries and the Indians of Canada in Encounters Since 1534*. Toronto: University of Toronto Press, 1984.

Grant, S.D. "Indian Affairs Under Duncan Campbell Scott: The Plains Cree of Saskatchewan, 1913-1931." *Journal of Canadian Studies* 18, no. 3 (Autumn 1983).

Gresko, Jacqueline. "White 'Rites' and Indian 'Rites': Indian Education and Native Responses in the West, 1870-1910," in A.W. Rasporich ed., *Western Canada: Past and Present*. Calgary: McClelland and Stewart West, 1975.

Gwyn, Sandra. *The Private Capital: Love and Ambition in the Age of Macdonald and Laurier*. Toronto: McClelland and Stewart, 1984.

Hall, D.J. "Clifford Sifton and Canadian Indian Administration, 1896-1905." *Prairie Forum* 2, nos. 1-2 (1977).

Halliday, W.M. *Potlatch and Totem: The Recollections of an Indian Agent*. Toronto: J.M. Dent, 1935.

Hanks, Lucien M., and Jane R. Hanks. *Tribe Under Trust: A Study of the Blackfoot Reserve in Alberta.* Toronto: University of Toronto Press, 1950.

Harper, Allan G. "Canada's Indian Administration; Basic Concepts and Objectives." *America Indigena* 5, no. 2 (April 1945).

———. "Canada's Indian Administration: The Treaty System." *America Indigena* 7, no. 2 (April 1947).

Hawthorn, H.B., C.S. Belshaw, and S.M. Jamieson. *The Indians of British Columbia.* Toronto: University of Toronto Press, 1958.

Hiriano, Keiichi. "The Aborigine in Canadian Literature: Notes by a Japanese." *Canadian Literature* 14 (Autumn 1962).

The Historical Development of the Indian Act. Research Branch, Department of Indian and Northern Affairs, 1978.

Hodgetts, J.E. *Pioneer Public Service: An Administrative History of the United Canadas.* Toronto: University of Toronto Press, 1955.

Howay, F.W. "The Settlement and Progress of British Columbia, 1871-1914," in J. Friesen, and H.K. Ralston, eds. *Historical Essays on British Columbia.* Toronto: McClelland and Stewart, 1976.

Hungry Wolf, Adolf. *The Blood People.* New York: Harper and Row, 1977.

Jenness, Diamond. "Canada's Indian Policy Yesterday. What of Today?" *Canadian Journal of Economics and Political Science* 20, no. 1 (February 1954).

Jones, David C. *Midways, Judges, and Smooth-Tongued Fakirs: The Illustrated Story of Country Fairs in the Prairie West.* Saskatoon: Western Producer Prairie Books, 1983.

Katz, Michael, and Paul H. Mattingly. *Education and Social Change: Themes from Ontario's Past.* New York: New York University Press, 1975.

Klinck, Carl F., ed. *Literary History of Canada*, vol. 1. Toronto: University of Toronto Press, 1976.

Koester, C.B. *Mr. Davin, M.P.* Saskatoon: Western Producer Prairie Books, 1980.

Larmour, Jean. "Edgar Dewdney: Indian Commissioner in the Transition Period of Indian Settlement, 1879-1884". *Saskatchewan History* 33 (1980).

LaViolette, Forest E. *The Struggle for Survival: Indian Cultures and the Protestant Ethic in British Columbia.* Toronto: University of Toronto Press, 1961.

Leighton, Douglas. "A Victorian Civil Servant at Work: Lawrence Vankoughnet and the Canadian Indian Department, 1874-1893," in I.A.L. Getty and A.S. Lussier, eds. *As Long as the Sun Shines and Water Flows.* Vancouver: University of British Columbia Press, 1983.

Livesay, Dorothy. "The Native People in Our Canadian Literature." *The English Quarterly* 4, no. 1 (Spring 1971).

Long, John. *Treaty No. 9: The Half-Breed Question, 1902-1910.* Cobalt, ONT: Highway Bookshop, 1978.

———. *Treaty No. 9: The Indian Petitions, 1889-1927.* Cobalt, ONT: Highway Bookshop, 1978.

———. *Treaty No. 9: The Negotiations, 1901-1928.* Cobalt, ONT: Highway Bookshop, 1978.

Loram, C.T., and McIlwraith, T.F., eds. *The North American Indian Today.* Toronto: University of Toronto Press, 1943.

Lynch, Gerald. "An Endless Flow: D.C. Scott's Indian Poems." *Studies in Canadian Literature* 7, no. 1 (1982).

MacBeth, Madge. *Over My Shoulder*. Toronto: Ryerson Press, 1953.

MacInnes, T.R.L. "History of Indian Administration in Canada." *Canadian Journal of Economics and Political Science* 12 (February 1946).

Macleod, H.C. *The North-West Mounted Police and Law Enforcement, 1873-1905*. Toronto: University of Toronto Press, 1976.

Mandlebaum, David. *The Plains Cree: An Ethnographic, Historical and Comparative Study*. Regina: Canadian Plains Research Centre, University of Regina, 1979.

McDougall, Robert L. *The Poet and the Critic: A Literary Correspondence between D.C. Scott and E.K. Brown*. Ottawa: Carleton University Press, 1983.

McFeat, Tom, ed. *Indians of the North Pacific Coast*. Toronto: McClelland and Stewart, 1966.

McGee, H.F., ed. *The Native Peoples of Atlantic Canada*. Toronto: McClelland and Stewart, 1974.

McGregor, James G. *A History of Alberta*. Edmonton: Hurtig, 1972.

McNab, David T. "Herman Merivale and Colonial Office Indian Policy in the Mid-Nineteenth Century" in I.A.L. Getty and A.S. Lussier, eds. *As Long as the Sun Shines and Water Flows*. Vancouver: University of British Columbia Press, 1983.

Meckler, Lee B. "Rabbit-Skin Robes and Mink-Traps: Indian and European in 'The Forsaken.'" *Canadian Poetry* 1 (Fall/Winter 1977).

Milloy, John S. "The Early Indian Acts: Developmental Strategy and Constitutional Change," in I.A.L. Getty and A.S. Lussier, eds. *As Long As the Sun Shines and Water Flows*. Vancouver: University of British Columbia Press, 1983.

Monkman, Leslie. *A Native Heritage: Images of the Indian in English-Canadian Literature*. Toronto: University of Toronto Press, 1981.

Montgomery, Malcolm. "The Legal Status of the Six Nations Indians in Canada." *Ontario History* 55. no. 2 (1983).

_____. "The Six Nations Indians and the Macdonald Franchise". *Ontario History* 57, no. 1 (1985).

Morton, Desmond and Glenn Wright. "The Bonus Campaign, 1919-1921: Veterans and the Campaign for Re-establishment." *Canadian Historical Review* 64, no. 2 (June 1983).

Mountain Horse, Mike. *My People the Bloods*. Calgary: Glenbow-Alberta Institute and Standoff, AB: Blood Tribal Council, 1979.

Ormsby, Margaret. *British Columbia: A History*. Toronto: Macmillan, 1958.

Pain, A.S. *The Way North*. Toronto: Ryerson Press, 1964.

Patterson, E. Palmer II. "Andrew Paull (1892-1959): Finding a Voice for the New Indian." *Western Canadian Journal of Anthropology* 6, no. 2 (1976).

_____. "Arthur E.O'Meara, Friend of the Indians". *Pacific Northwest Quarterly* 58, no. 2 (April 1967).

_____. "A Decade of Change: Origins of the Nishga and Tsimshian Land Protests in the 1880's". *Journal of Canadian Studies* 18, no. 3 (Autumn 1983).

_____. "The Poet and the Indian: Indian Themes in the Poetry of Duncan Campbell Scott and John Collier." *Ontario History* 59, (June 1967).

Pettigrew, Eileen. *The Silent Enemy*. Saskatoon: Western Producer Prairie Books, 1983.

Ponting, J.R., and R. Gibbins. *Out of Irrelevance: A Socio-Political Introduction to Indian Affairs in Canada*. Toronto: Butterworth, 1980.

Postal, Susan K. "Hoax Nativism at Caughnawaga: A Control Case for the Theory of Revitalization." *Ethnology* 4, no. 3 (July 1965).

Price, Richard, ed. *The Spirit of the Alberta Indian Treaties*. Montreal: Institute for Research on Public Policy, 1980.

Rasporich, A.W., ed. *Western Canada: Past and Present*. Calgary: McClelland and Stewart West, 1975.

Ray, G. Ross. *Le Sentiment de la nature dans la poésie canadienne anglaise, 1807-1918*. Paris: A.G. Nizet, 1961.

Redford, James. "Attendance at Indian Residential Schools in British Columbia, 1890-1920." *B.C. Studies* 44 (Winter 1979-80).

Sanders, Doug. "The Nishga Case." *B.C. Studies* 19 (Autumn 1973).

Scott, Duncan Campbell. *The Administration of Indian Affairs in Canada*. Toronto: Canadian Institute of International Affairs, 1931.

_____. *Beauty and Life*. Toronto: McClelland and Stewart, 1921.

_____. *The Circle of Affection*. Toronto: McClelland and Stewart, 1947.

_____. *The Green Cloister*. Toronto: McClelland and Stewart, 1935.

_____. "Indian Affairs, 1763-1841," in Adam Shortt and Arthur G. Doughty, eds. *Canada and Its Provinces* (Vol. 4, Section 2, Part 2, *British Dominion*). Toronto: Glasgow, Brook and Co., 1914.

_____. "Indian Affairs, 1840-1867," in A. Shortt and A.G. Doughty, *Canada and Its Provinces* (Vol. 5, Section 3, *United Canada*). Toronto: Glasgow, Brook and Co., 1914.

_____. "Indian Affairs, 1867-1912," in A Shortt and A.G. Doughty, *Canada and Its Provinces* (Vol. 7, Section 4, *The Dominion*). Toronto: Glasgow, Brook and Co., 1914.

_____. *In the Village of Viger and Other Stories*. Toronto: McClelland and Stewart, 1973.

_____. "Introduction" to Amelia Paget, *People of the Plains*. Toronto: W. Briggs, 1909.

_____. *John Graves Simcoe*. London: Oxford Unversity Press, 1927.

_____. *Labour and the Angel*. Boston: Copeland and Day, 1898.

_____. *Lundy's Lane and Other Poems*. New York: Doran, 1916.

_____. *The Magic House and Other Poems*. Ottawa: Durie, 1893.

_____. *New World Lyrics and Ballads*. Toronto: Morang, 1905.

_____. *The Poems of Duncan Campbell Scott*. Toronto: McClelland and Stewart, 1926.

_____. "Traditional History of the Confederacy of the Six Nations." Royal Society of Canada, *Transactions*, Section 2, 19 May 1911.

_____. *Via Borealis*. Toronto: Tyrell, 1906.

_____. *The Witching of Elspie*. New York: Doran, 1923.

Sluman, Norma, and Jean Goodwill. *John Tootoosis: Biography of a Cree Leader*. Ottawa: Golden Dog Press, 1982.

Smith, Donald B. *Long Lance: The True Story of an Imposter*. Toronto: Macmillan, 1982.

Snow, John. *These Mountains Are Our Sacred Places: The Story of the Stoney Indians*. Toronto: Samuel Stevens, 1977.

Stanley, G.F.G. "As Long as the Sun Shines and Water Flows: An Historical Comment," in I.A.L. Getty and A.S. Lussier, eds. *As Long as the Sun Shines and Water Flows*. Vancouver: University of British Columbia Press, 1983.

_____. *The Birth of Western Canada*. Toronto: University of Toronto Press, 1960.

Stich, K.P., ed. *The Duncan Campbell Scott Symposium*. Ottawa: University of Ottawa Press, 1980.

Stow, Glenys. "The Wound under the Feathers: Scott's "Discontinuities," in George Woodcock, ed. *Colony and Confederation: Early Canadian Poets and Their Background*.

Vancouver: University of British Columbia Press, 1974.

Sylvestre, G., B. Conron, and C. Klinck, eds. *Canadian Writers/Ecrivains Canadians.* Toronto: Ryerson Press, 1964.

Tennant, Paul. "Native Indian Political Organizations in British Columbia, 1900-1969: A Response to Internal Colonialism." *B.C. Studies* 55 (Autumn 1982).

Titley, E. Brian. "Indian Industrial Schools in Western Canada," in N. Sheehan, D. Jones and J.D. Wilson, eds. *Schools in the West: Essays on Canadian Educational History.* Calgary: Detselig, 1986.

———. "W.M. Graham: Indian Agent Extraordinaire." *Prairie Forum* 8, no. 1 (1983).

Tobias, John L. "Canada's Subjugation of the Plains Crees, 1879-1885." *Canadian Historical Review* 64, no. 4 (December 1983).

———. "Protection, Civilization, Assimilation: An Outline History of Canadian Indian Policy." *Western Canadian Journal of Anthropology* 4, no. 2 (1976).

Tooker, Elisabeth. "On the New Religion of Handsome Lake." *Anthropological Quarterly* 41, no. 4 (October 1968).

———. "The Iroquois White Dog Sacrifice in the Latter Part of the Eighteenth Century." *Ethnohistory* 12, no. 2 (Spring 1965).

Upton, L.F.S. "Colonists and Micmacs." *Journal of Canadian Studies* 10, no. 3 (August 1975).

———. "Indian Affairs in Colonial Nova Scotia, 1783-1871." *Acadiensis* 3 (Spring 1974).

———. "Indian Affairs in Colonial Nova Scotia, 1783-1871." *Acadiensis* 4 (Autumn 1975).

———. *Micmacs and Colonists: Indian-White Relations in the Maritimes, 1713-1867.* Vancouver: University of British Columbia Press, 1979.

———. "The Origins of Canadian Indian Policy." *Journal of Canadian Studies* 8, no. 4 (November 1973).

Veatch, Richard. *Canada and the League of Nations.* Toronto: University of Toronto Press, 1975.

Ware, Reuben. *The Lands We Lost.* Vancouver: Union of B.C. Indian Chiefs, 1974.

Wilbur, Richard. *H.H. Stevens, 1878-1973.* Toronto: University of Toronto Press, 1977.

Williams, David R. *The Man for a New Country: Sir Matthew Baillie Begbie.* Sidney, BC: Grey's Publishing, 1977.

Woodcock, George, ed. *Colony and Confederation: Early Canadian Poets and Their Background.* Vancouver: University of British Columbia Press, 1974.

Zazlow, Morris. *The Opening of the Canadian North, 1870-1914.* Toronto: McClelland and Stewart, 1971.

Index